Office Space Planning

Office Space Planning

DESIGNING FOR TOMORROW'S WORKPLACE

Alexi Marmot

Joanna Eley

McGraw-Hill

New York San Francisco Washington, D.C. Auckland Bogotá
Caracas Lisbon London Madrid Mexico City Milan
Montreal New Delhi San Juan Singapore
Sydney Tokyo Toronto

Library of Congress Cataloging-in-Publication Data

Marmot, Alexi.
    Office space planning : designing for tomorrow's workplace / Alexi Marmot, Joanna Eley.
      p.cm.
    Includes index.
    ISBN 0-07-134199-4
    1. Office layout. I. Eley, Joanna. II. Title.
    HF5547.2.M37 2000
    658.2'3—dc21   00-036123
                                        CIP

McGraw-Hill

A Division of The **McGraw·Hill** *Companies*

1 2 3 4 5 6 7 8 9 0 PBT/PBT 9 0 9 8 7 6 5 4 3 2 1 0 9

ISBN 0-07-134199-4

The sponsoring editor for this book was Wendy Lochner, the editing supervisor was Caroline Levine, and the production supervisor was Sherri Souffrance. It was set in Matte Antique by Kim Sheran of McGraw-Hill's Professional Book Group composition unit, Hightstown, New Jersey.

Printed and bound by Phoenix Book Technolgoy

This book is printed on recycled, acid-free paper containing a minimum of 50% recycled, de-inked fiber.

This book is for office workers whose work environment needs constant vigilance to help improve their working lives.

Contents

Chapter 3 Reengineering Space Allocation   83

Chapter 4 Individual Office or Open Plan: Which Works for You   105

Chapter 8 Technology in Office Buildings   233

Chapter 9 Office Moves and Change Management   259

Case Histories

Acknowledgments

*O*ur earlier book *Understanding Offices: What Every Manager Needs to Know about Office Buildings* was so enthusiastically received that we have expanded and updated the material for a North American and international readership.

We have spent many days inside other people's offices where we have met fascinating people in a wide variety of organizations. From all of them we have learned a great deal about the successes and failures of today's office environment. We have shared their vision that good offices are an important part of shaping a successful business. We wish to thank all the clients we have worked with at AMA and the thousands of people who have described their working lives to us, for the rich insights they have provided. Many designers, their clients, and their photographers have generously allowed us to use material about their buildings in this book. Cartoonists Darius and Louis Hellman created cartoons that greatly enliven the text. Our families have tolerated patiently and supported enthusiastically our commitment to shaping this book. Particular thanks are due to our researcher, Judith Abell, whose considerable skills and good cheer helped to draw the book together.

The following people were particularly helpful in providing information for each of the case studies:

4 Times Square, New York City. Kirsten Sibilia, Michael Cala

Alcoa Corporate Centre, Pittsburgh, Pennsylvania. Anne Lehman, Joyce Saltzman

Arthur Andersen, Human Capital Services, Chicago, Illinois. Phillip Deneau, Sarah Wortman

Arthur Andersen LLP, Boston, Massachusetts. Helen Novak, Steve Basque, Richard S. Mandelkom

Andersen Consulting, Wellesley, Massachusetts. Lara Neubauer, David Manfredi, Elizabeth Lowry Clapp, and Howard Elkus

Bank of America Dealer Loan Center, Las Vegas, Nevada. Karen Van Ert, Charles Uehrke

Bates USA, New York, New York. Kris Kemmerer, Todd De Garmo, Andrew Bordwin, and Megan Kenny

BBDO West, Los Angeles, California. Candice Kessler, Michael Beckson, Steven Heisler, and Tom Bonner

British Airways Waterside, London Heathrow. Alison Kedrick, Hilary Henning

Campbell-Ewald West, Los Angeles, California. Mary Lissone, Benny Chan

Commerzbank HQ. Elizabeth Walker, Nicola Rains, Ian Lambot

Education First, Cambridge Massachusetts. Lara Neubauer, David Manfredi

Excite Headquarters, Redwood City, California. Michelle Gong, Erik Sueberkrop and David Sabalvaro

First Data Investment Services Group, Westborough, Massachusetts. Helen Novak, John Uzee

MCI Telecommunications, Rally Center Project, Boston, Massachusetts. Ethan Anthony, S.G. Bradford

Metropolitan Life. Daniel May, Pat Brady (Metropolitan Life Archive)

Turnstones/Steelcase. John Malnor, Craig DeDamos, Alan Rhealt

National Electronic Warranty Co., Great Falls, Montana. Robin L. Cary, Peter Hapstak, Dale Stewart, and Michael Moran

National Minority Aids Council, Washington, D.C. Robin L. Cary, Peter Hapstak, Dale Stewart, and Michael Moran

Nortel Networks, Brampton, Ontario. Beth Kapusta

PricewaterhouseCoopers—The Zone, Philadelphia, Pennsylvania. Barbara McCarthy, Scott Van Valkenburg, Michele G. Sheehan

Publicis & Hal Riney, San Francisco, California. Briggs McDonald, Michelle Hill, Karla Erovick

Rhino Entertainment, Los Angeles, California. Candice Kessler, Michael Beckson, Steven Heisler, and Tom Bonner

Silicon Graphics, Inc., Redwood City, California. Michelle Gong, Erik Sueberkrop, and David Sabalvaro

TBWA/Chiat/Day, Playa Vista, Los Angeles, California. Jane Wuu, Clive Wilkinson, Jeremy Miller, Benny Chan

West Group, Egan, Minnesota. Marcia Malinowski, Dan Spencer, Dave Paeper, Lisa Pool, Joe Hamilton, Cory B. Rettke, Dana Wheelock, Jerry Hass

World Neighbors, Oklahoma City, Oklahoma. Leslie Goode

Cartoonists. Louis Hellman, Darius Gilmont, Peter Waddington

INTRODUCTION:
Offices for Business Needs

CASE HISTORIES

See Case Histories 1, 2, and 3 on pages 281–300

After 100 years of progress the verdict is "Could do better"

Workers in Metropolitan Life Insurance Building, New York, 1896

Source: MetLife Archives

Call Centre, UK, 1999

Photographer: Don McPhee, copyright *The Guardian*

The flex-firm concept does not imply structurelessness; it does suggest that a company, in being reborn, may cease to be a mule and turn into a team consisting of a tiger, a school of piranhas, a mini-mule or two, and who knows, maybe even a swarm of information sucking bees. The image underlines the point. The business of tomorrow may embody many different formats within a single frame. It may function as a kind of Noah's Ark.

—A. TOFFLER, *POWERSHIFT*

So where are the instructions for building and sailing Toffler's Ark?

You have attended the conferences and learned what the new business looks like; your organization *is* on the right track to meet the challenges of the twenty-first century; you *have* identified the opportunities and made the changes.

But do you know what sort of building you should be in, and how to use and manage it when you've got it? Do you know whether it will be an office building or something else altogether? Will each office worker get more or less space in future? Will open plan and air-conditioning fall out of favor as people return to cellular offices and openable windows? Will office buildings fill with leisure and family-support facilities, so that people can spend all their waking hours there, or will they become clubs for an occasional visit?

Management books abound, describing how to lead, how to make one-minute decisions, how to manage difficult people, how to recognize—or reorganize into—a shamrock or a doughnut organization, how to thrive on chaos. Not many of them describe *where* all this takes place—the physical realities that support the business. Material written about buildings is directed either at facilities managers, concerned with running buildings, or at the specialist concerns of designers, property agents, and builders.

Office workers are increasingly important in the running of the economy. They make up half of all those in active work. Their importance will increase as many other jobs decline absolutely in advanced economies. In the United States, 50 million office workers occupy around 10 billion ft^2 (1 billion m^2) representing about $10,000 billion. In the United Kingdom alone there are now over 10 million office workers. They work in 2,000 million ft^2 gross of office space (200 million m^2) representing about $200 billion (£120 billion) of capital investment. Just to heat, clean, manage, and insure this space annually costs on the order of £10 billion.

Office buildings abound, large and small, old and new, in urban and out-of-town locations, in single- and multi-occupancy, purpose built and converted from other uses. Some office work takes place in specialized buildings, such as hospitals, schools, theaters, museums, airports, factories, warehouses, and shops. All these places are where white-collar workers spend much of their time and find at least part of their identity. The many organizations using office buildings constantly adapt and change them to suit their evolving needs or build new ones if nothing already available will do. This book has been written for designers and managers. It will help managers to understand their office space, making it easier for them to get the best out of their buildings, to use the precious, scarce resource of built space efficiently, and to create a good-quality environment in which their staff can work effectively. It will help designers of office buildings, their interiors and furniture, by sharpening their sensitivity to the needs of business and employees. The knowledge and skills required to get the best out of office buildings can be applied to all building types where office activities are housed. But first a question must also be asked: What is the future need for offices likely to be?

The Office of the Future, or the Future of the Office?

The business of the future may be run by executives who are scarcely ever in each other's physical presence. It will not even have an address or a central office—only the equivalent of a telephone number. For its files and records will be space rented in the memory units of computers that could be located anywhere on Earth,...vast memory banks beneath the Arizona desert...or wherever land is cheap and useless for any other purpose?
—ARTHUR C. CLARKE, *PROFILES OF THE FUTURE*

A new generation of changed organizational patterns and social consequences is upon us. In the age of e-commerce, we have to re-examine what we need offices for, what we can justify in their name. If information handling is carried out more efficiently by dispersed groups networked to powerful computers, why should we need offices? If we cannot stop them guzzling so much energy, will we still be able to afford offices? Can we make sure that they are located where they can be reached without a two-hour journey in overcrowded transport or by car with a single occupant? Will people still want to come to office buildings? Will all future offices have to have a "green agenda"? Will there actually be office buildings in the future?

Offices have flowered as a building form, and a social structure, for a fairly short, intense period. They seem to have permeated totally our understanding of the world of work. But they could be a short-lived phenomenon, a transitional stage in economic evolution. Agriculture had its buildings—barns, byres, warehouses, transport depots. Then, for manufacturing, factories and power stations were invented. The "new industrial state" needed office buildings, and they were built by the thousands, ripping the factories and warehouses out of urban centers and creating the new image of the skyscraper city in the twentieth century. Now we are moving to a new economic structure based on information and intellectual products in which the buildings that will be needed are unknown, a phase of information manipulation that will require networks of wires and waves linking networks of buildings unlike any we have now. What forces might encourage office buildings to disappear? What forces might keep them alive and well and living in the future? The number of people working in offices has grown throughout this century, as shown in Figures I.1 and I.2. This trend is slowing, may stop, or even reverse.

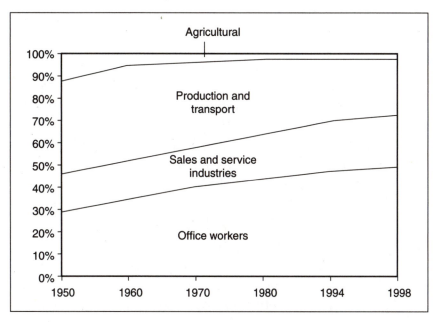

Figure I.1 Distribution of the U.S. workforce by occupation, 1950 to 1998.

[U.S. Bureau of Labor Statistics (BLS), historic and current data accessed from the BLS Web site http://www.bls.gov and the U.S. Bureau of Census Web page http://www.census.gov.]

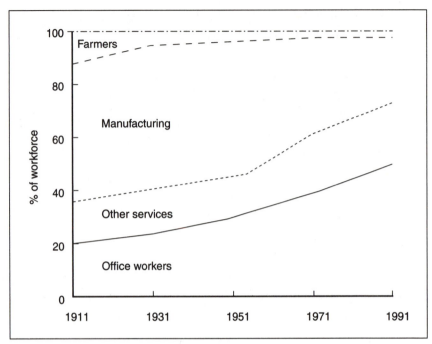

Figure I.2   Distribution of the UK workforce by occupation, 1950 to 1998.

[Data cited for 1911 to 1971 from G. Routh, *Occupation and Pay in Great Britain* (London: Macmillan, 1980), p. 11. Data cited for 1991 from OPCS, 1993, *Census Report for Great Britain*, Part 2 (London: HMSO), Table 74.]

Redundant churches have been adapted to emerge as theaters, gymnasiums, community halls, video studios, and flats. Is this a pattern that can dimly be seen to have parallels in the office world? Will our present office buildings become redundant, reused for other activities, while office activities are scattered elsewhere? The vision painted by Clarke decades ago, which he placed a century into the future, around 2060, is already easy to picture given the nature of current equipment.

Still, it is hard to imagine administration, government, and organizational management being carried out entirely through computer networks between remote individuals without places where people come together to work, resembling in essentials the offices we know today. The routines involved in governing large groups of people, supplying them with the goods and services they need for survival and demand for enjoyment, require cooperation. It is in order to enhance the necessary cooperation that offices will continue to exist. Corporate culture needs to be transmitted to new recruits. People need to be trained to enable them to work effectively. Some of this training will take place in offices. Home video training, corporate conferences, or computer courseware will not achieve this unaided. When people are physically together, they can best get to know each other, understand each other's skills and weaknesses, learn by example, find those people with whom they work best, and discover in what type of work they themselves excel. Once trained, socialized into cooperation, many people can be liberated to work in a wide variety of locations, some of which will be offices. Only a few of those so liberated will actually want to take up the freedom wholesale. Others will need the companionship and constancy of an office routine, for some or all of the time.

Though offices will continue to be needed, it will be for a different working population. At present around half of the workforce within developed western economies has office-based white-collar jobs. The full extent to which this will change can only be guessed. The overall numbers are likely to increase—office-based work still has some sources of growth, even while other sectors of the economy are likely to stagnate or decline. Despite this, the need for office floor area will decline as a result of a drive for economy and the fact that the office workforce spends less time in offices. Already some users occupy an office for very few of the available hours. The building is always present, every hour of every day of its long life. Office workers spend a very small proportion of time there. They are away from the building because of weekends, leave, and sickness, because the working days use only 8 of the available 24 hours, and because office hours are spent elsewhere for meetings, training, or work in other locations. In some cases workers may spend as little as 5 percent of the available hours in their office building. This sounds ridiculous, but for someone who is habitually out of the office for an average three and a half days per week and who takes a full complement of annual leave, that is what is happening. These people are not freaks; many jobs involve this sort of work pattern, from those of sales representatives to senior executives, from two-day-a-week academics to expensive management consultants. How far the provision of buildings for such a work pattern can be justified is one of the issues that must be and is being addressed.

The percentage of available time spent in offices is declining. According to present trends, the proportion of a white-collar person's working life spent in an office will decline, even in the case of those people whose jobs keep them at their office desk all of every working day. The length of a person's working life has been shrinking, absolutely and relatively. The average length of life is increasing, but young people are in education for longer, so they start working later, and retire earlier. The number of days of annual holiday to which people are entitled has expanded, with the two-day weekend replacing the single day or one and a half days, the increased number of public holidays, and the longer personal holiday allowances being offered by many organizations. The length of the working day has also been gradually reduced. In Europe the Economic Community has introduced "The Working Time Directive" to cap the number of working hours. If these trends continue, offices will change, as they will provide for a different amount of an individual's time and serve different aspects of their identity. These trends are of great importance to women who make up most of the office workforce. There have always been large numbers of women in the most lowly clerical capacity. Many once worked only while young and childless. More women these days continue to work after starting a family. Their requirements are for shorter journeys to work and part-time work or job sharing that allows them to combine work with child care. Office technology liberates them from a fixed location, allowing offices in or near their homes to function as well as central ones.

Places where people can come together and marshal, exchange, and use information will still be needed, even for a smaller workforce, which spends fewer hours per year in office buildings. What will these buildings be like? There are various problems that exist in the office buildings already: Employees dislike air-conditioning, there is a risk from bombs, and there is a need for huge transport infrastructures to support them. Suggestions for alternatives include satellite or neighborhood offices and business parks. Suggestions in Chapter 1 are for alternate offices in vogue with those who focus on the mobile workforce. The *club,* the relaxed lounge with refreshments and interesting discussions with colleagues, is the favorite image. In fact, the old Lloyds Coffee House in the City of London, the birthplace of huge insurance offices, is back in favor. Club offices would serve a much larger number of people than current office buildings because so many people would be away at any one time. This is one way of improving the use made of a building. Individuals would be away from the office more, allowing them to integrate their personal lives with their working lives.

Another image is the *work palace,* a building with a range of excellent and exclusive facilities so that staff could spend the whole day there, using the office to support personal life, leisure, entertainment, and family care—making use of infant care or even granny care units. This would also help to make better use of the building as a whole, even while the hours spent on paid work are reduced.

Another possibility is the *technoemporium,* a building that acts as a repository of electronic gadgets, where desks groan under ever more exotic equipment. Such offices could be much smaller, used in short, sharp bursts when large, expensive, nonportable equipment is required. There would be shelves in the stockroom dispensing the latest pocket-sized gizmo to use away from the office. All of these are, of course, caricatures—recognizable ones, bits of which exist already.

A patchwork is the most likely outcome, with different emphases on these various outcomes, brought together in the mix that works best for each organization, in buildings that are "intelligent" or "forgiving" enough to accommodate them in changing proportions over time, without too much strain. The emphasis will always be on how to make good use of expensive building measures, which is an expensive resource, to serve more people for longer and to accommodate activities that cannot easily take place elsewhere.

Location, Location, and Location

The three most important factors ("location, location, and location") that real estate agents have told us for years matter most when selecting office buildings have meant, until now, that desirable locations are the ones that other people have already chosen. As a result, they are densely developed, expensive, and often entail a tedious and stressful journey from where most people live. Such locations are also vulnerable to disruption on a massive scale—when transport systems break down through strikes, severe weather, or technical failure, or when terrorists decide to hit. The simple principle "Don't put all your eggs in one basket" has an important place in planning office accommodation, if only to alert companies to the need for disaster planning.

Location and transport are intimately linked, and there are real opportunities for major energy savings by reducing or eliminating the journey to work. This saving is gained on behalf of the community rather than reaped directly by the organization. If private-car commuting is the predominant mode of travel, then locating an office to which people can walk, bike, or take a local bus will make enormous energy savings. This fact is behind some of the changes in office-work patterns that have taken place in the United States. In Los Angeles, to reduce energy consumption, several government office organizations are reducing the number of commuter journeys by encouraging some staff to work at home for one or two days a week. Local offices have been developed where people can go to work if they prefer not to work in their own homes. The location equation is changing to help reduce national levels of energy consumption and pollution.

The new way of working described in Chapter 1, the freedom from dependence on location, has been well explored in the press from the point of view of an individual office worker. Fewer people are willing to stand up and be counted when it comes to describing what this will really mean for the locations of the office buildings of the future. Will they migrate to residential neighborhoods or to motorway intersections? Will the new locations be served by public transport? If people can work anywhere, will they insist on working in a convenient place? If so, convenient for what? Home or urban facilities? Will management seek cheaper locations and forgo the face-to-face opportunities of densely packed urban areas? Will city centers continue to be office locations in the future? The forces that centralized large parts of the office population in major cities, in densely developed locations, acted over many decades. A slow reversal seems to be taking place. What could speed things up would be a change in the amount of pressure applied to organizations to act in environmentally responsible ways, as in California, where it is already happening. It may be greatly intensified. High costs associated with transporting big populations in individual cars can be measured and passed on to offending organizations. Alternatively, more office staff may vote with their feet, or their wheels, and accept only convenient jobs—close to the residential doorstep.

It Could Go Either Way

A hundred years from now, many office buildings that exist now will still be here though they may be different. They will have to be made as sustainable as possible in the design of upgrades and control of energy costs, and the tailoring of all consumable and management practices will need to meet acceptable standards of behavior.

That is, if people have not abandoned them. Cheap third-world labor, fewer regulations concerning working conditions, and the possibility of instantaneous information transfer make foreign office activities an attractive opportunity. Just as manufacturing has moved to developing countries, large parts of the office work currently carried out in attractive offices in western countries could be exported. This would render redundant many office buildings in the developed world. Only a few would be needed as offices. The rest would be converted, perhaps to housing or leisure facilities, or pulled down or, perhaps most likely, left to rot where they stand.

Immediate concerns must take precedence over imaginary future scenarios. There are plenty of opportunities at the moment to improve the office building, new or old, and make it a better place.

Why Does the Building Matter?

The office building is the Ark in which most business still sails. Good managers understand their building. They excel if their office building supports the way they want their firm to function, if it helps people to communicate, and if it gives customers the right image. They know that they have a competitive advantage if their building performs better than the norm through efficient design and space management. They seek to make the most of their property assets to support their core business.

Yet senior managers are often in the dark about their buildings. They are responsible for the mission statement for a business, but often they are not in close contact with the people whose job it is to see that a building, with its equipment and furnishing, properly supports the business to achieve this mission. Property directors are appointed in only a small percentage of companies. The director responsible for property is most likely to be a finance director. But finance directors have more important things to worry about than buildings. Even property directors are more likely to be expert in the financial side of property deals and asset management than in understanding what makes the property that they occupy useful and attractive, or inhibiting and unpleasant, for their organization.

Office is a very hard worked word. What does the word conjure up for you? Is your office the organization to which you belong in your work role? Or is it the building where you work, or perhaps your own little room in that building, or maybe the one at home where you retreat on Sunday afternoons? All these meanings, and a great many more, are perfectly valid as far as the dictionary is concerned. The word is used to refer to a role, the job that a person has in an "official" capacity. It is attached to the place where clerical activities are carried out, an office building. The place where specific activities are carried out in an organization—such as the "booking office" in a railway station—or whole organizations that have a particular role—such as the "Post Office"—have incorporated the word in their titles, implying both a role and an activity. *Office* is also used to mean all the people within an organization, and people from many organizations are sometimes referred to collectively as *office workers*. In this book, mostly we use the word *office* to mean "office building," though when discussing an enclosed, personal "office," it is also used to refer to rooms. We have done our best to make the various meanings clear as they shift and merge.

This book is about productive buildings for leading-edge organizations. We admire unreservedly office buildings of breathtaking architecture and rich interior design. But aesthetic concerns are the focus of other books. We adopt the view that office buildings can be analyzed rationally and sensible decisions can be taken if managers and designers only know the right questions. We believe designers can create better work environments if they know the main concerns of their clients. This book helps managers and designers formulate those questions as they determine the right solutions.

We have not prepared an exhaustive academic treatise on office design. This book seeks to demystify a technical subject for the benefit of people whose specialist skills lie in other fields but for whom this information is important. Many good ideas we have come across—those of clients, designers, managers, and colleagues from all over the world—have been pressed into service. We have used comments from the thousands of individuals whom we have observed or interviewed in our effort to understand their real needs while developing plans for their office. Clients in large and small organizations, public and private, in the United Kingdom and elsewhere, in lavish or humble premises, have provided us with insights and much of the material upon which this book is based. Rather than scatter footnotes throughout the book on the origin of each thought, we have collected key references to important reading material in a list at the end. No one should underestimate the contribution that these other writers and practitioners have made to our work. What we have made of their ideas is our own responsibility.

We have not attempted to make a space-planning expert out of every reader. Rather, our aim is to give insights about office buildings to managers and designers, even those who expect to leave building planning and management to others. Better decisions can be made if managers understand generic information about buildings and their fittings. They can then help to choose and use buildings that will serve the company mission well. Many issues are discussed in the context of existing premises occupied by existing organizations. Most people are in this situation most of the time. Yet it is at the time of a move that everyone wants the answers to many of the questions addressed here. Sometimes this is a good time to get people's attention and enable resources to be devoted to seeking answers and understanding their implication. Often it is not. At the moment of a move, everyone concerned has too many different agendas, too little time to think straight and too much to do. A move is threatening, and many people may find it hard to make constructive contributions. If some of the ideas discussed in this book can be considered in the relative calm of an existing building, the organization will be better equipped for a future move, should it arise, as well as getting more out of its current situation. Nonetheless, if a move is happening willy-nilly, this book can be used to clarify potential solutions in an as yet unselected building, to clarify objectives, to prepare the program, to help assess several existing buildings in order to make a suitable choice, or to define a new building.

Innovative ways of working are making news. Their consequences in making the best use of a building, in space and time, are explained in Chapter 1. But these apply to only some businesses all the time, even if they may eventually apply to all businesses some of the time. In all circumstances buildings need to be understood if they are to serve their users well. Fundamental information about the size, efficiency, and utility of a building is reviewed in Chapter 2. Space standards and the dichotomy of the desire for enclosed offices versus the benefits of open-space planning are covered in Chapters 3 and 4. Chapter 5 considers furniture, and Chapter 6 discusses the issues of sick-building syndrome and the comfort of occupants. Space that does

CHAPTER 1

Office Work
without Office Buildings

**See Case Histories 4 and 5
on pages 301–311**

Q: When is an office not an office?

A: When it's "hot," virtual, a twisted pair, or a gentleman's club.

This answer is directed at organizations with:

- A large proportion of office space empty much of the time.
- Sales representatives who should be with their customers, telesales people.
- Creative writers, software writers, journalists, and copyeditors who work odd hours in odd places.
- Consultants or auditors who work on client premises.
- Inspectors who must make visits.
- Sophisticated and widely distributed communications technology.
- A need to keep or attract valuable staff, which can be accomplished by allowing them to choose to work from home for at least some of the time.
- Other reasons to adopt new ways of working.

Your Office Is Where You Are

As we have become acclimatized to offices as places where many people gather to work on paper-related tasks, we have lost sight of earlier small-scale, individual places in which people worked. Now that image is being challenged.

Much has been written about the design of offices. Fortunes have been made and lost on the property market by creating, selling, or leasing buildings intended for office occupation. At the same time—unnoticed by the majority but accepted as unremarkable by those concerned—some white-collar office workers are not actually working much in their office buildings; instead, they are working wherever they are. Insurance representatives, for example, may have a filing cabinet in an office somewhere, but their real base is their car, their briefcase, and their laptop. They do not have an office to go back to.

As communications technology has grown more sophisticated and hardware has become truly portable, the reality of office work outside the office has flourished and acquired a glamorous veneer. Advertisers show limousines furnished as traveling meeting rooms—*office caravans*—for those valuable members of organizations who need to be several places on one day. Airline seats are sold with ads showing dynamic, upwardly mobile office people working on their laptop computers one moment, then dining on caviar and champagne the next, and sitting in the same seat throughout.

The next step is to make work look like a holiday—the laptop on the beach, business and pleasure combined as never before (Fig. 1.1). This is a big leap. A new icon represents "office work." It is not the office block—that focus of frenetic investment, the concrete-and-glass monument to commerce designed to house an ever-increasing army of office workers. Rather, it is a lightweight battery-powered "notebook" or "palmtop" and the mobile phone that you, a solitary individual, wrap in your bathing towel and return to after a dip in the sea.

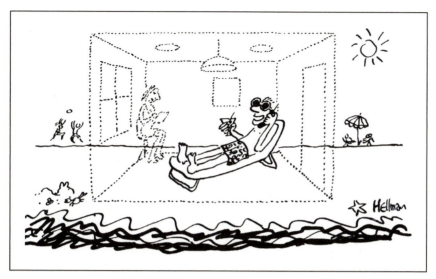

Figure 1.1 The virtual office.
(Louis Hellman.)

Dependence on the office building as a place has clearly been reduced. The reasons are not hard to find. The development of efficient offices, as we know them now, was much influenced by the development of equipment for communications; the typewriter and the telephone are obvious examples. They helped to bring people together in a single location, to "glue" them together to exploit the equipment and enhance the value that could be obtained from it. The very same equipment, in its latest versions, is now acting as a powerful "solvent." Information at the most sophisticated level of complex and subtle content can be carried over vast distances, instantly and cheaply.

Technological developments have resulted in equipment that is still capable of representing "glue," as did the first telephones or computers. Examples are large integrated machines that print or copy or fax in color or black and white, at record speeds, with high quality and at high capacity. But they are expensive and can best be exploited in a place were large groups of people can come together—an office.

At the same time various functions, such as computing, telephoning, faxing, and color copying, are being performed by cheap, miniature, portable versions of the more elaborate equipment. The solvent has developed from the glue technology, and it is being packaged and sold in a different way. Cables can now be used to transmit data as easily as speech. Now anything that can be rendered into digital signals can be sent anywhere and reconstituted on arrival for manipulation on a large, expensive, centralized piece of equipment or, almost as easily, on a small, cheap one that lives in the back of the car at the bottom of the suitcase, in the team room at the office or beside the TV at home.

New Ways of Working

"New ways of working" seems an unlikely topic for much excitement, yet the centrality of this subject must be appreciated. In our culture many measures of personal value are related to identity at work. This is why the debates about new ways of working, new solutions to the place, the rules, the trappings surrounding work, are of such interest—why a better grasp of the facts, as opposed to fantasies, is essential.

Responses to new technology in the office embrace a wide spectrum. A variety of new ways of working is practiced, to varying degrees, by different organizations. There are companies that do not acknowledge the changes in ways of working that technology has made possible. Like proverbial ostriches with their heads in the sand, they have not noticed changes, or they have seen and rejected them as of no interest or relevance, or they believe they cannot afford them. Others have started to challenge the conventions of the office hierarchy of status and rank.

A small but influential and growing number of people is enthusiastically and aggressively adopting changes that challenge the time and place constraints of office work.

They use the availability of cheap technology to liberate people from location and from the nine-to-five day. These organizations have espoused flexible and location-free working to a lesser or greater degree. New behavior patterns that attract attention are "flexible working," "telecommuting," and "hot-desking." These concepts have been variously defined and widely publicized, and they have been claimed to have great importance—flexible working because it offers employees control over their life/work balance; telecommuting because it will be practiced by many people; and hot-desking because it will save companies space and therefore money. These concepts depend on some office work taking place somewhere else than in the office building.

THE OFFICE: COMING TOGETHER

An office is assumed to be a well-understood type of place, office work an accepted and normal activity. In reality, office work, based in a place called an "office," is a relatively recent phenomenon. The need and ability to bring a number of people together in one place to work on information, on paper or, now, on computers is familiar to twenty-first-century town and city dwellers. It would have baffled a fifteenth-century craftsman, as would a nineteenth-century factory. The most officelike environment in the fifteenth century would have been a sort of factory, an assembly of monks and scribes perched at writing desks copying books, perhaps with one member of the group sitting at the front, reading an improving text to divert the minds, but not the hands, of the copyists—a bit like the "Muzak" broadcast throughout the factory floor. But the task would have been one of making books, not collecting and manipulating knowledge to further a separate business objective. Office work, dependent on collecting, ordering, manipulating, and passing on of information, was not a common part of that world. These functions were needed for some exceptional organizations—the Vatican or the Imperial Chinese Army. They were not part of everyday life.

About 150 years ago, when information-based activities had become more commonplace, the notion that "your office is where you are" would have been obvious. For example, the management of an estate took place in an "estate office" on a landlord's main premises, but the manager could and would carry all the necessary information with him to outlying properties and perform the paperwork tasks wherever he needed to be. Again, a member of the gentry wishing to see a lawyer would summon the lawyer to

(Continued)

THE OFFICE: COMING TOGETHER

(Continued)

him and see him in his own home, where the necessary business could be transacted, rather than making a trip to the solicitor's office. An architect's office in Dickens's time, where projects for clients were developed and training of hopeful new young architects took place was, generally, his own home.

As the number of people who were engaged in office work grew, there was increasingly a reason to bring them together in one place, an office. There they could share the ever-more-complicated paper tasks, divided into steps and stages, and they could be managed as a whole unit of production. Technologies to serve these activities were developed that involved capital outlay and bulky, heavy equipment such as typewriters or complex adding machines. The reasons to go to an office multiplied. There the tasks could be carried out with maximum efficiency and minimum outlay on the equipment, which could be shared by everyone. The telephone created a further powerful reason to come together in one place, where communications were at their most intense. Transport systems were developed to bring people from their homes to their offices and became another factor strengthening the concept of working together in offices, or "paper factories." To distinguish them from the workers in blue overalls in industrial factories, office workers became known as white-collar workers.

THE OFFICE: MOVING APART

The range of legitimate office environments has increased as a result of technological and organizational changes and the alternative work styles that have accompanied them. It is now accepted that office work takes place in different types of location and environment, according to the needs of the individual and the business.

Home office. A special study for one person, the corner of another room, the kitchen table, attic, or a space under the stairs—may be equipped with the full range of office machinery or occasionally set up with a laptop and a mobile phone. These home offices may be used for regular daily work—or for occasional heads-down work when exceptional concentration is needed.

Call centers. Reminiscent of an old-style factory with machinery that could not be turned off and needed people present at all times, teams of workers now respond to

(Continued)

THE OFFICE: MOVING APART

(Continued)

telephone calls in call centers, offering information, selling goods or services, and acting as help desks for almost every sphere of business. The extent to which these services are required by customers determines the size of the teams at different times of day. In some cases supplementary staff are connected to the centers from home-based work places at times of exceptional pressure. The service may be provided on a round-the-clock basis from a single location using early, late, or even night shifts. It is also possible to shift the work location, rather than the work time, for the staff and use teams on the other side of the world.

Satellite offices. The local outpost established by a larger business is acquiring an identity of its own. It may be set up for a variety of reasons—to exploit cheap space for activities that do not require central locations; to provide offices that are more accessible to employees' homes and enable them to avoid extensive commuting; or to set up in new locations, starting with modest premises, to test the local opportunities.

Business center. Simple or lavish, space can be rented for a few hours or for months, a single desk or several rooms for a team. Business centers can be part of large chains with multiple outlets in different cities and countries, or they can be single offices, either suburban or central. They are suitable for companies establishing a base in a new location or start-up firms. Services that emulate those in a large organization—reception, conference suites, and other client-focused facilities—are provided to be purchased on a take-only-as-much-as-you-need basis.

Client locations. Outsourcing and the need to buy in specialist services have fostered situations in which individuals or groups are regularly located not in their own office premises but in those of their clients. At the same time as all organizations grow increasingly conscious of the cost of providing and maintaining office space, so the balance between client and provider constantly shifts, no one wishing to be responsible for accommodations for which others can be persuaded to pay. Some of these implants are related to activities that need to be located in the office building, such as reception, security, catering, facilities management, IT-related troubleshooting, and helpdesks. Other typical interlopers are consultants providing an in-house role on a short-term basis, leading or manning project teams of defined duration, and contractors absorbed alongside company employees to maintain a reduced permanent headcount at a low level but enable fluctuations in workload to be managed.

Cybercafe. Ready access to computers, software specialists, and a good cup of coffee in sociable surroundings are available in cybercafes around the globe. While their primary market may be computer-poor youngsters and travelers, they also serve itinerant employees away from base.

(Continued)

THE OFFICE: MOVING APART

(Continued)

Airport lounge or hotel lobby. Space for clients and travelers to read, plug in laptops, use fax or telephones, and capture precious moments for work between other activities. Support staff may provide help, or the facility may simply give access to power, a table, space, and quiet.

Telecommuting

If people need to communicate at all with colleagues, using data links from afar (the *tele* in *telecommuting*) reduces their need to travel physically, that is, to commute, to work. *Telecommuting* does not always mean working from home, though it is often assumed to. The essential component is that work is being performed somewhere other than in an office building while connected to it. The father of telecommuting, Jack Nilles in California, predicted 10 years ago that many millions of people would be working this way by the year 2000. Since then every crystal-gazing organization has added its might to the hype, and it would by now be tempting to imagine that soon there will be no need for office buildings at all. The Henley Centre for Forecasting suggested that 4 percent of the UK workforce, 1.2 million people, already uses their home as an office, at least for part of the time, and Nilles suggests that 4 million are doing it in the United States. Organizations are encouraging staff to work from home some of the time, in order, among other reasons, to reduce the pollution, congestion, and energy waste caused by the wholesale movement of people on a daily basis from one building to another and back again. Public agencies in California, for example, have been participating in the California Telecommuting Project since 1985. They want staff to stay away from the office, doing what can be done anywhere with the right equipment.

All the data-carrier companies are striving hard to ensure that the equipment is indeed there by actively marketing equipment to home-based workers. Providers of home furniture market the home office desk, competing in their efforts with the office furniture suppliers who also market several versions. Shelves in the do-it-yourself (DIY) section of bookstores groan under the weight of manuals about creating the home office. Newsletters and Web sites for telecommuters explain how to discover the most useful equipment, publicizing the most recent successful spin-off of a group of employees into home-based independence. Associations of teleworkers aim to ensure that members have the right insurance coverage and to match work opportunities with teleworkers. Banks issue new small-business customers with home-based business machines. The focus of interest is workers who are able and willing to work in their own homes. The assumption behind much current management literature is that this is a potentially widespread phenomenon.

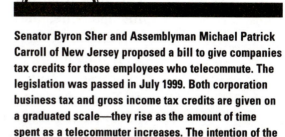

Senator Byron Sher and Assemblyman Michael Patrick Carroll of New Jersey proposed a bill to give companies tax credits for those employees who telecommute. The legislation was passed in July 1999. Both corporation business tax and gross income tax credits are given on a graduated scale—they rise as the amount of time spent as a telecommuter increases. The intention of the legislation is to reduce congestion and help alleviate road rage. Time will tell if the bureaucracy involved in calculating the tax credits outweighs the environmental benefits. And will the bureaucrats administering the legislation work from home or add to state congestion?

Charles Handy, in his book *The Empty Raincoat,* says:

> The new shape of work will center around small organizations, most of them in the service sector, with a small core of key people and a collection of stringers or portfolio workers in the space around the core....Software, telecommunications, environmental engineering, health products and services, and specialized education are increasingly the province of the tiny partnership. They are well suited to the portfolio worker, who costs much less if the firm does not have to house him or her.

No one would be surprised to find that these portfolio workers work from home with a personal computer, an answering machine, and a fax, and fill in their tax returns as self-employed individuals.

If they are not self-employed but still part of the company, these people may represent a problem for their employer. Some managers say that they find it harder to conceive of managing efficiently people who are out of sight. Managers seem to be afraid that if the workers are out of sight, the tasks will be out of mind. This is surely a management myth. People willing to work at home or away from the office are usually well able to complete tasks and to perform to a standard.

> **Q: *Do you not work at home, at least for some of the time?***
>
> **A: *Never. Of course, I could do much of my stuff there.***
>
> **Q: *So why don't you?***
>
> **A: *They won't let me.***
>
> *She pointed to the end of the room where, behind two large glass windows, sat the two deputy editors. "They like to have me where they can see me and shout at me."*
>
> **—ATLANTA JOURNALIST TALKING TO CHARLES HANDY,**
> **THE EMPTY RAINCOAT**

The real barrier may actually reside in the legal responsibility for an employer to see that staff are working in safe, healthy, insurable conditions wherever they may be. As discussed in later chapters, providing suitable furniture, lighting, and air quality in an office building is fraught with pitfalls. To do so in the homes of employees presents even more of an obstacle course unless the employees are fully self-certifying in health and safety.

Not all work, and not all homes, are suited to home-based work. Some organizations are seeking solutions where the commute is reduced but may not be eliminated; work takes place near but not at home. From Sweden to Hawaii via the Scottish Highlands, there are experiments with tele-cottages, neighborhood work centers. A *telecottage* is described as follows:

> A community centre, equipped with modern technology such as computers, fax and photocopiers, where local people can train or work using the resources provided....A community based workforce is a more committed workforce; this shows an increased motivation and productivity. City based companies are realizing this, and more and more work is being tendered out to telecottages, reversing the centralizing effects of the industrial revolution. (Source: Telecottage Wales).

There are countless examples of workforces located in unexpected, unconventional, non-office buildings, such as prisoners in an Irish jail handling the claims forms for an insurance company in the United States. One well-known, frequently quoted, and much researched organization in the United Kingdom, a pioneer of teleworking, is FInternational (FI), a computer programming company. It pioneered home-based working in the 1970s, being staffed by a group who preferred, and were able, to do part of their work in their own homes—women with children, whose high qualifications and expert skills might otherwise have been lost to the labor market. Interestingly, this group, once 600 staff with office space sufficient for only 60, has changed somewhat over time. It now has several office buildings; project teams are based in the FI offices more than on client premises or at home. The difference between this and many other consultancy organizations has diminished. The office building, and the scope it offers their functions, has been found to have a value.

Working from home sounds idyllic if the home is spacious, in a peaceful environment, and is well equipped. But many people prefer to keep a distance between their home life and their office. Home is less attractive for work if it is too small to provide a permanent place for the computer or it is filled with the noise of wailing two-year-olds or discontented teenagers out of work and into drum and base, or it is cold because day-long heating is too expensive. There are numerous difficulties to be resolved. Who pays the telephone bill? Do benefits, such as an agreement with the employer to pay a suitable proportion of the heating bill, have to be taxed? Who pays insurance, to cover what eventualities?

> *I would be quite happy to work from home. I don't particularly like coming into the office because it's particularly uncomfortable—it's very humid and gets very oppressive. It's also very noisy, so you can hear a phone conversation three, four, five desks away, and that can be very distracting.*
>
> *If I've got anything difficult to do, I stay at home—there's too many interruptions, it's too noisy in the office.*
>
> *I would kill to have a computer at home...and a printer.*

But on the other hand:

> *I view my home as somewhere in which the company doesn't intrude.*
>
> *I would not like to work at home; I like to keep home and work separate.*
>
> *I've got everything I need in the office, and I've got the people I need in the office. The remoteness of the home situation means I'd miss out on a lot of the informal side of things. I like the discipline.*
>
> —QUESTIONNAIRE RESPONSE ON HOME WORKING
> FROM MANAGEMENT CONSULTANTS

Will home office furniture have to comply with ergonomic requirements that are enforceable in an office setting? There are different home circumstances, different answers to

Figure 1.2   Going to work—at home.
(*Darius.*)

these questions given by each organization, and different individual temperaments, so people, even in a single organization, do not agree. Strong feelings are expressed on both sides of the argument (Fig. 1.2).

Alternate Officing

The world's largest accountancy firms and consultancy organizations, among others, are enthusiastically following another parallel avenue, that of "alternate officing," "desk sharing," or "hot-desking," as a way to acknowledge, and thereby exploit, the change in working patterns. With *desk sharing,* or *pooling,* someone who has just walked through the front door settles down at any one of the available desks. The term *hot-desking,* borrowed from "hot bunking" on submarines, assumes that the desk has just been vacated by a colleague and is reoccupied before the chair has had time to cool down. Desks are dubbed *touchdowns* when it is assumed that people settle there only briefly, like butterflies flitting in and out of the office. The people using these desks are variously described as *nomads, road warriors, peripatetic,* or merely *mobile.* Why even consider such a horrendous idea? Isn't it a thin disguise for squeezing people into unacceptably tight spaces? Who wants to give up the ownership of his or her desk? What lunatics are willing to give up their *own desks*? Who can stand sharing? Will any managers be willing to give up their *own offices*?

Desk sharing may or may not operate at the same time, or for the same individuals, as telecommuting. When one worker is at home or working on an airplane or a train, another one can be using the desk in the office. The convention whereby everyone is allocated a place of their own has been effectively challenged. What is new is that so much management attention is being applied to an alternative. But creating new conventions by overtly undoing the old is much more difficult than simply tolerating some unconventional groups on the fringes of the organization.

Not surprisingly, it is not just fashion that allows these threatening ideas to be considered. The search for an effective change in office conventions has developed from the realization that, for many types of so-called office work, the last place you would expect to find the worker is in the office. One of the best-known organizations to examine such possibilities is IBM, whose very existence has flourished by developing changes in the technology surrounding office work. IBM started its investigations in the United Kingdom, Canada, the United States, Japan, and Australia based on the supposition that its sales force should not be in the office. Sales representatives were meant to be maximizing "face time" with potential or existing clients. This is better done on a client's premises than in the sales representative's own office, the place where other salespeople are working on deals with the client's competitors. An active sales force results in a sea of empty desks, an expensive luxury at $50 to $150 per square foot per year (£300 to £1,000 per square meter per year.) The same holds true for other sales organizations. Other types of people are also often out of the office. Consultants, whose task is to get to know well the business of another organization, spend part, sometimes most, of their time on client premises. Other examples are inspectors checking that firms are following correctly the rules laid down by taxation and health and safety or other employment regulations, who often need to see the organizations actually at work, or journalists who must be away collecting material before crafting it into reports, or researchers in the field gathering data or interviewing people. All these are among the groups whose work takes them out of the office and may keep them out more than in.

The Space-Time Equation

In well-managed companies, the aim is now to make the best use of time as well as space in a building. The methods used to observe and document the use of space over time also allow managers to understand in more detail how staff spend their days. This can in itself be very helpful not only when replanning space but in other ways as well.

Managers or staff may know their general patterns of behavior, but they may give little serious thought to understanding the way in which people use buildings, so their knowledge is often mythological, only approximating to the truth. Careful documentation of whether and when people use their desks and offices can show startling results. Detailed observation may indicate that for as much as 80 percent of the working day, no use is made of the workplace provided. In effect, a person is in the office on average only one day in the week. While people may be aware that the nature of a job implies that this is likely to be the case, such knowledge is rarely translated into information bearing directly on the use of space.

Tools for looking at space use and deciding appropriate ratios of desks to staff numbers have been developed for, and used by, numerous organizations. They involve observers' recording use of space or activities that staff are engaged in. Records are made systematically, in a fashion similar to old time-and-motion studies. The outcome is a record of space productivity, or the way whole groups of people make use of space over time. Another source of information is diaries, filled in over a week or more, indicating where people have spent different parts of the working day. The results of these investigations give a graphic representation of where people need to be and what use is being made of office premises (Fig. 1.3).

It is easy to see why giving everyone their own desk may not make economic sense if people are rarely in the office. It is less easy to decide how many desks to distribute among how many people, what the rules should be about who gets priority of use, and how to deal with numerous practical details about sizes of groups, location of personal storage, the nature of equipment needed at the desk, and proximity to other office facilities. And what is the significance, if any, of the difference between pooled and shared desks?

What is well-occupied space? Other fields use various rules of thumb. Many airlines, theaters, and hotels find that 60 percent occupancy represents breakeven and that 70 percent is needed for a healthy financial position. Above that figure handsome profits accrue. To have hospital beds available for unexpected and emergency situations and for orderly changeover of patients, 5 percent must be empty at any one time. More vacancies increase the cost of health care; fewer mean that life-threatening shortages arise. In an

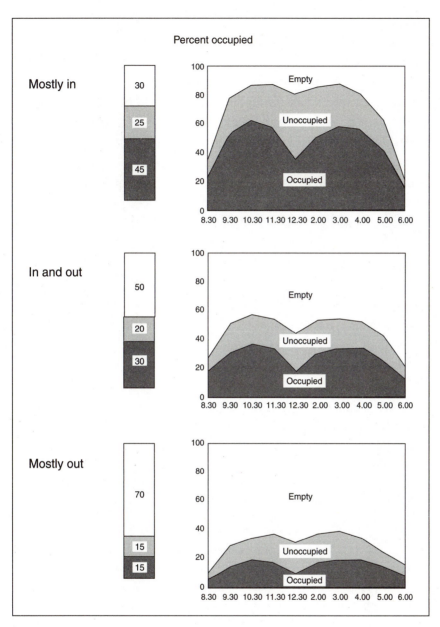

Figure 1.3 How different people use desks across the working day.

(*AMA, Alexi Marmot Associates.*)

office, if all employees always work at their desks when not on vacation or ill or in courses or training, they would be using the desk for only 75 to 85 percent of working days, depending on the holiday allowances and opportunities for training provided as part of their jobs. People who are additionally away from their desk for meetings or work outside the office with clients or traveling or are at home may be at their desks for only 10 to 20 percent of working days. So should your office be like a hotel and aim for 70 to 80 percent occupancy as a reasonably fully occupied desk pool? Or could you be more like a hospital and aim for 95 percent? The answer will vary according to the type of work that your organization does (Figs. 1.4 and 1.5).

Work Pattern	Typical Ratio of Desks to People	Percentage Desks
Mostly in	1:1	100
In and out	0.7:1 to 0.4:1	50–70%
Mostly out	0.3:1 to 0.1:1	10–30%

Figure 1.4   Planning the number of desks for mobile workers.

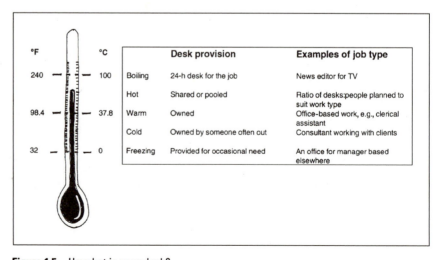

Figure 1.5   How hot is your desk?

To Share, to Pool, to Touch Down: That Is the Question

The way in which workplaces are allocated can vary. A "shared" desk implies that two or perhaps more individuals have the use of a single desk. This is initially an appealing and simple way to manage the problem of space. Similar to the concept of a timeshare vacation, this is a timeshare desk! The sharers can behave as if they owned the desk because their personal possessions can be stored there, they can agree with the colleagues with whom they share when they have the right to use it, who fills up the empty stapler, and whether to take each other's phone messages or tell callers when to phone again. The problem with this form of sharing is that some residual sense of ownership still operates. If each person's timetable cannot be fixed, then serious trouble can result. Coming into the office on an unplanned basis can produce the reaction, "Who's been sitting in *my* chair?" or the more disruptive, "Get out of my chair."

A "pool" of desks shared between a large group of people, who may sit at any desk in the pool, can avoid this problem but only at the expense of insisting that no one has a desk of which they own even a part share. The pool needs to be the right size; it needs to be managed so that the bullies do not corner their "own" desks where they always sit when they do come in. Furthermore, personal items have to be equally accessible to all the desks, yet not at any desk (Fig. 1.6).

Accessible touchdown desks can be provided for people who come in for very short periods. These are the equiv-

Figure 1.6
(Louis Hellman.)

alent of the stool at the restaurant counter where a snack takes a few minutes, rather than the table suitable for a longer meal. Restaurateurs know that, to function properly, tables must be cleared and salt, pepper, and sugar containers refilled. Some office organizations have taken similar steps for their liberated mobile workforce. Support staff replenish the stationery and supply the documents requested in advance by mobile workers. Not all managers are convinced that to provide and maintain communally owned staplers and other desk accessories is cost effective. The alternative is that all users of the desk bring their own desk accessories to it, either in their ordinary briefcase or in a desk tool kit that is stored nearby.

It is vitally important that personal storage for those who work at pooled desks is properly designed. Furniture manufacturers have started to consider the types of storage furniture suited to pooled-desk arrangements. The mobile personal pedestal and the part share in a communal cupboard have not proved totally successful; new designs are emerging constantly, and there is now a wide choice. Furniture available for this purpose is discussed in Chapter 5.

Enclosed offices can be pooled as well. The provision of fewer offices than people is far less widespread than desk sharing, though it occurs. Andersen Consulting, a large management consulting firm, has taken a radical step in this direction. In many of their locations there are enough consultants who would previously have been entitled to an owned office to allow a pool, at a ratio of one office per five people or more, to function effectively. Each office is identical; each is well decorated, with attractive pictures, desk accessories, and furniture. Just as consultants book hotel rooms in advance, so they book an office and, on arrival, find documents and mail already there and a telephone with their usual extension number on it. This system works only where there is a large number of cellular office users, most

Interpolis, an insurance organization in the Netherlands, has taken a bold step, deciding that their new premises would not provide an owned desk or office for any of their staff, regardless of the type of work they do. Instead, different work settings have been provided on each floor, allowing for open-plan work, group meetings, individual quiet work in tiny cells, relaxed coffee areas, and group and personal storage. Individuals take their personal work to the space of their choice for the day. They have compact wheeled storage cases—like a large briefcase fitted with hanging files and a stationery tray—for the items personal to themselves, and they make extensive use of IT and of the communal storage facilities. Adopting this approach has allowed the company to provide for all their staff in a single building rather than the two for which they had planned and budgeted. As a result, they have been able to provide many benefits for the staff: very high quality furniture, interesting interior environments with extensive planting and artworks, a variety of lighting and varied decor in shared areas, electrically operated height-adjustable desks, and individual opening windows in each small glass-enclosed work cell.

of whom are away a great deal. It also relies on effective secretarial backup that enables the right files and papers to reach offices in advance.

Even more important than the details of furniture and accessories is the development of clear rules about how people should use the pool of desks or offices and systems to ensure that everyone can be contacted effectively. These demand a mixture of management, spatial, and technical solutions. For example, touchdown and pooled desks must be obvious to the occasional user. Location and identity through color and style must help direct visitors and coworkers to these facilities, instructions for use must be obvious, clear, and simple, and operation by agreed rules must be encouraged and if necessary enforced. Communications systems—the telephone and message-transmission technologies—are being developed to serve situations in which people need to be contacted in different locations, within or outside the office. These are the foundations of the virtual office.

The Virtual Office

It doesn't matter whether you want to stay three months or just one day, whether you want the full office or just a token presence. Just walk in and you are in business.
—ADVERTISEMENT FOR CARLTON, THE INSTANT OFFICE NETWORK

The *virtual office* relies on the idea that technology is now capable of routing communications effectively to reach people, no matter where they are, so seamlessly that the people can behave as though they were physically nearby, as if in an old-style office building. The familiar certainty of location is effectively replaced by a new certainty, that of reaching *you,* as your office really is where you are. This is achieved at present by several strands of communications technology. Telephone systems can be rerouted to any location in a building if people stray from one desk or room to another, maintaining the telephone number as an adjunct of a person, not of any particular telephone. Radio links can extend communication beyond the building to the mobile phone that the caller assumes is in the office. Electronic mail and voice mail allow slightly disjointed but effective two-way communication between people on the move. Network connections, rapid and high-volume transmission of data, the development of video links all enable people out of the office—or without an office—to appear as if they are in one.

Many versions of virtual offices, known sometimes as "executive suites," exist. Some of the earliest were developed in airports, where busy executives could pay for secretarial help, photocopy and fax documents, and rent meeting space. They have spread to city centers and to suburbs, providing rooms, single rooms, suites, or sometimes only desks. Here an organization of 20, a one-man band, or the embryonic outpost of a large but distant parent company can access shared equipment and space for meetings, a shared reception and telephone system, and a complete

ANYWHERE OFFICE

The U.S. General Service Administration (GSA) has a new "product" to offer federal staff. The Anywhere Office is a division that provides remote-access systems to the growing federal mobile workforce. Wanda Smith is chief operations officer helping to solve the problems of applying the technology suitably. She says, "I tell the agencies that I don't think it's a question of whether we're going to do it. We're going to have to do it." There are already numerous examples of federal employees' using mobile equipment with appropriate systems and communications. Office of the Comptroller of the Currency examiners from the Treasury department collect data from banks around the nation to ensure that they meet federal standards. While on the road, they access the central database through their modems to upload data collected and stored in a mobile database. In a similar way Naval Quality Assurance inspectors now have the ability to use standardized equipment names to check and record data on palmtops while onboard ship, rather than on paper, and then to upload the data to a central database. This has greatly enhanced speed and accuracy.

smokescreen to hide the size of the organization or the identity of its next-door neighbor.

For a while a virtual office may be an apology for, or a concealment of, the fact of not being in a real one. In due course the term *office* is likely to be replaced or to change its connotations. It will be neither possible *nor desirable* to pretend that wherever you are is virtually an office. To be in an office akin to those of today will not be necessary for those companies that have shown that they do not need to be in such offices, that they function effectively in other modes. That some groups may remain in traditional office buildings for a long time to come will not invalidate new working methods.

"We Was Robbed!"

If you can work out the essential infrastructure and operational rules for a particular business, espousing new work practices and flexible approaches to office use, there is still a fundamental problem to be solved. That is the problem inherent in trying to change conventions and to create new relationships. Many people find it hard, even impossible, to feel positive about desk sharing or pooling or working in radically new ways with ground-breaking technology. The resistance is not simply to change. The difficulty is that the office is more than a job, the desk more than a tool for the task, and people feel deeply threatened by their loss. This is eloquently testified by the people quoted in the sidebar who were questioned six months after they had moved into a brand-new office with many improvements over the old one. As they are part of a group who have always spent most of their working time out of the office, their new desks are pooled and are no longer owned individually. From their reactions, clearly, the challenge is to find a way to realize the benefits of such a change without accruing a loss to employees and their productivity.

We was robbed! Why are we the only ones lumbered with this poor system? It wastes time, decreases feelings of personal involvement (I'm just a cog, I fit anywhere), reduces feelings of team involvement.

I do not like the shared-desk system. I am adapting to it. I understand the reasons for it....However, I think it is necessary for staff to have space that is their own. Work is an important part of most people's lives. It is their status, it is their source of livelihood, aspirations, and fulfillment. It is a very insecure world subject to many changes. I think that having one's own little reasonably secure space that can be personalized to a degree is psychologically very important to most people. From that "secure" space people can and do face "the rest" with more confidence. Although I can't prove it, and I doubt anyone else can, I think that one of the reasons for so much sickness since we moved is because the "secure" anchor has been removed. It is also a fact that many people use work as a "safe" haven from the pressures of domestic life. Their space at work is theirs—not the family's. It helps to keep the "stressors" in balance".

—QUESTIONNAIRE RESPONSES FROM PERSON IN A REFURBISHED OFFICE USING DESK POOLING

What Is the Office For If Everyone Is Working Somewhere Else?

In part, it's what it was always for, a place to come to for work. As important as the possibility of working away from the office is the change in the way office work is actually carried out within offices. The wholesale adoption of computers has meant that many office workers are far more productive but at the expense of being forced to adapt to using machines and subjected to discomfort and physical stress as a result. There is, as a result, more awareness of the tasks people actually accomplish during their time in an office and how the physical requirements of the tasks may differ. People think, write, record, and manipulate their own thoughts or information gleaned from other sources, talk on telephones or face to face, search files, and do many other varied activities in the course of a working day. All of these activities can, and do, take place in offices. The variety has become more widespread, applicable to a larger proportion of the workforce. More productive people make higher demands on their bosses for interesting and varied work. Greater understanding of physical stress related to computer work has stimulated the belief that variety in tasks is important for health. Faster communications between people has fostered the growth of more complex work interactions and helped to emphasize the value of teamwork. These developments mean that it is no longer appropriate to assume that a single type of workplace—an office or desk in one place in the building—is the best provision for a staff member in an office (Fig. 1.7).

Staff in organizations that have advanced down the route of new technologies, new organizational patterns, new ways of working, and flexible working may operate in a variety of ways, at different times in the working day. For different tasks, they may realistically need to move between distinct

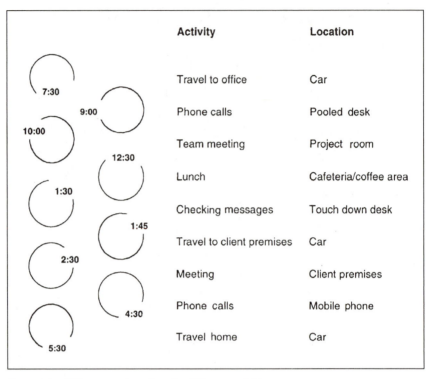

	Activity	Location
7:30	Travel to office	Car
9:00	Phone calls	Pooled desk
10:00	Team meeting	Project room
12:30	Lunch	Cafeteria/coffee area
1:30	Checking messages	Touch down desk
1:45	Travel to client premises	Car
2:30	Meeting	Client premises
4:30	Phone calls	Mobile phone
5:30	Travel home	Car

Figure 1.7 Different work settings for different activities.

locations, suited to the activity of the moment. This development changes the way offices are designed and equipped and judged to be good places to work.

If it is accepted that the office building cannot be designed equally well for all functions, on what should it concentrate? The concept that attracts the media is that of the club, the place where people come together not only for planned meetings and face-to-face teamwork but also for the important serendipitous benefits of unexpected meetings and the exchange of apparently unrelated ideas. You are a member; you don't have to attend from nine to five. You are there from choice because it serves your needs. The business lounge, the business-class waiting room of an airport, is the prototype of the office worker's club. The airline provides the receptionist who greets you, ensures that the

accommodate the needs of new work patterns as they emerge. The building and what it offers will need far more conscious and directed management if it is to support the needs of staff working in more flexible ways. The first-level benefits of reduced cost of space, of energy, and other running expenses, and the second-level benefits consequent on the new individual freedoms of personal time and space, are purchased at quite a high price. One obvious cost is that of installing efficient communications links. The entire project founders if the technology does not deliver what it has promised. Less frequently recognized is the need to train people to use the new technology and the new type of office space effectively and to nurse them carefully through the transitional phases. A new need must be recognized—to ensure that the building and the way it can be used are immediately understood by users. New signs and symbols need to be developed to combat unfamiliarity with the office building among infrequent users and the loss of a sense of personal or group identity. To meet this need requires knowledge and people: *knowledge* of how to provide and manage storage, how to choose the correct number and types of desks or offices, how to acknowledge rights and duties of staff in relation to these workplaces, and *people,* such as receptionists and backup staff to help those who are rarely present but need to access the hub of communications in order to support their work. These backup staff may get lonely, bored, or confused by seeing some people only rarely, and their needs too must be considered.

IBM UK took a very broad and comprehensive look at new ways of working. They created the SMART (Space, Morale and Remote Technology) program, and they worked as hard at the morale and remote technology elements as at the space issues. The early stages of the program followed a strict set of project principles, important to the success of new ventures. Data gathering in advance to determine appropriate ratios of people to workplaces was extensive.

User needs were carefully investigated. Trials were implemented and feedback gathered. Then the SMART approach was ready to go live. The effects were monitored, and the roll-out continued, allowing new technology to be used more extensively and many unwanted buildings to be emptied and sold. It evolved into the Teambase program that is now used in all IBM offices in Europe.

IBM's approach is one that needs to be considered for all such ground-breaking projects. Only when the ideas are common currency, when concepts such as pooling or ratios of desks to people are understood by managers and users alike, when the right furniture and telephone systems have been sold in their millions, will it be easy to embark on changed ways of providing office space without careful data, user consultation, and pilot trials.

Summary

This chapter helps to clarify how to accommodate your organization to exploit some of the new ways of working. It allows you to assess whether you need a traditional office building or something very different. The effects of new technology on office work patterns are discussed in relation to their impact on buildings. This is of particular relevance to the types of organizations listed at the start of the chapter.

Maximum publicity is being given to the concept of "location-free work." The development of communications technology first brought the office together and now is enabling it to drift apart. The extent to which this idea is accepted will vary according to how suitable it is for a particular organization.

Telecommuting describes the option to avoid the journey to the office by working elsewhere, be it at home or at a local office. Management does not always find it easy to accept that people will be sufficiently motivated to carry out their allotted tasks if they are not under its eye. Generally this has not been found to be a problem in practice. More difficult is that isolation may not suit everyone, and not all homes provide a good work environment.

Observations show that in some organizations desks may be unoccupied as much as 80 percent of the time. It is necessary to know what the actual pattern of use is before making plans; this requires methods for systematic observation. The trends and prospects for future change are equally important. New ways of providing furniture and equipment are being sought. Ways to organize the office for those who use it only occasionally are still being developed. The temptation to arrange for two or more people to share a specific desk should be resisted. Where possible, a pool of desks, available to a larger number of people on a first-come-first-served basis, is more likely to work. Any innovative solution will require more management time to be devoted to it than the traditional one person-one desk. In an extreme situation some people may have a virtual office and communications systems that enable them to simulate the fixed office when, in reality, they may be anywhere at all.

A new way of planning for people who are often out of the office may be well justified but is unlikely to be popular with everyone. It needs to be well prepared, implemented only for those to whom it is really suited, and taken seriously by managers to the extent that they also use pooled space if at all possible. Even when accepted, the real sense of loss that people experience must be understood and taken into account. There must be real advantages for the individuals involved as well as for the organization. If undertaken merely as a space-saving exercise, hot-desking is not likely to be a success.

Whatever changes are undertaken, the specific solutions for technology, furniture, plan layout, and management are crucial. These must be worked out carefully and based on good data.

CHAPTER 2

Know Your Organization and Know Your Building

CASE HISTORIES   See Case Histories 6, 7, and 8 on pages 313–331

O ffice buildings are a physical expression of the match between the needs of an organization and its functions. The success of the match depends on understanding both sides of the equation, the organization and the building.

Office work pervades every sector of the economy. It takes place in organizations that are public, private, locally based or global; profitable or unprofitable; creative or routine; tiny or vast; well managed or chaotic; steeped in tradition or avant garde; growing, stable, or declining. The conduct of work varies enormously in different organizations as does the pace of work, the way in which it happens, and how people relate to one another. Yet the argument of this book is that the spatial issues that must be addressed to create suitable work environments are constant. This is not to diminish the importance of the variety of different work cultures. Examples of that variety follow.

The Academic Office Environment

If you work in a university or college, you will find that much of the description below is about your offices:

- All academics want rooms of their own—space for heads-down, concentrated work is the main need. Offices shared by two or three are reluctantly accepted and open plans are strongly resisted.

- The hierarchy is very important and clearly marked out as space is allocated differently for full-tenured professors, assistant or associate professors, senior or junior lecturers, research associates or assistants, and administrative staff.

- Control of space is essential. Each department within the wider university or college tries to cling to its space denying other departments access. Without space the department cannot grow. Without growth, additional research projects cannot commence. Without new research projects, steps on the academic ladder cannot be reached.

- Computer power and connectivity is usually high.

- Walls of shelves and filing cabinets to store books and papers can never be too numerous.

- "Clean desk" policies can never be enforced.

- Budgets are always modest; furniture is functional; style is utilitarian; people are allowed to humanize and personalize their space in their own way.

Offices for Large Retail Organizations

Large retailers have small offices for local managers within each retail outlet, plus a central head office where all of the main business decisions are taken. The local offices tend to be hidden away in spare space behind the delivery bays and somewhere near a staff room where salespeople stop for their breaks. Head offices are more orderly and are characterized by the following:

- Large reception areas where suppliers gather before meeting buyers

- Generous offices for the top managers

- Small desks in open-plan layouts for buying departments

- Interspersed among the office space is storage space for setting out product lines from household items, clothing and small accessories, or food products to large bulky items like sofas and garden furniture

- Suites of meeting rooms well equipped for audiovisual presentations

- Some specialized rooms for storing perishable goods under refrigeration

Offices for Cultural Establishments

Museums, art galleries, libraries, and theaters all operate thanks to the work done by three populations: front-of-house staff who interact with the public; operational staff who look after the contents (conservation, cleaning, stage set building, framing and transportation of the artworks); and office-based staff who determine the direction of the establishment and its collection, keep the organization solvent, write catalogues, prepare performances or exhibitions, and inform the public of its contents. This third group may number several hundred in a large national museum or just a few people in a small organization. Whatever the size of the establishment, office space comes second to the space for the main activity (housing art, exhibitions, plays, or books). Offices tend to be found in "Cinderella" space—basements, annexes, old wings that are relatively inaccessible, new wings inserted to house a few more people, or short-term space rented down the road. These offices share the following characteristics:

- Communication among different departments is often a problem because of the scattered layout.

- Expenditure on office furniture and systems is rather modest.

- Management of the office space may be rather amateur as the main space management efforts are directed at the front of house.

- Some of the office staff prefer to work heads down in cells as they come from academic traditions.

- Others are more comfortable with team offices or open-plan arrangements for tasks such as cataloguing or finance.

- Storage of books and papers in vast quantities is common.

Offices for e-business and New-Technology Companies

The companies responsible for creating and marketing the new technologies and services in the Internet, computing, and telecommunications that influence everyone else's office work share common features in the way they house themselves:

- As the companies are quite youthful, they tend to have few outward shows of differences between top management and the most junior levels.

- Using the new technologies is common within them even if the best and latest is sometimes reserved for customers.

- Impressive showcases and training areas for customers, dealers, and staff form part of many of their buildings.

- Work mobility is common to the way sales teams operate, so the office for them is an occasional stopping point in a work rhythm that includes customer premises, cars, planes, trains, hotel rooms, and home.

- Storage is primarily electronic.

- The company image must be that of a functional, up-to-date, well-organized operation.

- To attract and retain excellent young staff, the buildings include many relaxed places for solo and teamwork plus some play space and relaxed catering areas.

Offices for Banks, Insurance Companies, and Other Financial Players

Financial institutions come in many shapes and forms from retail, commercial or investment banks, stockbrokers and trading houses, insurers and reinsurers, home loan mortgage companies, asset management operations, and credit card companies. Many are long-established companies that in one guise or another (and several mergers away) were founded more than a hundred years ago. Others are newcomers created to sell financial services directly to consumers through the telephone and Internet, thus avoiding much of the costly infrastructure of the older companies. Some of the characteristics of the offices are:

- A significant presence in the main trading centers of the world's finance capitals—Wall Street, London, Frankfurt, Tokyo, and Hong Kong

- Utter dependence on computers, hence a lot of office space for IT departments

- Trading floors for some of their staff consisting of tightly packed desks each equipped with multiple computer screens, creating an electronic bazaar for buying and selling stock

- Back-office clerical factories for processing transactions housing large numbers of relatively junior people

- Call centers where queries are answered, housed in suburban centers or office parks away from the expensive metropolitan centers

- Headquarter offices redolent of solidity, wealth, and history, with enough artworks and elegant meeting rooms to impress on key investors that the organization is long established, safe, and solvent

- Reduced reliance on paper processing as electronic records gradually dominate all transactions

- Growing introduction of remote work and home work for some parts of the organization—for example, insurance claims settled without any paperwork by roving inspectors reliant solely upon laptops operated from customer premises, cars, or their own homes

Offices of Large Accounting and Consulting Firms

The last 20 years have witnessed breathtaking growth in the dependence of public and private organizations on the services of a few vast international accounting firms with their allied consulting operations. Mergers now leave a handful of such partnership companies checking and advising others on how best to further their businesses. Their offices can be described as follows:

- Located in the major cities of the globe with growing presence in Asia, Africa, Latin America, and Eastern Europe.

- Path breakers in pushing the limits of efficient space use through implementing desk sharing for young audit trainees and hoteling for consultants.

- Struggling to define a balance between the space demands of partners (ideally large corner offices) and space efficiency (pooled offices and desks, as partners are often away).

- Suites of meeting rooms, some elegantly decorated to impress key clients.

- They are happy to announce their presence to the outside world with big lettering and neon signs atop their buildings.

- Traditionally they provide very clear space increments that parallel career advancement from trainee to auditor or consultant, managing consultant, partner, to senior partner, though this is breaking down as space efficiency increases.

Offices for Major Industries—Manufacturing, Energy, and Transportation

Offices in these companies are just a small part of the building stock that also comprises factories, research and development laboratories, processing plants, exploration bases, workshops and maintenance zones, and stations and terminals. Yet the headquarters and central office functions accommodate vast numbers of people to keep the organizations ticking. Offices need to house the board and top management, strategic departments who help define the future directions by examining trends and exploring new product concepts, sales and marketing operations, finance, human resource and training sections, information technology, and a miscellany of other central functions including communications and public relations, property and real estate, legal, purchasing, and health and safety departments.

These businesses deal with different preoccupations and locational imperatives. Some common themes typically emerge, however:

- Main headquarters are usually in the central city area of a major financial center.

- However, some have their HQ on or close to one of their major operational sites.

- Management is pressured to reduce the number of staff in the central operations and to reduce the costs of the HQ; hence, they may move to more suburban locations or office parks.

- Management may outsource some activities to other organizations to help the pace of downsizing the HQ.

- The HQ must look and feel suitably opulent.

- The culture of the company is often balancing the dominant culture of its skill base (e.g., chemistry, engineering, geology) with the multidisciplinary need of the business.

- Investment in new technology is essential; hence, office buildings and their contents are not allowed to fall too out of date.

- The company evolves through frequent mergers and acquisitions that require much effort to unite the image and processes between formerly discrete companies in different buildings.

- Corporate history is a source of pride and may demand space for displaying artifacts and an archive.

Offices for Creative Industries

Offices for creative industries are made up of a combination of routine and mainstream departments (finance and IT) plus departments that more directly shape the business. The overall image in such organizations is usually youthful and casual:

- Much creative work is done in teams, which requires that spaces be provided for teams to meet in conference rooms, project rooms, coffee bars, and chill-out areas.

- The corporate image is projected clearly from reception areas on through into the building. Depending on the industry, books will be displayed in every office, or a TV will broadcast, or music will be played, or posters displayed.

- Hierarchies tend to be unimportant in spatial terms.

- Apart from newspaper and TV, locations are usually within a few large cities filled with bright young people whose ideas dominate the cultural frontiers. New York, Los Angeles, London, and Boston play a significant role.

- Buildings are often outside the most expensive central areas, and creative management groups dare to take on slightly difficult structures, converting them to a space that expresses the corporate image.

- Materials, colors, and finishes are lighthearted and explorative. Cheap plastic or recycled manufactured goods may be used to create internal walls, ceilings (e.g., painted TV remote controls or crushed recycled aluminum soft drink cans).

Government Offices—Federal, State, and Local

Vast bureaucracies are essential to keep modern social and economic systems functional: to defend our countries; to ensure that taxes are paid; to educate the young; to ensure that the poor receive medical treatment, housing, and enough money for survival; to ensure that justice is served; to preserve the environment; and to regulate industries. At a state or local level, smaller bureaucracies are needed to run and maintain sanitary services, schools, libraries, street lighting, fire protection, roads, and highways. What are the peculiar characteristics of offices for the public employees helping to deliver our common infrastructure?

- They are housed in vast office building clusters, in small areas within the capital cities. The older of these buildings are likely to evoke associations of the classical

Empire of Rome—being built to impress. The modern buildings are more varied.

- Town halls and city administrative buildings similarly are built to impress, both internally and externally.

- The growth of public administration in this century will have resulted in the accumulation of many office properties close by serving to house back-office personnel or to foster new government initiatives.

- The ceremonial parts of government need their own spaces for elected representatives to meet in committees and in debating and voting chambers.

- Modest furnishings and fittings are the order of the day—public accountability suggests that overt signs of comfort and elegance should be avoided.

- Space allocation is governed by clear sets of principles laid down by bodies such as the General Services Administration. Status and job type dictate spatial provision.

- Vast amounts of paper filing are essential in most departments, though electronic record storage is starting to make inroads.

Legal Offices

If you are a lawyer or an attorney, you probably work in a partnership with many other lawyers, trainee lawyers, and support staff. And you probably have, demand, and cannot conceive of working without an office of your own. The typical spatial formula for large legal practices consists of the following:

- A location in one of the world's main financial or manufacturing centers or capitals

- Many small offices around the perimeter of the building for lawyers

- Open-plan or small-group offices for legal secretaries and other support staff

- A wing with the meeting rooms for clients, furnished tastefully with a balance between traditional (you can trust us with your affairs—we are solid and have been around a long time) and modern (yet we know the ways of the world and are up to date with every new twist of business, government, and society)

- Paper everywhere starting with a legal library, spreading into every office down into file rooms, basements, and off-site archival offices

- Space pressure due to growth, which may have required junior lawyers to share offices (They won't like it, but they will find that it still works.)

- In a few cases, experiments with fully open plan arrangements plus a number of small rooms for concentrated work (This arrangement is more common for the legal department within a large corporation, which in turn may have moved to an open plan throughout.)

- Space pressure and the desire to reduce overhead with the result of many more firms' reallocating their space, experimenting with more open space, more space sharing and mobile office work off site, perhaps at home, with clients, for best concentration

Know Your Building

Influencing behavior is almost all of what management is about, and buildings influence behavior. Failure to wring every benefit out of the most expensive capital asset most companies ever have would not be countenanced in any other aspect of corporate life.

—JOHN A. SEILER, "ARCHITECTURE AT WORK."
Harvard Business Review, 120, September–October 1984.

Are you a prisoner in your own building, or does it serve you? How well do you know your building? The first requirement for making the most of an asset is to know what the asset is. The next is to know how it may be used to your benefit. If you were asked a few basic questions about your building, could you answer them or, at least, get the right answer with a single telephone call? For example, how big is it? How much space do you have? What does it cost you, as a percentage of revenue and per person? When was it built, and with what form of construction? What kind of tenure do you have? Do you have an air-handling system and, if so, what type? Is your plant operating at optimum levels for your requirements? And so on. If information is not available, or is inaccurate, or is in the hands of others, you will have less power to make sensible decisions and be more likely to be maneuvered down routes chosen by others, which may not suit your needs.

It is commonplace to read that a business's greatest asset is its staff—so much so that it seems impossible to believe that there was ever a time when managers did not know this. It is well understood that there is considerable investment in people, that they take time to train, both in the ways of the business and in specific knowledge and skills in their particular field. The armed forces, for example, know that it takes 15 years to train a good officer. This being the case, one justifiably may wonder how they could ever have been so profligate as to throw away their investment by dismissing women officers when they became pregnant. The policy indicated that, at one time, the forces did not fully understand that their major asset is people. Such lack of understanding is no longer usual. Industry is increasingly knowledge based, and it is people who have the monopoly on the use of knowledge, so their importance is accepted.

After Salaries, What Costs Most?

Buildings do. The capital cost of buildings is not ignored but is viewed as a necessary evil, as an outlay up front or in the form of a loan or rent. Office buildings may also be treated as a potential crock of gold as a result of speculation in the property business. Neither view is complete; neither looks at the ways in which a building can best serve the needs of the organization. After staff salary costs, the next biggest bill for office-based organizations is that associated with buildings—renting, rating, running, and repairing them. Accommodating each member of staff typically costs between $2,500 and $15,000 per year. A wide variety of rents in different cities affects the cost (Fig. 2.1). To make the best use of this inevitable expense demands some knowledge of buildings on the part of management. Companies change rapidly—this is more and more of a truism—yet buildings last a long, long time. Buildings must continue, through many changes and adjustments, to be a valuable asset, to serve and protect organizations. They have the potential to do these things. Skill and understanding are needed to deliver them.

Yet business shelves in bookshops are strangely empty of texts that explain anything at all about buildings to managers of companies. Managers of the buildings are somewhat better served, but they do not manage the business. The skills associated with management of people and understanding business cultures are naturally the most important since people are a company's main asset and their biggest cost. Nonetheless, it seems reasonable that the next biggest cost item, the building, should not simply be regarded as a liability, a drain on resources. The scale of financial liability is considerable. An office may cost 10 to 20 percent of company revenue annually to acquire, operate, and repair. Its role as an asset is considerable. Its potential lies not only in the capital balance sheet but also in enhancing productivity and wellbeing. It can be a positive influence on behavior, an enabler or inhibitor, a tool to improve service to customers, and an influence on business cultures. These aspects should also be explored and understood in order to maximize benefits or, at the very least, to reduce waste.

In economic booms, the property market plays a major role in financial planning and management in many businesses. Managers within individual organizations, not merely property dealers and real estate agents, become aware of the asset values represented by buildings as never before. Large profits can be made from property deals. Some companies are bought simply to be acquired, and then

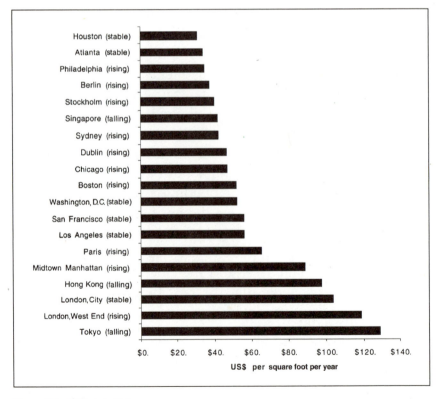

Figure 2.1   Office rents.

World Office Rents (July 1999) Richard Ellis, St. Quentin, London immediately sell their undervalued property holdings. In booms it seems as if the upward spiral of value cannot be halted. Some companies draw dangerous conclusions from what they see happening in the marketplace. They act as if their organizations are qualified to take on the role of a property development business merely because they are building owners or occupiers.

All organizations employ staff with financial skills or have a group of financial advisers with whom they are in regular contact. Finance directors, usually some of the most senior people in an organization, are able to assess advice on leases, taxation issues, and rents. However, finance directors frequently have a considerable gap in their knowledge of buildings and their contents. Generally these do not fall within the experience of senior management. Either senior management relies on specialized external expertise or, at the other end of the spectrum, assumes that anyone with common sense who has worked in an office has the necessary skills to make decisions about a building. Some businesses do consider the efficient running of their building to be a major concern. Specialized expertise is often employed within large organizations in a property or facilities department. Generally, however, the status of even the most senior people in that area is comparatively low. In large UK companies surveyed recently, none had its most senior property executive on the main board, although they generally agreed that these days the property department is a bit "less of a Cinderella." Frequently the role is shared in smaller companies, where it is often part of the responsibility of the finance director, with personnel or human resources involved to some extent. A current trend is to accept that management of the building is not core business and to decide that it should be left to experts in independent organizations hired to carry out the necessary functions. Facilities management companies are sprouting everywhere, ready to save you money on all aspects of building decisions and management. They probably can, but you are the one who holds the knowledge of what you really need.

The value of buildings to an organization is influenced, among other things, by whether they are efficient and appropriate and whether they project the right image to staff and clients. Senior managers need some knowledge of how such qualities may be achieved. They must be able to instruct and assess the specialists who understand buildings and interior outfitting and be able to check that decisions do not ignore important potential. Some of the vital characteristics of buildings can be readily measured, others less easily.

How Big Is It?

This sounds like a simple question and the answer so obvious that it must be unimportant. Not so. If it were so simple, everyone would have the right answer, but they do not. They often have no answer at all without asking their lawyer what they are paying rent for; and, if they do that, they may have no idea of what the answer really means. And it is not unimportant. Rent is usually related directly to floor area and is expressed in terms such as dollars per square foot or pounds per square meter. Other costs—local taxes, daily running and maintenance, the cost-in-use—are all dependent on the building size and design and can all be described in area-related terms. Value for money cannot be assessed in a vacuum; it concerns relative costs. Expression of cost per unit area allows relative costs for different buildings and for different ways of running buildings to be compared and the best ones for the purpose to be selected.

Information always helps people to make decisions. Consider energy costs. One of the easiest ways for an energy manager to achieve large savings for an organization is to learn how much energy is used, for example, to discover the peak electrical load that the company requires and to make sure that only the appropriate tariff is paid. Equally easily, money can be lost by, say, signing a long-term agreement for a rate based on inaccurate information, such as an assumed annual consumption that is higher than the actual one. The same is true of space. If total area is inaccurately measured or if the two parties to a contract are not measuring the same things, someone (usually the occupier) gets a bad deal.

A plan drawing of the building is an important starting point. The drawings must be to scale—any scale will do, provided it is stated on the drawings—and show the main building structure, the windows, the escape stairs, the elevators, the water closets (WCs), and, if possible, the electrical and other services. It does not matter if the wall partition and furniture layouts are not up-to-date. Changes in these are easily sketched on to a drawing that has the correct dimensions of the building's main features. Frequently managers lose track of where suitable plans can be found in buildings only a few years old, so that new ones have to be created from a fresh accurate survey. This is not difficult to do, but it costs time and money. It is astonishing how hard it often is to get hold of a proper scale drawing because, for example, "The architect came from out of state and anyway went out of business, so we have no drawings of the building." "We have CAD (computer-aided design) drawings on disk but we don't have the software to read them." People who deal with leases are content with rudimentary drawings or none at all. Maintenance engineers often have simplified sketches of the building, with electrical or heating information superimposed diagrammatically, which are adequate for their needs but not enough for decisions about space.

Even with a good plan, measuring a building is not simple because it has many layers, like an onion. There is one size when you measure round the outside, another when you measure around the inside of the outside walls, another when you exclude the space taken up by cores, which contain essential ducts and plant rooms, elevators, and fire stairs. The size of each layer is relevant for different reasons. Fortunately, there are rules that can be used to decide how each layer is defined. American National Standards Institute (ANSI) and Building Owners and Managers Association International (BOMA) published the *Standard Method for Measuring Floor Area in Office Buildings* in 1996, to define space measurements. Rules used in the United Kingdom emanate from the Royal Institute of Chartered Surveyors where real estate agents are born. Not surprisingly, these are the ones that matter most for rent. The inner layers are the ones that matter for the occupier, as they concern the areas that can be used for business purposes. Space planners and interior designers have been busy, in the last decade or so, refining rules that describe the inner layers.[1]

Terminology for Main Components of the Building Area and the Measurement Categories Used in This Book

Structure and core. Walls, columns, plant rooms, stairs, lifts, WCs, and lobbies.

Primary circulation. Main corridors; horizontal routes required for escape in case of fire.

Fit factor. Space that is unusable because of building peculiarities.

Support space. For all the building: cafeteria, library, reprographic services, and conference suite.

Ancillary space. For departments or groups: group files, local copier, and project area.

Workspace. Desks, offices, and the local circulation to reach them.

Gross external area (GEA). Whole building round the outside of the walls.

Gross internal area (GIA). Whole building to inside of outer walls.

(Continued)

---

[1]Numerous versions of the area measurement terms used here may be found in other books, and in the real estate planning and management documents of any organization. The principles outlined here remain the same, though the terminology and precise area definitions can vary.

Terminology for Main Components of the Building Area and the Measurement Categories Used in This Book

(Continued)

Net internal area (NIA). Gross internal area less all structure and cores; the area on which rent is usually paid (sometimes called the net lettable area, or **NLA**).

Net usable area (NUA). NIA less primary circulation.

Terminology used in the United States:

Gross building area. Measuring to outside finished surface of permanent outer walls.

Floor rentable area. Gross building area less major vertical penetrations (similar to, but larger than, NIA as it includes a proportionate share of the lobby and other shared elements).

Floor usable area. Office area as enclosed between finished surfaces of office area (similar to NUA).

As Bert Parfet, for the Building Owners and Managers Association International (BOMA) points out, the detailed differences in the way in which area is measured may mean that figures, such as rent per square foot, are not strictly comparable between countries. However, this does not affect the principles behind the argument.

Figure 2.2 indicates the different areas that are useful to measure on a building plan. The details of measurements of all the different layers need not be committed to memory, but the rules of thumb about efficiency, which express the relationship between the areas, are useful. Until you know the areas involved, you cannot determine how space efficient your building is.

It is instructive to check existing records of areas measured for different purposes and to ascertain that they have been clearly defined, that they match the areas described in the following paragraphs, and that those that should be the same actually are. For example, is the amount of space measured for a cleaning contract the same as the area rented? If they are identical, were they both measured independently, or was one inaccurate measure copied from the other? If they

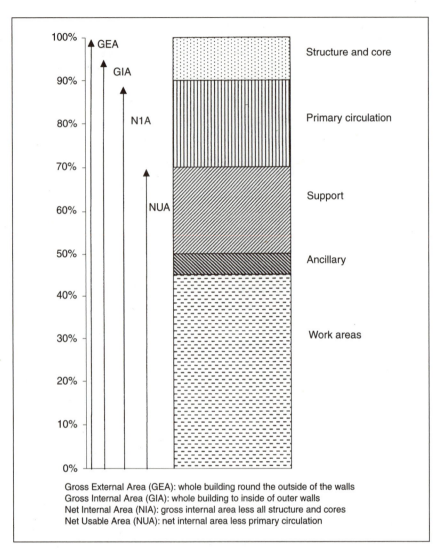

Figure 2.2   Know your building area.

(AMA Alexi Marmot Associates.)

differ, what is the reason? If the area cleaned is larger than that rented, are you cleaning someone else's space—say, the landlord's common areas? If so, is this reflected in rent or service charges? And so on. Someone must be sure of what areas have been measured before any of these questions can reliably be answered.

The first two items, core and structure, are givens in any building. Their efficiency is of concern to the owner of the capital tied up in the building. The third, primary circulation, falls within the *net lettable area* (NLA)[2]—the rented area—and yet it cannot be used except to move around the building. The larger it is in relation to the lettable area, the more rent is effectively being paid for the usable area. The shape of a building, as well as how it is used, has an effect on the necessary primary circulation routes.

The last three area categories—support, ancillary, and workspace—are what the occupier wants the building for. How the *net usable area* (NUA) is divided between these categories is in the hands of the user and will be considered in later chapters.

As a result of peculiarities of the building itself, to fit all the necessary uses into the building may require more space than at first seems the case. This is space that is effectively wasted. There is no standard term for this, but it can be thought of as *building-related waste.* It is high where irregular shapes cannot accommodate sensible furniture layouts, where perimeter space is wasted by intermittent radiators or air-handling units that prevent the use of a narrow fringe all round the space, where columns or structural walls break up useful areas into the wrong sizes. An example of the type of problem that occurs is seen in a recently designed office with distinctive curved bay windows on all upper floors. When you get inside, you find that the floor is raised by one step in the bays. The curved shape, although attractive, is in itself not much use for office furniture, so some space is inevitably wasted. To make matters worse, the raised area is too small to use for a desk or small meeting table so that

[2]Similar measurement conventions exist in the United States, published by ANSI/BOMA, Ref Z65.1-1996, "Standard Method for Measuring Floor Area in Office Buildings." It is an American National Standard, approved June 7, 1996. There are some differences from the standards used in this book.

the whole bay is difficult to use for anything other than having a potted plant or piles of old files. This problem is often serious in historic buildings, although a delightful environment can result from room sizes, structure, and many attractive architectural features that are inefficient and inconvenient for office planning.

Is It Efficient?

Space efficiency, thermal efficiency, maintainability, and so on are all aspects of efficiency. Here space efficiency is at issue; the others are considered later. Space efficiency is about how well a building is suited to office use, both for the occupants and for the working patterns of a particular organization. Space efficiency involves choosing well-designed space and making good use of it, *not* squeezing into space that is too small. It is always possible to cut down on area by providing minimal desks and no amenities. This is not efficient if it fails to deliver a good, productive working environment.

The relationships between the areas identified in Figure 2.2 is one way of measuring space efficiency. If the area on which you pay rent, the NLA, is large but the area you can actually use for accommodation of staff and equipment, the NUA, is very much smaller, then the building is inefficient for the user. The higher the rent paid per square meter, the worse is the value for money to the user of an inefficient building. As a rule of thumb, an acceptable building, from the tenants' point of view, is one in which the primary circulation represents between 15 and 20 percent of the lettable area, or, expressed another way, the ratio of usable to lettable space is between 85 and 80 percent. (Note: When primary circulation is 20 percent of NUA, it is only 15 percent of NLA, so keep checking the figures if using rules of thumb.) Where the primary circulation is less than 15 percent of the NLA, the building is efficient. Where it is more than 20 percent, it is poor. The difference may seem small, but take 5 percent of a 5,000-ft^2 area of office space—that is, 250 ft^2—at $40 per square foot per year (not an exceptionally high rent), and the saving on an efficient over an inefficient area is $7,500 to be paid year after year. In addition, with an extra 250 ft^2 of usable office floor, you could accommodate three or four more people. So space you cannot use is extremely expensive, in terms of both cash and opportunity lost. To justify the cumulative impact of paying for an inefficient building over many years, the building must offer other compensating factors, such as lower-than-average rent, terrific location, exceptional architectural quality, usable floors that are especially suited to departmental needs, or a combination of many plus factors. The compensating factors need to be kept constantly under review to check that they are still valid—for example, that the rent stays below average, that the location is still excellent.

The time to get the efficiency right is when making a move to a new or a refurbished building, as most of the relevant factors are fixed once the building is built. So if you got a bad bargain at your last move, there may be little to be done about it. Working out the efficiency of an existing building is still worthwhile. Really understanding the process of collecting and using measurements is invaluable when it comes to a move, and doing it is the best way to understand it. Knowing just how good—or bad—your current building is may help you to make the decision about whether or not to move and will provide a benchmark against which to judge future options.

Other area-efficiency calculations can be made. The area of the whole building, the gross internal area (GIA), includes all the internal structure, walls, and columns holding up the building inside the inner face of the outside walls, and the cores. If this area is very much larger than the area for which rent can be charged, then the building is inefficient for the owner. The larger the GIA, the more expensive (other things being equal) the building is to build and maintain. If it has a small lettable area, the capital outlay is not working as efficiently as it would for a building at the same rent level with a proportionately larger lettable area. For owner occupiers, the gross is effectively the same as the lettable area since that is what they are paying to run. But the two different measures of efficiency still need to be considered separately, based on the layers of the onion in Figure 2.2.

Does It Enhance Your Image?

The building does not need to be lavish for the answer to be yes. Danger lurks for the organization whose chief executive responds to the suggestion that elegance, not opulence, should be the objective of a new building design by saying, "There's nothing wrong with a bit of opulence if it is in the right place," and then proceeds to specify a 400-ft^2 office

Some Rules of Thumb for Guidance

Owner efficiency. When the ratio of lettable to gross internal area is 80 percent or more, it is good, and when it is 70 percent or less, it is poor.

Tenant efficiency. When the ratio of usable to lettable area is 85 percent or more, it is good, and when it is 75 percent or less, it is poor.

Primary circulation. Allow about 15 percent additional space over and above the area required for work, ancillary, and support activities. If you have a complicated floor plan, this percentage will increase. If you need much more than 20 percent, a change of layout may be indicated.

Fit factor. 3 percent or less of lettable area is good; 5 to 10 percent of lettable can easily happen. Over 10 percent is worth worrying about.

Internal partitions. 5 percent of lettable area occupied by partitions might occur even in an open-plan building; 15 percent of lettable area occupied by partitions could be the consequence of a highly cellularized building.

for himself with attached shower, WC, and kitchenette, plus a boardroom rarely used and able to accommodate only a custom-designed, crescent-shaped boardroom table. (This particular organization ended up having to vacate its building within a couple of years. Those special bits of tailor-made opulence proved the hardest part of the building to replan successfully for the leaner, fitter organization that took it over.) Office opulence may cost the director his job. The London headquarters for the European Bank for Reconstruction and Development were extravagantly designed, and large sums were spent in changing the almost new lavish reception area provided by the building owner. Once the renovation cost was made public, the fired director no longer had the opportunity to enjoy his new office.

A building needs to be able to accommodate the evolving needs of a business, so that organizational change is not held back or distorted by its limitations. It needs to support people, not frustrate them. When a building cannot support the work that is being done there because it is inadequate in size, shape, layout, or management, it shows. Furniture tends to become disorganized, desks and shelves fill up with papers, and the floor gets covered in piles of marginalized material. The building need not be state of the art; however it should signal to staff and visitors that they are valued and that their needs are well served. Its image should reinforce the impression that the organization wishes to make.

Image clearly resides in the reception area. To make a visitor feel at ease, the reception should be easy to find, sufficiently large, comfortable, have a good color scheme, be clean and congenially lit, and have enough chairs, access to WCs, and perhaps coffee. Welcoming reception staff are essential. The same features have a similar effect on staff, affording them pride in their organization and the expert attention it pays to the needs of its customers. Image cannot stop at the entrance and visitor areas. If the staff areas are, in stark contrast, dingy, cramped, positioned along murky passages, and inadequately furnished, then the very features that make a visitor feel cherished will add to the frustration of the staff. They will feel that money has been spent in the wrong place. If a building looks very lavish, a small or a young or public-sector organization will not wish to occupy it. Their managers believe, probably correctly, that customers and auditors will think that money is being spent on the wrong things—the look of the place, rather than on high-quality staff. They seek a more ordinary but businesslike look.

Many factors combine to make a building one that bolsters your image and makes staff and visitors feel that they are held in esteem: the amount of space given to each person, whether individuals have enclosed offices, whether the facilities available are suitable for the work people do, the type of amenities provided, the colors and finishes of the building and its furniture, the quality and amount of IT, the standard to which the building is cleaned and managed, whether it reflects people's wish to be responsible to the environment, and a host of others. Many of these subjects are considered in subsequent chapters.

> *Most people still consider the quality of accommodation a reflection of the esteem in which the firm holds them.*

> *There's no pride in these offices. It starts with the firm. It's shabby, so individuals accept clutter. It's a bloody shambles actually....You don't bring people into your office.*
> —QUESTIONNAIRE RESPONSES FROM MANAGEMENT CONSULTANT IN LARGE ACCOUNTING FIRM

> *This is the first time since I've worked in this organization that I've wanted to invite my wife and kids to see where I work.*
> —COMMENT MADE DURING A REVIEW OF NEW PREMISES

Sound management decisions cannot be made solely on the basis of what people say they want, such as lots of space or a solo office for everyone, but they must take account of how people feel. When organizations move or adapt their buildings, some, if not most, decisions are made to take account of change. Change may seem to disadvantage some staff. Change is, in itself, often threatening rather than stimulating. To set about implementing change without knowing what people want is to start from a position of weakness, making it hard to carry out decisions in a way that convinces those that matter, and the staff in general, that they are indeed valued. Not to know what people are using the building for, not to understand how well they feel it supports their needs may be the start of making the wrong decision. Finding out how people feel about their place of work, and why, is an important part of managing it well. Ways to make sure that management knows include using questionnaires or suggestion boxes so that people can say what they think, holding workshops and group meetings, watching and collecting real information about what they do and where, asking staff to fill in diaries indicating where they work at different times of day, having people available who know how to listen, directly or in passing and can act on what they hear. All these methods are used to find out how people use and feel about the building, and why. They are particularly valuable techniques to help plan for future needs and to create the program for relocation (see Chapter 9).

Does the Building Encourage Communication?

The building plan can influence the ease with which people talk to each other. If you seek a highly interactive environment, steer away from buildings with features such as long, dark corridors with enclosed offices on each side; fire doors that inhibit people in one wing of a building ever moving into another; a restaurant or cafeteria located inconveniently far from workspaces, or of unattractive design; stairs and elevators that are hard to find or badly designed so that people will think twice before going down to another floor; security systems that demand digipads or card swipes on doors into every floor. Conversely, communication will be eased in buildings without many doors or with fire doors held open permanently (except in case of fire when their electromagnetic closures come into play); open-plan stairs that invite people to travel between one floor and the next even for a very short conversation; buildings with an atrium where lots of activity occurs overlooked by people on other floors who can rush over to catch the person with whom they would like to chat; glass partitions separating enclosed offices from corridors so that you can readily see who is in and who is out; catering facilities that attract people to eat in them; and sufficient space in tea-making areas for an easy conversation to take place without being overheard. In short, seek buildings with few visual or mechanical barriers.

Is It a Good Shape for Your Organization?

The efficiencies intrinsic to the building as a whole, the various areas available, are determined very largely by the design: the shape of each floor, the location of cores on those floors, the number of floors, and the spacing and design of windows. These determine the fit factor and primary circulation routes. Possible ways to use a building are also determined by size and shape. A long, thin bedroom might be suitable for bunks but would not set off a four-poster bed to advantage. Similarly, the shape of a building fixes the ways in which it can be planned. As an example, a building on a college campus known as "the Cheesebox" has a shape that has very little going for it. It is small, eight-sided, with a central column to support a frilly roof. It got its name because every room is shaped like a triangular wedge of processed cheese. There are very few possible ways of using it, as no activities are well suited to this dominant shape, and space is likely to be wasted in most furniture arrangements. Strong shapes such as triangles, circles, or hexagons for parts of or whole buildings share these problems, especially in small rooms or small floor plans.

Simple circulation routes do not squander space. The routes must connect entrances to all activities and, vitally, in case of fire let people reach safe exits from wherever they are. The position of enclosed rooms affects possible routes, and sensible sizes and shapes for such rooms need to be considered when assessing the overall shape of the building. Even with its simple circulation, the poor Cheesebox achieves a low efficiency level of 71 percent. This is because it is so small. In a larger building of the same shape, an identical route would be more efficient as well as serving larger, more useful, and pleasant rooms.

There is an infinity of possible shapes despite the almost irresistible urge to think of office blocks as simple rectangular prisms (Fig. 2.3). The shape and size of a building can tell you a lot about how and when it was built and the underlying assumptions about the way it would be used. Buildings vary according to prevailing office technologies and the type of work layouts favored, as well as the construction technologies available in the place and at the time of construction. The hallmark of office buildings erected since the 1980s is the *atrium,* an internal covered courtyard running vertically through the middle of the building. The atrium developed in response to the desire for construction economy—the walls around the atrium are cheap to build as they are not fully weatherproof or soundproof—and economy in air-conditioning—the atrium is often not a fully conditioned environment. It is usually designed as a grand and glamorous space and gives people working next to it a view—"outside awareness" in trade jargon. Where culture or the law, as in Northern Europe, demands that no one is ever farther from a window than 6 meters or the depth of one other person's workplace, or where natural ventilation is a prerequisite, a deep landscaped office is not a possibility. The building must be no more than, say, 30 to 50 ft from window to window. The financial dealing sector in London, New York, Frankfurt, or Tokyo depends on the adrenalin rush that a large, busy group can create. Windows would be an undesirable distraction, and very deep floor plates, perhaps 60 to 100 ft from window wall to window wall, are favored. The maximum number of stories that can be built depends on construction materials and methods, on elevator technology, and on the restrictions of planning departments and neighbors. The number of floors that may be desired by the building's owner depends on land values and that required by the occupiers on how well the organization can function when located on different floors. There are still technical limits of height; 100-story buildings are still fairly rare because of the costs and problems associated with their construction.

Buildings used for offices have often had previous uses. Elegant eighteenth- and nineteenth-century homes, more modest urban houses, converted warehouses, and old schools are all used, with and without extensions. They may have unusual room sizes, types of window, floor-to-ceiling heights, and, of course, services. Sometimes they are of historic interest, with restrictions on how many alterations are permissible, but people show great ingenuity in converting them to offices. Many of the construction and planning details differ from those of buildings purposefully designed as offices.

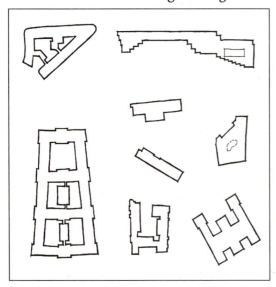

Figure 2.3 Offices of every shape and size, to the same scale and orientation. Each has its own characteristics.

(AMA Alexi Marmot Associates.)

Understanding whether the shape of a building is suitable for an organization's needs is a prerequisite to choosing the right one or finding the right way to use an existing one. A major retailer leased office space in a well-located building with a hidden disadvantage: the shape of the site. This led to an irregular, seven-sided courtyard building. It was laid out with many small individual offices, leaving inefficient areas for open-plan use. A reassessment of the spatial properties of the building revolutionized the floor layouts. With the new layout and changed circulation to improve the space efficiency, the response of the users was extremely positive—more people were accommodated, with more light, in more attractive space.

The decision to create a particular shape for a new building is complex and influenced by many considerations. It is essential to review a possible shape and evaluate the consequences that it has for an organization, before embarking on a major building project. Even for a building that you are not planning to change immediately, evaluation may indicate things that could be improved later, when an opportunity arises. Remember to consider both exit and expansion strategies—how you can shrink into less space or grow into more. There are a

One young and rapidly growing company took on a five-story building—a center city converted house. Each floor was big enough for a single department, and the ground floor was suitable for shared facilities and reception. Occupying this building "killed the company by slow death," according to a manager who left while it was dying. Separation by floor prevented the vital interaction needed so much during the period of change and growth. The required building would have allowed several, if not all, departments to be together on one floor, with additional space for future growth. Some sacrifices would almost certainly have been required to achieve this—for example, the company might have elected to accept loss of identity or prestige by accepting a tenancy in a larger building rather than ownership of a whole one, or a less central location in order to be able to afford enough space for growth and change. The priorities were wrong when the choice was made because the decision makers were unaware of the effect that an inappropriate building can have.

number of basic spatial properties to consider. The more important ones are covered here, in an indicative rather than an exhaustive list.

- *Location and size of cores, entrances, and fire stairs.* Can the entrances serve separate organizations and make each feel they have a real identity? Do the positions of fire stairs relate well to the natural locations of primary circulation routes? Do the cores break up the space so that you never get the benefit of the maximum dimensions and areas? Are the cores adequate in size and planning to contain all the services, such as ducts, cupboards, and WCs, that are needed to sustain the building?

- *Depth of the floor plate—distance from window to window or to blind wall.* How many people can work near windows with the type of layout you need? If the space is deep—over, say, 50 ft (18 m) between window walls—so that many people are far from windows, are there adequate compensations, such as being able to accommodate large groups or easy communication between groups? Can the inner areas be reached by the building services? Will ventilation be adequate? Can enough cables reach the positions where they will be needed?

- *Spacing of structure.* Is there always a column in the way of the desk arrangement you want to create? Or a window that cannot be subdivided when partitions need to be relocated? Is the clear space between fixed parts of the structure suitable for groups of desks? Does the geometry of the plan or the windows mean that rooms can only be an awkward shape, too small to be useful or so large that they are wasteful? Generally a grid that breaks down to 1.5-m lengths, both in plan and on the window elevation, is fairly flexible; 1.2 m can make planning difficult; and a larger one, such as

2.0 m, can lead to overlavish rooms when partitions are planned.

- *Structure and fabric.* Is the construction sound? Does it have potential problems, such as the difficulty of introducing cable routes, the presence of asbestos, or other characteristics needing remedial attention? Will it withstand bomb attacks? Are windows double-glazed or triple-glazed? Are the external fabric, walls, roof, and windows in good repair?

- *Circulation routes.* Can simple routes be planned without kinks and dog-legs? Can main routes be left open with fire doors held on magnetic closures? Are there wasteful parallel circulation routes in spaces requiring only one? What percentage of the overall area on a typical floor will have to be occupied by the primary circulation route? Is the building efficient? Can appropriate security access points be incorporated?

- *Edges, corners, and dead ends—"fit factor."* A large fit factor (a lot of space you cannot use because of details in the way the building is designed) is undesirable. An allowance needs to be made for some unusable space, but if too many factors combine, the penalties may be too great. A small test layout of half a dozen desks or rooms arranged the way you want them can help to show up unsuspected problems of fit. Do power and telephone cable routes make the fit bad by preventing desks from being placed wherever they may be needed?

- *Subdivision.* Can room sizes vary, and are they suited to the organization's needs? Check the size of the largest area of contiguous space and the smallest. Small increments in the length or depth of a space, resulting overall in a larger area, may not be particularly helpful in accommodating more people, as furniture comes only in a limited range of sizes. To fit in one more person, the extra cross-sectional dimensions have to be as big as a desk plus chair and its access. Can suitable room sizes be created, and can they be located in such a way that people in open-plan areas are not deprived of direct natural light?

Can It Adapt? Is It the Right Shape for the Future?

These issues are as important as any absolute measures of size or efficiency. Management literature stresses the great changes likely to be experienced by business survivors. Some changes will result in different ways to use office buildings, even when there is no significant change in staff numbers. The characteristics of shape need to be considered for the use initially intended but also whether they allow alternative scenarios with reasonable ease. Many of the different issues that become important as organizations change—such as alterations in space standards, the amount and type of cellularization, whether hot-desking will suit some or all of the staff, the introduction of new IT systems, or additional amenity areas—are considered in detail in other chapters. The ease with which any of these can be inserted into a building, and can continue to be fine-tuned to the organizational needs of the moment, relates to the design, the shape overall and in its parts, and the details of grids and service routes.

If your building turns out to be inefficient, inappropriate, or unadaptable, or it is giving you a bad name, should you fix it or move? If you decide to move, Chapter 9 discusses relocation. The chapters that follow explore in more detail various aspects of buildings that will help you to understand what decisions are needed to achieve maximum benefits from your building, whether you stay put or relocate.

Summary

This chapter sketches the very varied assumptions about the needs for office space in different types of organizations. It offers types by which you can recognize what habits and needs underlie the use of space in your organization. It gives you technical guidance to help you to decide if your buildings are efficient and suitable for your organization. As a good manager, you need to know something about buildings. Buildings represent a cost of 10 to 20 percent of revenue for a business. You need to understand how to make good use of them. Having the right information available when you need it is a key part of good management and decision making.

How much space you use, and what it costs, is basic information. Whether your building is space efficient, spatially appropriate, and projects the right image is important additional ammunition. A plan of the building is a fundamental tool for the purpose of good space information. Size is measured by specific rules that must be applied consistently if comparisons and targets are to be useful. Efficiency ratios are helpful as targets. As an owner, you need to seek a ratio of 85 percent of lettable to gross area. As a user, you need a ratio of 80 percent or more of usable to lettable area.

To be exploited as a positive asset, a building must make staff and visitors feel good rather than frustrated or undervalued. There are many management tools and techniques for discovering how to achieve this. The answers may sometimes be unexpected. The skill lies in matching the desired to the possible.

The size and number of floors need to be suitable for the groups and activities accommodated. However, there is more to a suitable building than getting the larger design right. Convenient entrances and routes in the building, access to windows, possible ways to carve up and subdivide space, the likelihood of wasting floor area — all relate to detailed aspects of the shape as well as to the general topology of the building. Without trying to know all the answers, a good manager must know the type of questions to ask about the different aspects of shape: cores, depth, structural grid, fit factor, circulation, and subdivision. These issues are particularly important when changes are made. Different ways of using the available space and the potential adaptability of the building must also be considered.

Reengineering
Space Allocation

CASE
HISTORIES

See Case Histories 9 and 10
on pages 333–342

Remember the last time you caught an airplane and sat in economy class—knees jammed up against the back of the seat in front, the newspaper opened on to the lap of your neighbor, wondering where to put your second foot after storing your bag under the seat in front? Didn't you feel wonderful that time you flew first class? Obviously there was more service, more hostess time, better cuisine, leg rests, a seat that converted to a bed, and your own video and telephone. You were not just more comfortable—you had *more than the others*.

One of the big questions every organization must answer is: How much space does each person merit? The cost of space per person is overtly reflected in different situations. Airline seats in the supereconomy section of the holiday charter night flight are much cheaper than those of the Concorde's first class. Part of the reason for that, you may say, is because of speed and convenience of service. But first-class seats on any train or plane are also more generous than standard or basic ones. Here the cost does not reflect a difference in speed and convenience. Space, as well as speed, has a price set on it by the transport business.

Should offices be planned so that the amount of space given to each individual reflects his or her worth to the organization? And, if so, how is worth measured? Does seniority automatically confer higher worth? Do status and authority need the support of extra space? Should higher responsibility be rewarded by an acknowledged privilege— extra space? Manifestly different amounts of space are allocated to different people in an organization, so extra money is being diverted to support those with the larger areas. Some office-based organizations, including government agencies have a sixfold differential in both salary and space allocation between the lowest and the highest grades, suggesting that space and salary are comparable measures of worth. Space in one such organization was carefully assessed on a cost-per-square-foot basis, demonstrating that the most highly paid people were clearly enjoying personal use of a much larger share of the accommodation cost. That same organization later started to rationalize space standards, so that relative space costs no longer matched salary. How far have the implications of the cost of space per person begun to have an influence on what organizations demand from their office buildings? How far should they? What are the space standards in your own organization, and have they responded to pressures of planning efficiency and cost per person?

Space Standards

A *space standard* defines how much space, how much of the area in the building, is given to each person working there. Standards have value as guides to estimating the size of the building that an organization should have, as design aids for a new project, as management tools to control the waste of space, and as ways to safeguard the interests of individuals.

The discipline of space planning, in which designers concentrate on planning the interiors of buildings, has developed in importance and has refined its working methods. As a result the concept of space standards has become increasingly important and useful to designers in two tasks: assessing overall space requirements for organizations and planning the use of buildings at a detailed level. Designers use space standards as a convenient aid for decision making in both these tasks. They are delighted to turn to a document provided by the user organization that lays down the rules about who gets what. Such documents are not likely to exist in small organizations, though they are fairly common in large, mature ones. The politics of who gets how much space, decisions about how much is the right amount, and why, need to be codified to create such documents. This process provides an opportunity to assess whether the right priorities are being met.

Deciding on the organization's space standards is one way of making sure that an office building is used to its best advantage, as it reduces the likelihood of wasteful, unproductive, ad hoc decisions about space. Standards should, however, be framed as guidance, not seen as rights cast in concrete, even though one of their uses is to safeguard individuals from overcrowding and inadequate provision. In some situations they cannot be met exactly, and then there is the possibility that they will be used as a lever by those who wish to find fault. This is not a reason for doing without them, but it is an incentive to devise a sensible set of standards allied to an agreed approach to flexibility in their use.

Average Lettable Area Per Person

The simplest standard to guide an organization on how much space it requires is the average *net lettable area* (NLA) that is required per person. *Person* is the term used here since traditionally it has been considered that each person has an assigned workplace, and each workplace is occupied by a person. Chapter 1 outlines the alternatives that are emerging where this is no longer the case, and for some circumstances in practice a clear distinction must be drawn between space per person and space per workplace. The average NLA per person bears little resemblance to the workplace, the area in which each person has to work, which is considered later in this chapter. As seen in Figure 2.2, the lettable area not only includes these working areas but also support and ancillary space—which are discussed later in this chapter and in Chapter 7—as well as primary circulation (see Chapter 1). The average is reached by dividing the whole lettable area by the number of people working in the building. Average lettable area per person varies considerably for a number of reasons. Even when working areas are planned with identical desk and office layouts, an organization with high requirements for support or ancillary areas uses more space per person than one with lower requirements. Individual working areas may be more generous in some organizations; proportions of large and small work areas vary.

The range of average space per person found in different offices is wide. This is true even within a particular type of organization, such as investment banks or solicitors' offices. The lower end of the scale is represented by about 100 ft^2 (9 m^2) lettable area per person, implying modest working areas for each of the few senior people in the office, few amenities, and perhaps a degree of desk sharing. At the high end is an average area of around 350 to 400 ft^2 (30 to 35 m^2) per person, nearly four times as much, implying large amounts of space for each individual and lavish shared space and amenities. These differences arise from different company styles, organizational needs, and building decisions as well as from different national practices. The smaller allowance is not intrinsically better or worse, though it is by definition cheaper. It may or may not be appropriate for a specific organization. In the United States and Canada, a typical figure is 200 to 250 ft^2 (20 to 25 m^2) lettable area per person for a medium-sized organization with a range of different levels of seniority in the staff. In the United Kingdom an average figure of about 150 to 170 ft^2 (14 to 16 m^2) is fairly typical. In Scandinavian countries 300 ft^2 is not atypical.

If the average space per person is excessive, considerable extra costs are incurred. For a hundred people, a reduction in the average lettable area per person of 10 ft^2 (3 m^2) saves not only the initial capital or rental outlay on 1,000 ft^2 (300 m^2) but also running costs each year and periodic upgrade costs. This mounts up fast to a worthwhile saving when construction costs are \$150 per square foot and running costs are, say, \$8 per square foot per year. An efficient building delivers a lower average area per person. Space can be sensibly reduced, without squeezing individual areas or being stingy with necessary support areas or desirable amenities, by systematically reducing ad hoc decisions and by planning the relationships of the individual work areas carefully, avoiding typical space wasters such as, for example, double circulation routes.

Space Standards: Many, Few, or One Standard for All?

The second use by office planners of the term *space standards* or *space guidelines* indicates the area allowance for each person on the working floors of the office building. This is the area taken up by the *footprint* of the working furniture, the desk, chair, storage, and the access route to get to and use them. It is shown by a plan view of the space taken up by the items of furniture or the size of the personal enclosed office. It is associated with the net usable area rather than the lettable area. Primary circulation is not included in the workplace footprint. For most organizations the way in which a job has been defined is linked indissolubly to grade or status. Generally the higher the grade, the larger the amount of space people are given, the larger their space standard—the footprint of their workplace or room size. Space is often taken to be an entitlement, particularly in companies with active unions and the more so if the space is called "a standard." If you are a customer service manager, should you expect a larger amount of space than a customer service assistant? Should it be different if you have many or only one person working for you? On what should any difference in space allowance be based? Is a standard an entitlement for staff, a goal for the organization to aspire to, or a convenience that need bear no direct relationship to the specific area occupied by particular individuals once layouts are planned?

Three different approaches can be adopted when deciding individual space standards. The outcome of the different approaches is shown in Figure 3.1. Hierarchy may be of great significance to the organization, expressed in space standards as well as job titles, grade numbers, salary, and, perhaps, location within the building, degree of enclosure, access to amenities, number of days of annual leave. With a long list of different grades, there may be many individual standards—10 or more. A functional approach is to reduce the number to a few, differentiated perhaps on the basis of the specific job requirements of individuals, which results in between 3 and 5 different standards. This approach implies not that there is no hierarchy but that seniority or responsibility are not recognized through allocation of space. Another approach provides all individuals identical workspace, a single space standard. This is how, for example, a typical headquarters building in Stockholm might be planned, giving each person a small individual office of about 120 ft^2 (12 m^2). Typical young telecommunications or IT companies give all but the few top people an equal open-plan workstation of around 65 ft^2 (6 m^2).

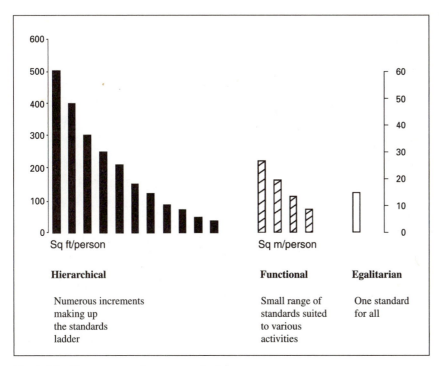

Figure 3.1 Three ranges of space standards.

(AMA Alexi Marmot Associates.)

When Grade Sets the Standards

Until recently grade was a widely, almost universally, accepted way to establish space standards. Government departments and international agencies have often been careful to set down such standards. The GSA has a set of eight current workplace standards for U.S. federal officers ranging from 60 to 400 ft² set out in federal property regulations. The regulations limit excesses in space for top grade officials by stating whether or not private conference rooms or private kitchen and dining areas, toilets, sinks, or showers or wood paneling are allowed. Since 1997 the GSA aims for an average no more than 200 ft² per person (18.5 m²) usable space, which is a benchmark in the public sector. Canada's Public Works and Government Services has guidelines amounting to 170 ft^2 (16 m^2) per person usable floor area. Australia's "Office wise" standards are for a minimum 65 ft^2 (6 m^2) workstation footprint. The British Civil Service had a grade-related set of standards abolished in 1990. There was an entire suite of 22 spaces to match the full range of administrative and executive grades. The largest size to which one grade was entitled was usually less than, or equal to, the smallest size available to the person on the next rung up the ladder. The top standard was about 500 ft^2 (45 m^2) for those managing entire departments, responsible directly to the politicians. The lowest was around 45 ft^2 (4 m^2) for clerks and typists. This has been supplemented by departmental standards based on the needs of the jobs people do.

A distinction based on grade does have its uses. Promotion can be marked by an upgrade in space, so fellow members of the office are made aware subtly of enhanced status. Space can be thought of as a perk, so the pay rise may possibly be smaller than it otherwise would be. However, some of the attendant disadvantages can be ignored only if buildings are treated as "free goods." When someone is promoted, under an agreed set of space standards, the higher grade rates a larger space. To provide this can be disruptive, especially if walls have to be moved. The disruption caused by a single promotion, however, is often insignificant. As promotion may mean a change of department, it is likely that a space of the right size has just been vacated, causing the need for the promotion, and eliminating the need to change desk layouts or partitions. Larger-scale changes, related to general reorganization, major growth (or decline), or market shifts, are more complicated. As groups evolve, the mix of grades does not remain static, so either people have to use standards that are, in fact, not the ones applicable to their grades, thus nullifying the point of the standards, or changes that cost time and money have to be made overall to take account of the grade changes. Many organizations that have experienced dramatic change, or anticipate upheaval in the future, have reexamined their approach to the number of standards they are using, reducing the number from, say, eight to four or fewer.

"Less Is More"

Adherence to fewer rather than smaller standards makes the office more flexible and more cost effective.

Reorganization of the office layout, so that standards are adhered to in the event of organizational changes, does not necessarily happen at each change, but when it does happen, it is costly and is not necessarily justified. *Churn* is the name given to the relocation of people within a building. Annual churn of 100 percent is a way of saying that, on average, each person moves to a new location in the same building, or to another building, once a year. The rate can be higher than 100 percent, implying that some people move twice or more in the year. High churn rates are common in rapidly changing organizations. Some reorganization of the layout is bound to be needed with high churn. In one of IBM's national headquarters buildings, the annual churn rate was about 66 percent, that is, about 2,000 people moved out of 3,000, an average of about 40 people every week throughout the year. A major finance and insurance company nearly fell apart in a year when its churn rate was 190 percent and most of its 3,000 staff moved twice in one year. Churn rates appear to be rising. The International Facilities Management Association (IFMA) reported in *Benchmarks 111* in 1997 that the average rate of churn for all industries has risen to 44 percent from 30 percent in 1988. In nonheadquarters offices this is even higher, an average of 66 percent being reported. Despite differences in the way these figures are collected and reported, they are an indication of the stress that a business has to cope with, especially as a major reason for churn is change in the structure of the business, itself a stressful process.

Office moves are expensive. First they involve management time in taking move decisions. Then they involve moving walls, desks, reorganizing telephones and computers, sorting out relocated storage units, and moving files. This can cost in the order of $2,000 per person moved. Part of this cost is incurred because disruptive moves should be, and usually are, done on the weekend, which entails payment at double and triple time for IT and telephone communications specialists as well as removal crews. Fortunately these days moves can cost much less. If workplaces are generally the same size, moves become both cheaper and less disruptive and can even be carried out during the working day. Moving people around simply involves a small hiatus while the telephone numbers are rerouted, so that Jones keeps his extension number when he moves, taking a short time to wheel a pedestal full of files to his new location. In this situation the cost falls to an acceptable $150 per head or lower, depending on the building and the types of services that have to be rerouted. Uniformity of servicing to desks can be an additional cost saver if the capital outlay can be justified. Even with reasonable costs per person, the disruption of churn needs to be controlled.

A reduced range of standards allows flexibility that is more than merely physical. When there are fewer formal distinctions, it is less significant if individuals deviate a little from the standard. If the same standard applies to many grades, then slight variations do not carry overtones of promotion or demotion. Reshaping work groups need not have so many barriers to acceptance. It can happen when business requirements dictate. It does not have to wait while large sums are saved to pay for it or while prolonged negotiations take place with staff who may resist a different space allowance for themselves or rail against the fact that their neighbors are going to get more space than in the last layout.

However, where they are fewer, standards are more significant. Where there are few well-differentiated standards, the differences are clear for all to see, and, if wrongly applied, the effects are obvious. If they are inappropriate, everyone is affected. If standards are too small, overall performance in the office may be badly affected; opportunities to accommodate minor changes in staff numbers by slipping in an extra desk or two may be inhibited; and morale may be low. If they are too large, the additional amount of space consumed by the organization rapidly adds up to a big rent and running-cost bill.

A Shallower Pyramid

The organizations that will survive and prosper are described in management literature as "leaner and meaner." For many this implies a reduction in the layers of hierarchy they have inherited. Being meaner, they also appreciate the cost benefits of a reduced number of office space standards. So in many such organizations the hierarchy is becoming flatter and the space pyramid shallower. The trend is toward fewer space standards, with a smaller differential between the lowest and the highest. Even where the hierarchy remains, several levels are given the same space standards. Reduced disruption and cost have helped to establish the logic of having fewer standards and hence less upheaval as group structures and numbers change, and less wasted space where the standards were larger than necessary in order to signal status differential. Typically, a forward-looking commercial organization has no more than three to five different space standards, matching a shallower hierarchical pyramid, as indicated in Figure 3.2. The most radical have moved to a single standard.

Changing space standards can seem to be synonymous with reducing them. A reduction in the number of standards, creating a shallower pyramid, is used as an opportunity to seek a lower common denominator. There is a danger in this. Standards should be sufficiently large to accommodate the

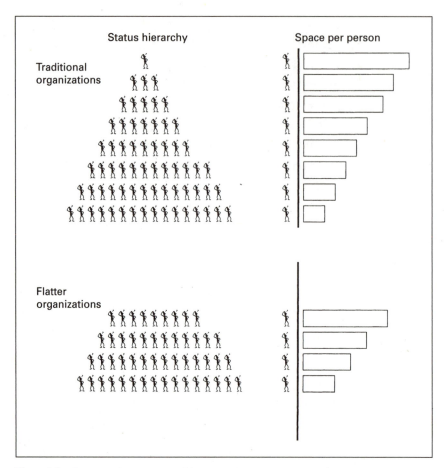

Figure 3.2   Status and space pyramids.

A Universal Work Space

At Lexis Nexis Corporation in Dayton, Ohio, the 72 percent churn rate was stretching resources to the breaking point. It has sought to minimize the effects of churn by introducing an 8- by 8-ft (2.4- × 2.4-m) universal footprint. The challenge for them is how to allow each individual to customize a standard space to meet their particular needs.

work to be done at the relevant workplace and should not fall below reasonable levels. A swing of the pendulum, as well as the quest for cost efficiency, is a possible reason why changes in space standards tend to reduce work areas. The last few decades have witnessed an increase in average space per person. Figures collected for offices in the City of London, for example, show a 40 percent increase in space per person over a 20-year period, so perhaps it is time to tighten belts a little. This increase reflects larger individual workplace standards, designed to accommodate computers at individual desks, and also increased ancillary and support space.

Sensible Workplace Standards

Buildings are now expected to perform more efficiently on behalf of the occupiers. Setting space standards sensibly, and then sticking to them, is a way of ensuring this. What is included in a space standard? How do you know when a standard is sensible?

A hierarchical approach to space standards is still common in traditional organizations. It makes a clear statement to staff and visitors about relative status and perceived worth.

Regulations prevent exploitation and overcrowding in offices. In the United Kingdom, guidance from the Health and Safety Executive, suggests a minimum volume per person of 390 ft³ (11 m³), which in typical offices would imply an

A city council department occupied an old building with gracious rooms. On each of two floors there was a room of identical size and shape with a bay window. The one on the upper level had a view of the historic town center, and was occupied by the head of the department. In the room below, differing only by having a less dramatic view, 16 members of the department were squeezed in.

average floor area of about 50 ft^2 (4.6 m^2). This is based not on a concept of the space needed for the job but on consideration of hazards to life; it is to ensure adequate ventilation, to provide room to escape in case of fire, and to create a space that is not too crowded and stressful.

Any sensible organization provides adequate space for doing the job. Work spaces needed for most jobs in offices must accommodate a desk, a chair, and maybe some storage, as well as allow the occupants access to their individual desks once they leave the main circulation routes. In addition to tasks carried out individually, space is needed for shared activities, for several people to meet together. The space required at workstations, for single tasks done by people who do not spend all their working day in that location, is surprisingly small. A bank teller's workstation at the cash counter is used for short spells of time and can be as small as 10 to 20 ft (1 to 2m^2). A work space used for most of the day needs to be larger—say, between 50 and 70 ft^2 (4.5 to 6.5 m^2). A desk for a manager who has to hold small, informal meetings around the desk needs even more space. The fashionable "tear-drop"-style desk additions, which are designed for these sort of meetings, create a footprint that takes up about 100 ft^2 (9 m^2). If a person needs full enclosure, it cannot sensibly be provided in a very small space except in spaces like a researcher's cubicle in a university. In an office setting, someone needing such enclosure generally requires enough space to accommodate special requirements for working on extensive confidential paperwork or holding frequent meetings for more than three people. These activities can take place comfortably in about 120 to 150 ft^2 (11 to 14 m^2). When still more space is needed for a single person, it falls into the category of status-related space. Sometimes this is appropriate for particular situations—for example, to create a necessary atmosphere of control, confidence, and confidentiality. Often it is not.

The footprints illustrated in Figure 3.3 have the advantage of being modular; that is, they fit together easily and can be exchanged when numbers change. Two × 65 square foot (6 m²) workplaces can be created when a 130 square foot (12 m²) office is eliminated or vice versa. Three of the smaller size are equivalent in area to two of the medium ones. Modularity is not essential, and different areas may be chosen as standards for many reasons. However, where it can be achieved, especially if the areas can easily be created within the building grids, the interchangeability of spaces can be a significant help for replanning.

Ancillary and Support Areas

In one organization the staff dubbed the local support zone for everyone in one area of the building the "village pump."

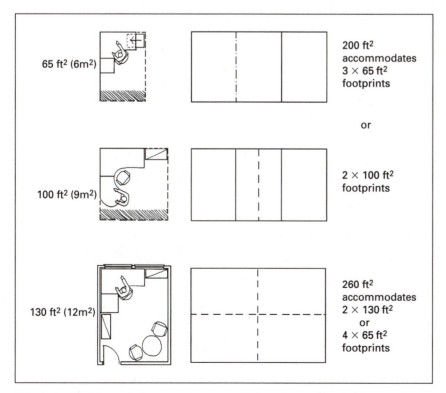

Figure 3.3 Modular workplace footprints are readily interchangeable when layouts change.

It contains items such as copiers, faxes, and shared printers as well as vending machines and notice boards. It is acknowledged as a necessary fount of information and local gossip. The "village pump" is shared by people in a team and is referred to here as *ancillary space*. When a service, such as a library or a computer suite or a reprographics facility, is there for the benefit of all the organization, it is called *support* (see Fig. 2.2). Ancillary areas that are generally needed near working groups include storage accessed by all group members, coat closets, equipment such as photocopiers and printers, shared computers with specialized functions, faxes, and microfiche readers, which are used by all but belong to no particular individual. Each group has different requirements; the areas needed must be assessed for each organization and each type of group. Typically, ancillary areas add between 5 and 15 ft^2(1.5 and 4.5m^2) per person to the space requirement in the working areas, and that figure is growing. Individual work areas, in particular the very largest, have reduced, and the office has become more of a shared resource and less of a place to come to sit at a desk for the whole day. This makes it even more important that it is easy to exchange different types of area to adapt the layout as the organizational needs change with business requirements.

Modularity is useful for ancillary or support areas as well as for workplaces. If they can share dimensions with the workplace standards, this further increases flexibility. If a 130-ft^2 (12 m^2) area can contain equally well an enclosed office, a photocopier, and a stationery area, the village pump, a computer store room, or a library facility, then as one requirement increases and another shrinks, the spaces can be interchanged. The areas taken up by workplace footprints and ancillary and support space are included in the usable area and have to be established for each organization according to the way in which its work is carried out. Generally, there has been a trend for the amount of ancillary space in relation to work areas to increase.

An 80-ft² Module

In General Motors' Truck Product Center in Pontiac, Michigan, modular thinking has been adopted. The standard 8- by 10-ft (2.4-by 3-m²) space is provided for everyone from the vice president down. Other spaces have the same footprint—for example, a small meeting area or a shared filing space. This means that different functions are readily interchangeable and substantial office reorganizations will be much easier.

Densities and Space Audits

When each person has a single space that they generally use and it is of a standard size, it is comparatively easy to work out the density or average lettable area per person. This is a useful concept to relate to the average cost of office space per person. It can also be calculated excluding the shared areas like cafeterias and photocopiers, to give an idea of local density of occupation. High local densities, while they may help to keep the adrenaline levels high for telesales people and dealing-room junkies, are generally associated with low status and low job satisfaction. This is the logical consequence of bringing together a large group of people with a low individual space standard, who are traditionally the lowest grade in a hierarchical organization.

Chapter 1 described new ways of working for people housed in various different places, performing different roles often away from their offices. For them the concept of density is no longer what it was. Global averages can still be calculated, but the relationship of density to office costs, or workers' health, or a real-time view of whether people are working in unacceptably closely packed situations is less clear. If at any particular moment a large proportion of people are working outside the building in which they are based, then a small average lettable area per employee, a low average space cost, says little about the quality of the working area. A more detailed view may be needed. A *space audit,* in which the space being used for specific activities can be measured and reviewed in the light of the type, importance, and frequency of those activities, is a valuable tool for understanding the building. Time is now a much more important dimension in providing space than it was in the past.

Space and Time Again

Space allocation today is more closely related to the work to be done in it divorced from the grade of the person doing the job. Alternative officing concepts expect people to exploit information technology and work when and where it is most suitable and have been combined with ideas about simplification that permit flexibility and cost control. From this has developed the concept of spaces for particular tasks: areas or rooms that have no particular individual's name attached to them, typical amounts of space for typical activities, not individual allowances for each member of the clerical, managerial, or professional staff. Common terms in space planning today are *quiet rooms, war rooms, project rooms, team areas, group bases, work lounges, huddle rooms, chill-out rooms,* and *commons.* All these apply to spaces used by people for different tasks at different times and in different combinations.

It is suddenly more complicated. This approach allows office buildings to be viewed in the same way as, say, hospitals or universities. In these sorts of organization, spaces are assigned to different activities that are not always performed in by the same people. Conversely, people are liable to use different spaces at different times. Offices have begun to behave more like these sorts of organizations. It is now necessary to consider how much time people spend in a traditional workplace, what part of their function is carried out there, and how large the area should be to fulfill this function. Standards for all the other spaces required by the organization must also be considered. To provide enough, but not too many, spaces for each activity requires a secure knowledge of use patterns, so that a mismatch between need and available space happens only on an acceptable number of occasions and in circumstances in which an alternative solution can be provided. If meeting rooms are wanted, what is the typical size of group they should be planned for? Room size could simply be set to cater to the largest gathering that takes place, so that it never fails. This is an extravagant approach if the big meetings happen only once a quarter, while considerably smaller ones take place weekly or daily. If meetings rooms are big enough only for small meetings, another space (say, a staff lounge) may need to be used, by arrangement, for that big quarterly meeting.

The amount of time over which particular activities take place should be included as part of the equation. Space needs to match the most typical extent of the activities if it is to be used most cost effectively, and it must be used enough of the time to justify its provision. "Utilization" is a useful concept. It describes how many people use the space in relation to its potential capacity and for what proportion of the available time. Use needs to be monitored in an existing situation and possible future changes taken into account to establish utilization rates:

$$\text{Percent utilization} = \frac{\text{number of people using the space}}{\text{capacity}} \times \frac{\text{hours used}}{\text{hours available}} \times 100$$

In one organization a major conference and training facility and staff meeting rooms were carefully and regularly monitored. It transpired that most rooms had utilization rates of between 10 and 15 percent during the workday. The most utilized room, the smoking room, had a 25 percent utilization rate. These figures were surprising, even shocking, to the managers. On the basis of these data, the company was able to replan the facilities to make better use of them over time. Some special needs may be so essential that, even though they occur only rarely, tailor-made space needs to be provided. It gets harder and harder to justify such uses, so examples no longer abound. The board room may be the last survivor.

Organizations have more complex and subtle space requirements than they had a few decades ago. What actually goes on in the office needs to be fully understood before a decision is made about how space should be divided up, and the people in the organization are as important as outside experts in deciding what is needed. Advice may be required, but it need not be in the form of hiring an outside team to plan and execute a project. It may be available in the form of a brief consultation to enable in-house people to devise and implement suitable solutions. For a small organization one day of expert help—sorting priorities, devising a strategic approach, and indicating particular strengths and weaknesses of current space use—may be all that is needed. Common sense can carry you a long way once you understand the possibilities inherent in buildings.

Summary

This chapter helps to address how much space should be given to each person and to each activity. It provides reasons for reducing the number of space standards to no more than three or four for most organizations.

How much space each person is worth needs to be determined. Space standards are used to answer this question. They are of great assistance both in estimating space requirements and in planning the use of space. An average lettable area per person of about 200 to 250 ft^2(19 to 23m^2) is fairly typical for an ordinary office building in the United States, less in the United Kingdom, though in the Scandinavian countries it is typically more.

Individual space standards deal with the workplace footprint. In the past standards have been defined by grade; the higher the grade, the larger the space. So there have been few people at the largest standard and many at much lower allowances.

The trend is toward fewer standards, with less difference between them—a shallower pyramid, even in some cases to a single standard. This allows for a more flexible approach to fitting floor layouts to an organization's needs and helps change to be more easily absorbed. Typical standards are now based more often on the amount of space needed for the job. Four or five different workstation layouts are likely to cover most needs in any organization. A good set on which to start to base a family of space standards is 65, 100, and 130 ft^2 (6, 9, and 12 m^2). Modularity between space standards, so that they relate to each other, is likely to help in planning a building.

Space per person, as an average figure over an entire building, is an important measure. It can be used to relate the cost of a building to the people it houses. Density of occupation, a slightly different concept, is more relevant when applied to working areas. These measures must be reevaluated in organizations where the population present in the building may vary from day to day and the places in which they work may vary depending on current tasks.

The importance of time as well as space has begun to be recognized. Priorities are established by how often a space is needed for a particular use as well as by how important that use actually is.

Individual Offices or Open Plan: Which Works for You?

See Case Histories 11, 12, and 13 on pages 343–367

Monica, who worked in Personnel, took me from the plastic mahogany and subdued lighting of the executive floor to the metal desks and neon operations (Settlements) two floors below. About 30 people sat at metal desks, shuffling and ticking and passing and sorting piles of paper. Some of them gazed into computer screens as if they were crystal balls. No one seemed to be speaking but it was noisy and confusing....We went through a pair of fire doors into another large office (Accounts). This one was divided up by freestanding partitions into a complicated maze, like a puzzle where you have to get a silver ball to the middle. The partitions were covered in a fuzzy brown material, repulsive to the touch, to deaden sound....Why did disembodied hands rise above the furry walls with files and papers, why did disembodied heads peep round the sides?

—JOHN MOLE, *BRITS AT WORK*

John Mole's evocative description of this first office in which he, an ex-senior manager turned writer, decided to find out what employment in the ranks was like, indicates clearly that there are various layers of privacy and different types of enclosure. People can be located on separate floors—the bosses are often at the top of the building—or they may be in separate rooms, or merely screened from each other in cubes in drab colors as Mole describes or, of course, in an open plan, not separated at all. In many organizations it is assumed that seniority brings with it a right to privacy and a luxurious environment. Junior status suggests being in the open.

Why is there so much open plan these days? Who gets an enclosed office? Does this reflect more than status? How far is enclosure or openness a necessary part of the way in which work is carried out? Should the use of enclosure take account of the way work is currently carried out, or of how you would prefer work to be carried out, or of space costs? Does the layout of a suite of offices influence the behavior of the occupants? Are changes easy to bring about? And what happens if you try?

Work Organization and Buildings

The debate about open-plan office buildings, where large groups occupy big spaces, versus highly cellularized ones, where many or most people have individual rooms, could take place only after office buildings with large open-floor areas had become a technical reality. When masonry load-bearing walls and timber ceiling joists were the form of construction used, only small rooms were possible. They were hard to change and encouraged static arrangements. They generally provided natural light and ventilation in each room because of the small dimensions of the rooms. New building technologies changed all this. Steel columns, joists and trusses, and then reinforced-concrete frames, liberated space, which might or might not be divided up by light-weight partitions. Rooms could be any size, *and there was no need to have rooms at all.* Buildings could be deep in plan if light and air could reach where they were needed. Walls could be made of glass and artificial lights could take care of the light. Fans and ductwork could push air into the middle of deep space.

So now buildings can be provided to suit a variety of office-work organizations. Different proportions of open to enclosed areas, areas of different sizes, especially very large ones, have become possible. Long, thin buildings, about 40 to 50 ft (12 to 15 m) wide, have a large perimeter in relation to their area, so cellular offices are easily planned without necessarily depriving other working areas of light and air. In such buildings, the main complaints are dismal, narrow corridors and isolation from other people.

Big, square buildings make large, open areas possible. Good light can be a problem, and ventilation a worse one—one that air-conditioning has failed to solve in many cases (see Chapter 6). The development of large, open-plan, "landscaped" office floors, the *Bürolandschaft* approach, with nonorthogonal furniture layouts and plenty of plants to soothe the eye and subtly subdivide the space, was promoted in Germany by the articulate, persuasive Quickborner team of designers in the 1950s. Privacy, particularly for the lower echelons of management and professional staff, was sacrificed to better communication among individuals and groups. Interaction was planned for, placing close together groups with a frequent need to contact each other. Only the most senior people kept their offices. It was recognized that if many offices were placed around the window walls, serving a fairly small proportion of the building population, the majority would be seriously disadvantaged, deprived of natural daylight, of views, and of any possibility of fresh air. Near total openness was hailed as a way to bring a sense of contact with the outside to as many people as possible. The alternative approach, putting the offices in the middle, away from the windows, is possible but rarely popular with bosses.

Other approaches to enclosure have been developed to express the right balance between hierarchy and privacy in different organizations. Private space for concentrated work, allied to shared areas to bring about communication, results in the Swedish *Combi office*. This is popular in northern Europe, though it has not caught on in North America or the United Kingdom. It uses a very large average amount of space, about 380 ft^2 (35 m^2) of lettable area per person, which tempers its popularity where space is costly. The widely admired SAS building in Stockholm represents a version of this prototype for an office building. It gives a private office to each person for concentrated work and small-group spaces for teams of about 24 people. It also creates a large and beautiful covered street linking parts of the building and providing many opportunities for interaction.

Open-Plan Versus Cellular Offices

Once choice is available, decisions, however tricky, need to be made, and there are more factors to be considered than the physical possibilities of the building. Privacy may be desirable; solitude can be a problem. Ample individual space may be pleasant; the cost may be prohibitive. The tension between satisfaction for the company and personal dissatisfaction is a key issue to be resolved.

Much discussion of the merits of open-plan versus enclosed offices takes place among designers. Management literature, on the other hand, rarely discusses this in depth, although there is often a tacit assumption that a manager has a private office. The basis for the decision about how much a building should be subdivided into separate offices is related to organizational culture and to need. Different design approaches have been developed, seeking to fit the

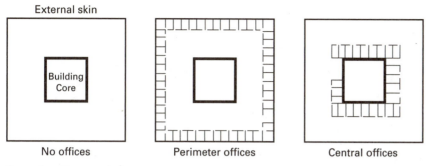

Figure 4.1 Fit the organization to the building. Locate enclosed offices nowhere, around the edges, or in the middle.

organizational needs to the amount and type of separation (Fig. 4.1).

A simplified analysis of organizations can enable spatial organization to be seen as a reflection of the business organization. Where there is a great degree of hierarchy, status is marked out by spatial devices, size, and subdivision, so that senior people have enclosed offices, and the more senior they are, the larger these offices. By contrast, the juniors are accommodated in open areas. Walls can inhibit communication. Where there is little need for communication or where it may be damaging because of breach of privacy or loss of concentration, there is subdivision into single-person offices. This is the situation in most solicitors' offices. Where the need for interaction is urgent and the benefits of communication are great, as in the media industry, in advertising, or in a creative design office, there are few spatial divisions. These relationships assume that buildings are responsive to the types of pressure described, that organizational culture creates spatial character. Though this can and does happen, it is fallacious to assume the reverse, that spatial reorganization will, of itself, bring about organizational rebirth.

A variety of factors influences choices about enclosure. The benefits of one approach rather than another are not always simple to evaluate, but some insights can be achieved by considering other building types. Take hospital buildings. They demonstrate some of the reasons for, and effects of, enclosure. You are given an enclosed room if you are critically ill, or if your condition needs isolation, or if you can afford one and would prefer it. In open-plan Nightingale wards, beds in rows in a large room are screened from each other by curtains. In some hospital designs, small rooms, for between two and six people, are used. These design options have followed changes in the philosophy of how patients should be cared for. Monasteries, which supplied the model for and the origin of collegiate living, vary according to the rules of behavior of the order. A silent order provides cells for solitary meditation rather than a shared dormitory. Hotels offer, at a range of prices, many grades and sizes of individual rooms, with the option to include an extra family member for a marginal extra cost. Youth hostels, on the other hand, accommodate people of limited resources by offering dormitories, frequently with bunk beds.

Open plan for office design is no longer a new idea. Many accept it as inevitable. Walls are coming down, Jericho-like, in most office buildings. But an open, exposed expanse of office floor is far from universally popular with the majority stranded out there on the plain. Furniture manufacturers have responded with system furniture, suitable for large-scale landscaped offices. In the case of system furniture desks, storage and dividing screens come with rules, like those for a child's construction toy, so that they fit together to create individual workstations. The resulting layouts, the "bull-pen" office full of cubes, provides an approximate, though debased, version of cellularization within the open area and creates John Mole's maze in the Accounts Department, at a high furniture cost but a low building cost. This can have interesting financial effects when revenue and capital expenditure are distinguished. Accountants have invested many happy hours refining such calculations.

A change to open plan brings with it benefits as well as problems. Where the benefits are clearly perceived by all affected, where senior managers show by their actions that they are as committed as they expect their juniors to be, where everyone is willing to learn to adapt, it can be well justified. Such conditions for success are by no means easy to achieve. Where they are ignored or forgotten over time, the difficulties most complained about become significant. Some of these are discussed below. Newer ideas about the effects of open-plan offices are also being considered by designers and social analysts. Where people have a disturbing impact on each other, this may intensify their reduced sense of control over their environment. A sense of control appears to be of importance and is being examined by researchers looking at sick-building syndrome (see Chapter 6). Providing environmental control for individuals in open plan is cumbersome and expensive. When 20 lights are controlled by a single switch, there is no way for individuals to control the one light affecting their workplace. By contrast, a light switch for an enclosed room is simple to provide and is also easy to switch off—it is by the door as you leave the room, so it is an efficient, simple, energy-saving device. There are real design as well as management problems to be solved for offices where the decision for cost, for communication, or for functional reasons is to provide open-plan working areas for large numbers of staff. Layout, type and placement of partitions, the height of screens between desks where these are used, and light-switching devices are all important design issues.

What Does It Cost?

One reason for the spread of open-plan office buildings is that this type of accommodation costs less per square foot to install, maintain, and replan, and you need less of it for a given number of staff. Each of the different office plans in Figure 4.1 can be viewed as a diagram showing the relative importance of bureaucracy and interaction in an organization. As far as the bottom line is concerned, they each have space-per-person and fitting out implications that have a significant impact on cost. Added costs are entailed by partitions, doors and their ironmongery, and individually controlled lighting and heating, and in finishes for smaller spaces. Though important, fitting-out costs have less impact than space-per-person costs, which recur annually.

The average amount of space per person depends in part on the level of enclosure. In open plan a desk can occupy 50 ft^2 (5 m^2) of open space or less. In cellular arrangements the individual's desk must be replaced by at least 100 ft^2 (9 m^2), a minimal room. This increases the average space per person. The Combi office has an even higher allocation of space per person because shared areas for a group are added. Total space requirements for an organization are built up as shown in Figure 2.2. The average space per person for a hypothetical group, based on the workplace standards illustrated in Figure 3.3 and including primary circulation, varies with different arrangements. With more individual or small-group rooms, primary circulation routes increase in length and hence in area. On this basis the average lettable space per person in open plan is about 75 ft^2 (7 m^2); for group offices for six people it rises to about 85 ft^2 (8 m^2), and for two-person offices to nearly 100 ft^2 (9 m^2) per person. Where all have their own office, it goes up to about 140 ft^2 (13 m^2) per person, and in an arrangement like a Combi office, it rises to 170 ft^2 (15 m^2) per person, for this hypothetical group.

A need to contain the cost of space should not dictate the type of office plan, the degree of enclosure, chosen to support your business. Neither should it be ignored. The costs locked up in the space equation can be affected in several ways; limiting the amount of enclosure is only one. Omitting partitions makes less saving than seeking competitively priced furniture and finishes. It could cost 25 to 30 percent more to outfit space to a similar standard for cellular space than for open plan, whereas costs could double between a basic provision and a high-quality one. Adopting new ways of working, and thus sharing space in different ways, may be more economical. Location decisions may be changed. A central, expensive location may be less important than lots of space and high levels of enclosure—unless, of course, you can afford both space and place, now and in the anticipated future.

Change, Churn, and Communication

Modern organizations must be fleet of foot if they are to survive. Change is the watchword, so churn must follow. Open-plan space needs minimal reorganization. It easily accepts newly constituted groups, especially if a limited number of dimensionally related space standards, as described in the last chapter, are used. This may be a very good reason for adopting it but not necessarily the decisive one. Communication may be more important. Both should be taken into account. In times of rapid change, when new organizational structures are being implemented and frequently modified, the locations where people work in a building change. Mergers and growth in boom periods are followed by downsizing and streamlining in recessions. Team structures and members are constantly on the move. Reengineering will undoubtedly lead to moves of individuals and groups as the entire way in which organizations work is subjected to radical change.

Fundamental space-planning policies—decisions about how much enclosure is required—have a major contribution to make. The less specific the subdivision of the space is to the particular group sizes that obtain at any time, the fewer partitions have to be moved to relocate differently structured groups. Fewer changes mean less cost and disruption. Moving partitions is disruptive at any time. In some buildings it is worse than others.

In the headquarters building of a major oil exploration company, a plan was put forward to reorganize an area, move a partition, and allow a stranded secretary to work more closely with her group. Engineers calculated that, as a consequence, the location of an air-conditioning unit would have to be changed and the cost would be $10,000. Even making an opening in the partition for visual links would unbalance the air-conditioning. The change was vetoed. The building, through the design of its partition layout and air-conditioning system, dictated a work pattern that the manager and his group knew would be less productive, not to mention less pleasant for the secretary.

Open plan can aid communication and interaction. Management gurus stress the importance of new communication patterns, the prominence of teamwork, the liberating effects of new technology. The possibility must at least be considered that a manager behind his or her own office door, even when it is an open door, is less likely to anticipate and adapt to the ever-more-ambiguous and fast-changing world. Office walls are themselves a form of insulation, if not against seeing the need for others to change, still often against having to change oneself. For a team to work together, its members must be in communication. One simple way to achieve this is for all the members of the team to share a work room or space that helps to foster communication. The landscaped office was promoted on the assumption that increased interaction would result from its use.

Researchers have begun to look at communication in more detail. Rather than simple openness, high levels of interaction seem to be encouraged in locations where lines of sight and access routes on the office floor link many workplaces. A topology that allows this is not always open plan. Equally, some open-plan layouts are such that this aim is not achieved. For organizations on several floors, interaction can be enhanced if the routes between floors are simple and as short as possible, with few direction changes. This idea is based on evaluating whether people are likely to interact with each other as they walk about in specific layouts, rather than assuming that openness creates interaction.

The people serving in reengineered organizations are less likely to be described as "managers" than before the changes, but are more likely to be given considerable autonomy and responsibility for their own actions. Yet the reward for taking on responsibility is not an office of their own, as it might well have been when middle managers were in fashion. In the interests of improved teamwork, these new-style workers may have had to give up the offices they once occupied, or at least forgo any expectation of promotion to an office.

Does it work? Are the benefits worth the deprivation? Where interaction is desired, it is often achieved in open plan. Freely offered comment from office workers questioned about their office building suggests that the theory that open plan aids teamwork and communication is borne out in practice, though there are also penalties.

I prefer the open-plan system. It is easier to be close to staff that you deal with on a regular basis. You are able to keep in touch with what is happening.

Togetherness creates team spirit. The major benefit of this office is the mixing of staff due to the open-plan arrangement. The drawback is the noise level when concentration on work is necessary.

—QUESTIONNAIRE RESPONSES FROM STAFF IN OFFICES THAT HAD CHANGED TO OPEN PLAN FROM GROUP ROOMS

Group Rooms

The choice may be wider than between a personal private office or a perch in a battery henhouse. Open plan is not precisely defined in a dictionary. Between two and four people in a room hardly seems to justify the term *open plan,* but it seems reasonable to consider a room with more than 10 people as an open-plan office. There are ways to space plan a group of this size so that people are clustered in smaller numbers, though the whole area may still be, in effect, open plan. People in a large survey were asked to state with how many people they shared their room. They sometimes opted for the size of a small local group within a larger space rather than indicating that the area where they worked was essentially a vast open plan area of up to 100 people. They may have suffered from some of the disadvantages of open plan, but their perception was that they were in a small area, usually accommodating 3 or 4 people.

A group room or a shared room, containing about four people, has several of the prized attributes of a personal office. Every occupant is close to a window, and the noise and disturbance to which they are subjected is from a small, defined group. The group can reach agreement about acceptable telephone behavior, at-the-desk meetings, or other sources of distraction. Conversely, they may sometimes find it hard to ignore completely the conversation of a few colleagues, whereas the general noise level in a large open-plan area can mask individual conversations. In a group room people can agree whether the window should be open, the lights on, or the blinds closed. The distraction caused by the movement of people around the office as a whole is muted by the separating walls and door. Rooms for small groups are common in office buildings. They are congenial in many respects, but from a layout and management point of view, they have some of the disadvantages of single-person offices in cost with respect to both capital and replanning costs. They have a particularly rigidifying effect, making it hard to create new groups, dissolve old ones, and bring people together in different forms—an aim that is important to the way some modern companies work. If the room prescribes the size of group, say, four or five people, because additional desks simply cannot be fitted in, this can be even more difficult to overcome than creating good working teams of varying sizes with people in individual or two-person offices (Fig. 4.2).

Figure 4.2 I *need* to be alone.
(*Darius.*)

I *Need* My Own Office

Q: *What can reduce grown men to tears?*

A: *Having to give up their own office.*

Space is the most emotional thing in the whole of the company....Half the power base is having an office.
—INTERVIEW COMMENT PRIOR TO THE PILOTING OF A CHANGED
OFFICE LAYOUT

A Room with a View, The L-Shaped Room: These are novels, not books about offices, but their titles convey the notion that a room can evoke strong feelings and be important for generating a sense of identity, security, and role. The reasons given by those working in their own offices for continuing in solitary splendor are pretty consistent: seniority, confidentiality, concentration, and the need to hold meetings. The assumption that seniority confers a right to an enclosed office is not always made explicit. There is tacit recognition that in times of change this may be a weak argument, though in reality it is often a strongly held view. Personnel officers say that privacy is essential to allow private matters to be discussed with staff. Lawyers claim client confidentiality. Academics, curators, and editors want isolation for concentration and walls for books and paper storage. They forget that space is not a free good. Senior executives assume that company strategy must be a matter for security. Statements made in defense of retaining personal offices imply that most telephone calls, however innocently they start, end up discussing matters that would be dynamite if they leaked out, that most one-to-one conversations with subordinates end in tears, and that the constantly frustrated goal of most office dwellers is to get their heads down to write or calculate in uninterrupted creative silence—not to mention the fact that they also need to hold private meetings in their offices.

Of course, all these things take place. What is hard to learn is the truth about how often they happen, how unpredictable they are, and whether, if known about in advance, they should, or at least could, take place in an enclosed room that is not a personal office. When pressed, people who "need" their own offices may admit that unexpected developments during telephone conversations that result in a need for the highest discretion are not a daily, perhaps not even a weekly, not even a monthly, occurrence. Most of the interviews that will end in tears can be predicted. Many people actually do their most creative work at home or on the train anyway. When a few colleagues are gathered together in a meeting, they are, of course, using only one private office for the purpose, so the others are empty. In strictly functional terms, much work could take place somewhere other than in an enclosed personal office.

Status, tradition, and identity also influence the desire for an office. Considerable persuasion may be required to alter entrenched views. Consider a hypothetical discussion between the chief executive of J. Robinson Foods and his finance director, recently hired from an organization that has benefited from more open planning.

J. ROBINSON III: My father had this office, all my friends have large offices, and I don't see why I can't have one too.

FINANCE DIRECTOR: Let's look at the reasons why chief executive or other senior directors might need a lavish office. First, for *status*, to protect their image in the eyes of the outside world and people in their own organization. Second, because they may have many large *meetings*, either with their own staff or with senior managers from other companies, and they wish to entertain them in their own office. Third, because space and *quiet* might be necessary for their work. Fourth, because matters they deal with may be *confidential*.

But let us also consider why they might not have one. First, it is expensive; the company may not be able to afford it, and such waste may create a bad impression. Second, it sets a precedent; all of their staff may aspire to offices of their own and feel aggrieved if they do not have one. Third, large meetings happen infrequently; most of the time the office contains only one person or is empty. Fourth, chief executives tend to travel a great deal to meetings elsewhere. Fifth, when they hold meetings in their own offices, they are interrupted by their staff giving them messages or asking them to sign documents or answer urgent calls. An individual large office is not necessarily the right solution.

J. ROBINSON III: I accept your points, but I still want my own office...because...well, because I *want* my own office.

FINANCE DIRECTOR: You talk like most senior directors. But in some organizations they have been asked to rethink their need for large offices. Let me tell you what some of them say after relinquishing them. They say that they communicate better with staff. They say that they understand far more about the workings of their organization. They say that they need fewer meetings, and those they have are shorter because they already know what is going on. They say that they feel part of a team instead of being isolated at the top.

J. ROBINSON III: But surely they feel they have given up something very important?

FINANCE DIRECTOR: They admit that sometimes they miss the splendid isolation of their lost offices, that sometimes they cannot concentrate properly on their work because of the distractions, that they may have lost some of their air of authority. The ones who seem most satisfied are those who instead have created a series of conference and entertainment rooms, available when they need them, used by others when they do not, rooms of beauty and on a generous scale, which are tidier and more dignified than their own messy offices. There they can talk to guests and staff when occasion demands. Some have kept an office just big enough for solo work or for meetings with one or two others. Give me a chance to show you that your authority will not be diminished, and your productivity may even be increased, by a different attitude to offices.

J. ROBINSON III: You speak persuasively. Perhaps we can think again about the number, size, and type of offices.

I might be able to manage without one, or anyway with only a small one.

Some people do need an office, if not an ultralavish one, and this can apply even in an organization committed to open plan. As suggested by J. Robinson's finance director, status, meetings, quiet, and confidentiality are all valid reasons in the right circumstances. There may well be people whose need for enclosure really *is* a reflection of status that should be emphasized and must be provided for. Others have a genuine need for frequent meetings, attended by several people, that would be disturbing if held in the open plan, and there may not be meeting rooms available. Quiet concentration may be essential for large parts of the day—academics are a case in point. Such people are often surrounded by more papers and reference material than normal and need wall space against which they can be stored. The most senior people in an organization—the governor of the National Bank, for instance—may deal with genuinely confidential material on computers or paper that is hard to keep "for your eyes only" during a normal office day without separation by walls and a door. Some people depend on being able to reassure clients or informants to whom they speak on the telephone that conversations are fully confidential. Lawyers are frequently cited as an obvious group, although there are examples of shared rooms, and even shared desks, for legal professionals, so merely being a partner in a large law firm need not be an automatic passport to an office of one's own.

Where should the cellular office be located if it is used? How should a manager's office relate to the workplaces occupied by the team? It is common, especially in North American buildings, for individual offices to occupy the window walls, enclosing a group of junior staff and secretaries in the dark middle of the building (see Fig. 4.1). This is a poor environmental solution, though the team's location in relation to managers may be good. In some organizations the principle has been reversed, so that managers occupy the artificially lit interior and their staff are near the windows. The justification for this is that the senior staff have the benefit of more space and are less often at their desks. Another arrangement designed to place managers next to their teams results in a scatter of offices along window walls. If carefully planned, these offices may give the additional benefit of screening small sections of open space from each other.

Where their relationship with each other is very important, several managers can be grouped together, even if it places them away from their teams. At the most extreme is the *top-floor syndrome,* where the directors inhabit a stratospheric area, far above the masses, surrounded by conference facilities, executive dining rooms, thick carpet, wood paneling, and original works of art. In a prominent headquarters of a San Francisco bank, the windows on that elevated floor are cleaned twice as often as those below. This way of allocating space is not as common as it once was, but it is useful where relationships between top managers and the outside world, or with each other, are paramount.

Space for the Top Team

"The best work environment I ever had before now," muses Bernard Fournier, chief executive of Xerox International, "was a long time ago when I worked with three others in an open office. For most of my career since then, I've worked in enclosed offices as I kept moving up the executive ladder." At the Xerox International headquarters in Marlow, he felt that the office inhibited communication and slowed down decisions. All directors sat in enclosed monastic cells protected by personal secretaries. Interaction happened according to the dictate of diaries full of meetings. It was effective for concentrated, heads-down work, but a barrier to work which is heads up or heads together, precisely those areas in which the company needed to develop.

(Continued)

(Continued)

Fournier felt the building needed a change to support the company's program of improvement. Xerox needed to become less hierarchical, develop a flatter organization, do more team-based work demanding participation and communication. Change needed to start at the top. Fournier picked up a pen and began to sketch a concept. The elements are simple—a large oval table shared by the top directors and fringed by four "glass boxes" into which they can retreat. The sketch has been built. Most walls have been removed—those that remain are ethereal glass walls without visible frames, and they act only as sound barriers, not as visual screens. Directors and support people sit together in the open. The concept is that everyone should be visible most of the time they are in the office.

The office works absolutely as intended. Decisions are speeded up, and the top team does communicate more effectively. They are each aware of what is happening, and they are more visible and more approachable. Formal meetings are reduced. Most work takes place at the oval table for ease of decision making. Casual meetings and interaction support planned meetings. Space has been saved. Is there any one thing he would wish to improve? Absolutely none. He is very happy with the way it has turned out.

The Trauma of Change

Maybe J. Robinson III followed his finance director's advice. Maybe not. Whatever the rights and wrongs of open-plan working areas, people's initial reaction is that they are suffering if asked to change from enclosed offices to open plan. Even those who formerly shared with two or three other people can resent a move to larger open-plan rooms. The trauma of change is not mentioned when the change is in the opposite direction. When staff previously in open plan are given offices of their own, stories are rarely heard of their suffering from isolation or their grief for companions they once enjoyed. So one must accept that there are real problems to be dealt with in the move to open plan.

Serious attention must be given to ensuring that people are not made to feel that they are being demoted by a change to open plan. The loss of an enclosed office happens naturally when a senior member of staff in a regional office is recruited to the central headquarters—rather like moving from the top of the primary to the bottom of the secondary school. Acclimatization can be difficult, but resentment is not usually a central reaction. A change from an enclosed office to large open-plan spaces is less well accepted by existing job holders if it is not shared by senior staff. It is hard to accept that loss of an office is not equivalent to loss of status if there are others whose seniority apparently entitles them to an office. The more general the change, the more levels in the organization it affects, the less likely it is to give anyone a sense of personal inferiority.

If the most senior manager can accept open-plan working, adapt to the fact of being potentially under scrutiny at all times, and maintain a managerial role without the support of clear spatial definition, it is easier for others to acknowledge that their own worth is not in question. If senior people indicate the value to be gained from openness, encourage interaction between hitherto separate groups and functions, and lead the change from in front, open-plan benefits will be maximized and will help to cushion the trauma of change. Bosses who take the lead and embrace the change personally can have a powerful psychological effect. Senior managers who go open plan at the same time as all the rest of the staff are on higher moral ground—important in a situation with such significant psychological dimension. In a practical sense, they are also more likely to make sure that the disadvantages are minimized and the bugs in the planning ironed out, as they are affected personally by the success or failure of the way the open area functions.

Regardless of how many others suffer the same change, bitterness is still aroused when people who expected to be given an office of their own upon reaching a particular level in the organization see that privilege disappear just before, or just after, attaining that status. The gap between expectation, which may have played a strong motivational role, and reality, is like waking up and realizing that something pleasant was actually only a dream. It is an emotional, rather than a functional, shock.

For some, however, there are functional problems as well: those whose work habits are based on the availability of a personal office. There is the loud-telephone-voice habit, which does not move easily into open plan. There is the occupant who is proud to be able to navigate unerringly through the layer of papers, several months deep, on every available surface in the room. This is a form of "horizontal" filing for which open plan cannot offer sufficient space or clearly defined boundaries, even if the squalor can be tolerated. These are real difficulties for which there are no easy solutions. Each group of people has different causes for concern, and each case deserves attention about how to overcome the problems. Some people are very hostile to change, even when the change is soundly based. They can grumble incessantly and cause an atmosphere that makes the change harder for everyone, even for those people who thought they would benefit from it. Such people need individual consideration, which must take the form of helping them to adapt without reducing their ability to function rather than adapting the proposed change to suit them at expense of others or of the office function as a whole.

Giving Something Back in Return

There is some scope for compensation when open plan is introduced. The environment can be made attractive with plants, artwork, and good lighting. Efficient and stylish new furniture can be offered. Other amenities may be provided for which there was previously no space (see Chapter 7). Portable computers, mobile phones, and the opportunity to work a more flexible day or week may help to soften the blow. Some organizations have taken very seriously the need to make better use of their space and to promote better communication within the office. They have decided to place all staff, even the most senior managers, in open plan as a matter of principle. When this has disrupted a long tradition of hierarchy, compensation has been made to those affected, and, as a consequence, some of the measures listed above have been successfully adopted. For others engaged in creative design or media activities, the benefits of interaction have always been appreciated. Even the most senior directors in such organizations have always worked in the open, making excellent use of shared meeting and interview rooms for the times when people need to be private.

The provision of alternative enclosed rooms, if people cease to have enclosed offices, must be carefully considered. As well as rooms needed for meetings, conveniently located near the working areas, there may be a need for interview rooms, to be used during recruiting sessions or staff reviews. Whether designated specifically as interview rooms or not, these can be located near the personnel or human resources team, who have frequent need for such spaces. The amount of time spent in meetings in their own offices is exaggerated by many managers. Typically senior managers have about three meetings a day, but only one in their own offices. Surveys in a wide range of organizations have shown that in situations where about 10 percent of the staff have enclosed offices, meetings are held in them only about 15 percent of the working day. If everyone were in open-plan settings, even this level of use would require several dedicated meeting rooms to allow for overlapping schedules.

Conference or meeting rooms may be grouped in a suite to which several teams within the organization have access. Flexibility can be added by folding doors, though good ones that are adequately soundproof and do not look temporary are expensive and hard to source. A suite of rooms used primarily for meetings with people from outside the organization, can be placed near reception to avoid the disturbance and security risk of outsiders entering the main working part of the office. They can be serviced efficiently for coffee and even meals if they are located near the kitchens or have a local serving pantry. Quiet rooms, small booths, carrells, or library and reference areas may be provided to satisfy the need for separation and quiet, and these may be even better suited to total concentration than enclosed offices, where people can telephone or drop in.

Control Noise and Distraction

A total open-plan system is not conducive to concentration. This needs urgent action. The noise at times is appalling. Interruptions are frequent and unnecessary.

The office can be noisy for telephone calls due to open plan.

The open-plan concept has failed. People feel cramped for space, and the noise levels cause constant distractions.

Open plan is like trying to have a pee in an open field. There's nowhere to hide.
—QUESTIONNAIRE RESPONSES FROM STAFF WHO HAD CHANGED TO OPEN PLAN FROM GROUP ROOMS

Status-related issues and individual functional idiosyncrasies are only part of the problem of open-plan environments. A perennial complaint is the inability to concentrate because of the noise created by others on the telephone or in conversation with people at their desks and the distracting effect of seeing people move around. This is, to some extent, always going to present difficulties. Soft surfaces, acoustic ceilings, carpets, upholstered chairs, and fabric-covered acoustic screens can all help to reduce sound levels. A very thick carpet, laid over a very thick underlay, can reduce ambient sound by as much as 70 percent. Many carpets in offices do not reach this standard, and even where they do, a 70 percent reduction in noise can still leave a very distracting residue. Screens that are described as acoustically efficient should absorb 85 percent of the sound hitting them. Again, this seems an impressive figure, but most of the sound that causes disturbance will not actually hit the screen; it will go over or bounce around. *White noise*—an indistinguishable background sound intended to cover and disguise sharper, random sounds—can be introduced. But no sound deadening wholly prevents the hypersensitive from being disturbed by the noise made by their colleagues, particularly if they are predisposed to be disturbed because of their dislike of the open-plan arrangement. The distance between people is important, so the area allocated to each person—that is, the density of occupation—affects how disturbing someone else's conversation may be. Whether they are facing each other is even more significant, so if the people are within 5 to 10 ft (2 to 3 m) of each other, positioning their desks at 90 degrees to each other may help reduce the problem.

Movement catches the eye, and people passing by do easily distract. If desks are placed so the occupants face a busy corridor or a center of activity such as a photocopier, their work may suffer. The value of being able to hear what others are saying—to be aware of developments, to make unplanned contributions, to know who is doing what—is part of what the improved communications of the open plan is about. This should not be taken to mean that all distractions are productive and must be tolerated uncritically. They need to be understood and controlled, in just the way that time-and-motion studies sought understanding and control of fragmented production processes.

A new management task is to observe and understand the dynamics of whatever degree of openness is deemed best for the activities being carried out in order to get the best out of the benefits and control the disadvantages. Only with knowledge of what happens in different physical arrangements can sensible decisions be made. It seems as if no thought had been given to the needs of settlements and accounts in John Mole's example but rather that decisions had been based on tradition and clout. Accounts were spiritually or habitually closer to the finance director and thus merited more subdivision, although in practice they did not want to be cut off by the high screens.

Two types of input are needed to create successful open-plan offices: first, design input to provide the correct layout, screens, and quiet places of escape, and second, management input to help people to use the space effectively and to feel comfortable in it. Much can be done to train people to be considerate—for example, to lower their voice when on the telephone, to sit down when talking to colleagues so that the sound does not travel far, to turn the bell on the telephone to the quietest ring, to move to a quiet room when concentration is essential. A clean-desk policy and good facilities management to ensure that tops of cupboards, spaces by fire doors, and corners under the desks do not fill up with surplus piles of paper can be very effective in creating an attractive atmosphere.

In a government office that took the radical step of putting everyone, including the most senior manager who is in charge of 1,000 people, into an open plan, rules have been devised to ensure good open-plan manners. Any visitor who stops to ask a member of staff a quick question is automatically asked to sit down. This stops sound traveling far and greatly reduces the disturbance of their chat.

Walls, Partitions, and Screens

Four walls and a door make a room. There are usually at least a few enclosed offices. There are always some rooms with walls, even in organizations where senior staff work in open plan, for such areas as conference rooms, group rooms, and stationery or computer rooms. There are several ways to build the separation. Walls can be built on site, fixed and solid, whether timber or masonry. They may be factory-made partitions constructed in a wide variety of ways and designed to be relocated. The nearest equivalent in the open plan is screens reaching up to somewhere between desk and ceiling height.

Functional, financial, and aesthetic considerations need to be borne in mind when making a choice of partition. This choice may be overt when planning and commissioning a new layout, or it may be tacit when deciding to move to an office building where a particular partition type has already been chosen and installed. The main issues are: Should the partitions be permanently fixed and built solidly as part of the building or be movable to some degree? And should they be partially, completely, or not at all glazed? How soundproof should they be?

For confidentiality, sound deadening is important. Measurements of sound levels make use of a logarithmic scale, so that twice as much sound raises the noise level by only a few decibels. Control of sound has to take into account the frequencies of the sound, the noisiness of the location, the quietness desired, and the distances between the sound and the person to be protected. A reduction of about 40 decibels reduces adjacent conversation to an unobjectionable level on a fairly noisy site. The sound deadening offered by different types of partition needs to be reviewed. As sound travels, it leaks above suspended ceilings and light fittings, below raised floors, through the cracks around apparently well fitting doors, and past poorly fitted partition systems. All things being equal, however, weight helps to reduce sound transmission. Solid walls, permanently fixed, are likely to be heavier than partition systems and may be cheaper to build in the first place. On the other hand, for an office layout that can be expected to change within a few months or a year, lighter partitions that can be easily removed and may also be relocatable reduce the disruption and cost of such changes. For many organizations this consideration is far more important than achieving the highest level of sound deadening.

Glazing can be used to reduce the claustrophobic effects of corridors, to allow "borrowed" light to reach interior spaces and to enhance communication when visual links are helpful—for instance, it allows people to see that the occupant is busy before bursting in. Some glazing is normally required for fire safety, although this may be as small as a porthole in a door. Larger areas of glass may be provided as panels in doors or partitions, or as full-height glass partitions. Blinds can act as screens when it is preferable for people not to be able to see into rooms. Etched glass allows visual privacy without blocking light, though many types are easily marked when touched and can look rather unkempt, as greasy marks are often hard to remove. Sound reduction can be achieved by double glazing with a wide gap of about 6 in (150 mm).

Screens—normally fabric-covered panels stopping short of the ceiling and separating one person from another—are the compromise eagerly grasped by those groups whose need for defined personal space cannot be met in truly open layouts. Beware of free-standing screens that can be moved from place to place. Not only do they usually have feet that stick out to trip the unwary, but also the bullies, the self-important, and the truly antisocial manage to acquire these as efficiently as magnets attract iron filings and create enclosures and empires quite irrelevant to the smooth working of the whole organization.

Screens connected to desks come in two distinct types. Some of them are essential to hold up the desk; others stand hard up against a desk that supports itself. The latter may be needed to act as a *modesty panel,* a low-level screen to stop drafts and discourage the guys from staring at nylon-sheathed legs across the room. The part that sticks up above the desk can be used or abused. It may function merely to stop papers from dropping off the desk onto the floor. It may rescue people who work face to face from eye contact or from staring into the rear end of their opposite number's computer. Even if acoustically efficient, it may not prevent noise from traveling but then a part of the distraction of someone else's conversation is being aware of what they are doing while they talk. A screen can act as a support from which to hang shelves and telephone stands or a surface on which to pin working material—say, maps of sales areas, administrative aids like telephone lists, or family photos and certificates of job achievement. Many types of screen can give you a bruised thumb if you try to stick in a push pin, so if they are really wanted as display surfaces, check that they are suitably constructed.

Different heights have different uses. Cubes or cubicles, shielded by 5 ft (1.5 m) high screens, are common in the United States, uncommon in Europe. As screens get higher, they cut out more and more light and air, so the pleasant expansive feeling that can be one of the benefits of open-plan space is replaced by a gloomy maze. Plan layouts of screens so that those parallel to the window wall are minimal in height, say, around 1 ft (300 mm) above the desk surface. Reduce to a minimum the number that are treated as a substitute for full-height partitions. They nearly always enclose an area that is smaller than it would be if it were a real room. In addition, there is a danger that there may be several layers of screened workstations between the window and a circulation route, so the overall effect can easily become poky and confusing, the very opposite of the open-plan, interactive environment. Dispose of any free-standing ones left over from the last office-planning exercise.

A Move Back to Cellular Offices?

The dislike, felt by many, of open plan, the feeling that it may alienate people at least as much as it allows them greater opportunities for communication, has fueled active discussion of the possibility of returning to the older pattern of more highly cellularized buildings. In Europe cellular offices have been popular for some time. The influence of North America has been in the opposite direction. Although *Bürolandschaft*—free-flowing layouts, and plenty of plants on vast office floors—is associated with Germany, the open-plan office was really a big hit in America. North Americans have little experience of long, narrow buildings or ones with a maze of tiny rooms clustered around a honeycomb of light wells. The North American urban legacy has few old buildings constructed before big spans were possible; hence its office buildings are large and high, with elevators to carry people up 20, then 40, then a hundred stories, and readily suited to open plan. Much of the development capital that fueled office-building booms in Britain after 1945 was influenced, even provided, by American companies. The style to which they had grown accustomed across the Atlantic was replicated, albeit not very lavishly. Recently the importance of international cooperation between European companies has become more significant. Other office cultures and ways of working have come to the notice of users and designers. There are, for example, rules in France about how far from a window your desk can be. This reduces the depth of buildings and immediately reduces the benefits of open plan. The Scandinavians, the French, the Dutch, and the Germans show a preference for enclosed, cellular office planning. Since people in other countries would like this too, there is a possibility that more new buildings will be constructed on models that at least allow for a high level of cellularization, even if they do not demand it. There is still, however, a huge stock of office buildings that will not work well with a high percentage of cellularized space, so many people will be working in open plan for a long time to come, and care in fitting out will be well repaid.

Summary

This chapter helps you to think through how much space should be allocated to enclosed private offices and how much should be open plan. It suggests approaches that may ease the transition to more open plan if that becomes the policy of the organization.

Enclosed offices were the norm until office buildings were built with minimal internal structural divisions. The prevalent assumption is that seniority confers a right to privacy even when construction enables everyone to be in the open plan. There are situations where enclosure is suitable and necessary. Open-plan office floors have encouraged the development of system furniture, which is often used to give an illusion of enclosure.

Enclosed offices cost more to provide. The average space per person is larger, and the capital and replanning cost is higher. Open plan facilitates change, making it easier as well as cheaper. It is often adopted in order to improve communications. Interaction is increased if the plan enables direct visual and physical communication between people. For appropriate groups, the benefits that this brings are much appreciated.

Those whose status, expectations, and habits of self-importance lead them to believe that they need their own office can be hard to convince. There are good arguments for adopting more open solutions even among senior people, whose example will ease the disruptive and distressing effects of change for other staff.

The benefits of open plan are often jeopardized by noise and distraction. Awareness of this problem, careful space planning, the introduction of special quiet areas where justified, and the use of sound-deadening finishes, white noise, and staff training, can all help.

Where enclosure must be provided, there is a choice between full-height separation in the form of partitions or walls and lower division provided by screens. Different partition types have varied levels of permanence, but the heavier they are, the more efficiently they intercept sound. The spaces above and below ceilings and floors can allow sound to leak if they are not carefully designed. Screens are least successful if they are treated as "almost partitions." Heights need to be controlled to allow light and openness to be enjoyed generally.

There is a belief that, as many people prefer enclosed offices and they are commonly provided in continental European countries, there will be a shift toward providing more buildings that may be highly cellularized. The trend for rapid communication between different teams and rapid regrouping of teams is a powerful driver to keep pulling down walls. The proper planning and management of open-plan space will be a valuable skill for some time to come.

CHAPTER 5

Furniture for Function, Fashion, and Finance

CASE HISTORIES

See Case History 14
on pages 369–376

The furniture looks very pretty but isn't functional. Many of the locks haven't worked since day 1. Drawers do not fit properly and are constantly coming off runners. Chances are that in five years' time we will be left with a pile of rubble.

—QUESTIONNAIRE RESPONSE FROM OCCUPANT IN AN OFFICE WITH NEW FURNITURE

Note: Some of the material in this chapter first appeared in *Space Management,* 1997–1998, Eclipse.

There are literally hundreds of companies making office furniture. Can they really all be making different things? At office furniture exhibitions, hundreds of firms exhibit desks, screens, tables and chairs. Office furniture is big business. The U.S.A. market has been steadily growing in real-dollar costs by an average of 5 percent per year for 20 years and is now around $13 billion per year. Competition is fierce, and the result is unlimited choice in a partially fashion driven environment in which poor purchases are made as easily as good ones, unless you know what you are doing.

A Desk Is Not Just a Desk

[For the executives] furniture tends to be of a higher quality than elsewhere in the organization....

—FRITZ STEELE, "THE ECOLOGY OF EXECUTIVE TEAMS: A NEW VIEW OF THE TOP"

People react to furniture as a symbol of many things; they do not merely take a rational view of how useful an item will be. Marketing information exploits this, as managers well know. Catalogues gloss over useful technical information and instead provide images of a lifestyle. The boss gets rosewood; the open-plan secretarial area gets a color scheme suited to a spring collection of ladies' separates in a department store.

There are ways to bring order to chaos and isolate important information from the noise of marketing. The most common furniture items, used by nearly all office staff, are a desk, a chair, and local storage units. Specialized items, like tables and chairs for conference rooms, cashier points, dealing desks, and bulk-storage systems, are sometimes needed. They are important, often sophisticated and expensive, but do not, for most organizations, represent the main part of the furniture budget. Take stock first, therefore, of just the desk, the chair, and local storage. This combination of items is called here a *workstation*.

Several aesthetics are to be found. There are ethereal, slim, high-tech items that hover on a single supporting beam that is all important structurally but hidden discretely under the desk surface. There are sturdy cubes carefully designed and coordinated with a place for everything, from trays for product literature, pens, and company stationery to a hook for a coat and a bracket for the telephone. There are total workstations that fold away into a cupboard, or open out like flower petals to reveal high and low work surfaces, storage spaces, and computer shelves. There are simple desks supported on metal or wooden legs or frames, which vary considerably in elegance. Do-it-yourself, self-assembly, and bargain items, affordable but flimsy and short-lived, are another solution. Practical, cheap, and without a claim to being furniture are desks made of a flush door balanced across two metal filing cabinets from a second-hand outlet dealing in bankrupt stock. This was the solution used by Jeff Bezos, the founder of Amazon Books. In the early days of his business, he said, "We have the best software, and the best people, but we don't spend money on things that don't matter much."

Many furniture lines are based on a wooden construction, and their suppliers have had the monopoly until recently in supplying chief executives' furniture. Utilitarian metal furniture was initially provided for the clerical masses and formed the basis of the business of, say, Steelcase in the United States, the largest furniture supplier in the world. Now the new designs in metal furniture have increasingly come to be accepted as high quality and form the basis of most office interiors. There are workstations majoring on ergonomic adjustability with clever levers and ratchets or motorized means of altering heights, angles, or slopes to suit different users. European manufacturers lay particular stress on adjustability though essential height adjustability can normally be provided by chairs. Refinements in manufacturing techniques have allowed for more interesting shapes, so now the fashion is for curves, waves, D ends, tear drops, and add-on meeting or computer spaces to replace rectilinear desks and for slim, bevelled edges to replace flat ones.

Two general philosophies about how workstation furniture can be provided are represented by stand-alone and integrated systems (Fig. 5.1). Some firms make single stand-alone items, perhaps only desks or cupboards or chairs. Others make versions of all three items so that an entire office building can be furnished fully with their products. Furniture standing in an environment provided by the building is the traditional end of the market. Then there are firms that manufacture system furniture. All the parts that make up the desk and local storage are ingeniously fixed together, with additional items like dividing screens, cable ways, and task lighting, even perhaps local air-conditioning. The furniture itself creates the environment that happens to be housed in the building. (The office chair, thank goodness, is still separate and mobile, not the fixed cafeteria arrangement where you slide into a seat growing out of the table or bolted to the floor.) Herman Miller produced the first commercially successful system furniture for offices in the 1960s. Since then the market has expanded enormously. In between these extremes there is a gray area, where parts blend into systems. Furniture designed to be assembled from a range of components, so that in different combinations a wide variety of end results can be achieved, is becoming more and more common. Accessories that go with the furniture, such as task lights, are optional.

The choice of a fully interlocking furniture system commits the user to continued use of the same system, so it must be one that serves its purpose and is liked by user groups. New items are restricted to the range supplied with the system, so unforeseen changes may be hard to deal with. On the other hand, the choice of unrelated items from the same

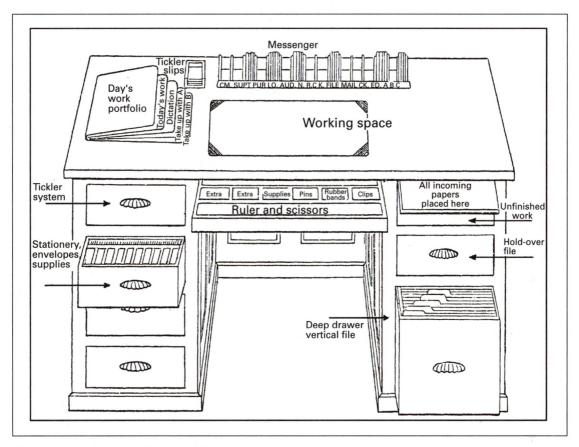

Figure 5.1   The choice of a desk to suit the task has always been important.

[The System Company, Chicago and New York, *How to Systematize the Day's Work*, London, 1911, p. 24.]

or different suppliers makes coordination difficult. In aesthetic terms it is hard to create a sense of unity; in a practical sense the dimensions of different items may not fit well together, leaving little gaps or overlapping parts that are hard to clean and make for wasteful use of space. Component ranges can offer a compromise—unity without a full straightjacket, coordinated dimensions and style that do not allow the furniture to take over the whole environment. This type of furniture is not problem free. To allow for choice, the components are often complex and specific and may involve keeping stocks of many different parts if the potential for flexibility is to be exploited.

Size, Shape, and Mobility

A variation increasingly found in many ranges is the addition of wheels to create options for complete rearrangement of working areas with minimum effort. The wheels range from the discrete carpet-friendly casters now accepted as a requirement for workplace chairs and as commonplace for desk pedestals, to large pushchair wheels on tables, or the newer personal units that are more than a storage pedestal but less than a desk. Any and every sort of office furniture can now be found in a wheeled version. Most common are work surfaces of various sizes and shapes, to be pulled into place when papers spill over or when a small group wishes to meet around the desk. These mobile surfaces often add color and interest to the working environment. At the same time they pose the problem of what to do with them when they are not in use.

Some ranges have developed a folding version, especially of the larger tables, so that they can be neatly stored when not in use. This is less common for the smaller ones. Thus, if these are to be used, "parking spaces" must be planned as well as appropriate width and route for circulation to allow them to be moved easily. Commonly nonrectilinear, they may not fit easily into the small out-of-the-way corner you had in mind for them. The advantages of mobility continue to be assiduously explored, such as entire desks made mobile with the addition of wheels. New devices, in the form of special miniature forklifts have been designed to move large filing cabinets even when fully loaded. An essential feature of effective mobile furniture is the ease of using the brakes and their efficiency.

Vertical mobility has not been forgotten. As with casters, chairs have been well in the forefront, exploiting gas lift height adjustability as a common solution for the needs of a workforce widely ranging in size and shape. The desk's top has followed more slowly. Height adjustment by a crank handle has never been a spectacular success. Electronically controlled gas-lift height adjustability could become sufficiently attractive, to justify the additional cost, especially where mobile workers use different desks each day. At the most extreme end of vertical mobility is the much illustrated Digital Equipment Company office in Sweden that enabled workers to pull a PC down from above as and when required and which could be set at whatever convenient height was desired. This is unlikely to become a standard type of solution but should be remembered as an example of the fact that most problems can be solved in a variety of ways.

In order to maximize flexibility, consider a desk to which a *separate* "return" can be added (Fig. 5.2). When an L-shaped arrangement is created out of a single item, the return is fixed on one side. In other words, the desk top is "handed," and left- and right-hand versions are needed. The alternative, to create the L shape with two separate items, must be balanced against the higher cost of two surfaces and the fact that a single item has the advantage of having no joint or crack in the work top. The choice depends in part on the extent to which future changes are likely to require revised desk layouts or to mean moving people rather than desks. It is also necessary to be aware of the changes that will result from the introduction of flat screens. Instead of needing a deep corner on which a cathode-ray screen can be placed, which has led to many versions of the "curved L" over the last decade or so, a simple rectangular table top or "wave" shape will comfortably hold the flat screen and keyboard in a good position, which may lead to changes in the preferred desk shapes in future.

Quality and value for money are everyone's objectives. They may be achieved by free-standing or system furniture, the latter generally being more expensive. This may

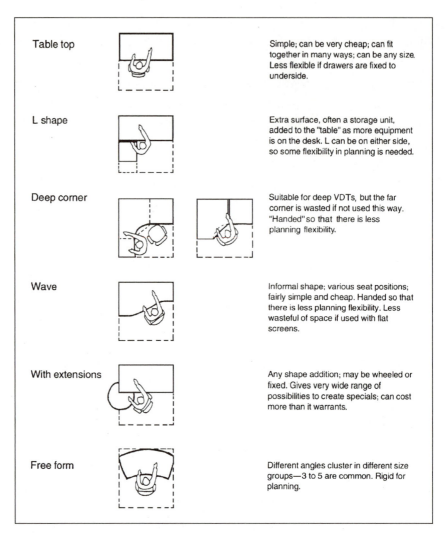

Table top — Simple; can be very cheap; can fit together in many ways; can be any size. Less flexible if drawers are fixed to underside.

L shape — Extra surface, often a storage unit, added to the "table" as more equipment is on the desk. L can be on either side, so some flexibility in planning is needed.

Deep corner — Suitable for deep VDTs, but the far corner is wasted if not used this way. "Handed" so that there is less planning flexibility.

Wave — Informal shape; various seat positions; fairly simple and cheap. Handed so that there is less planning flexibility. Less wasteful of space if used with flat screens.

With extensions — Any shape addition; may be wheeled or fixed. Gives very wide range of possibilities to create specials; can cost more than it warrants.

Free form — Different angles cluster in different size groups—3 to 5 are common. Rigid for planning.

Figure 5.2 Desk top shapes vary.

(*AMA Alexi Marmot Associates.*)

be reasonable, as it aims to do more, creating a whole environment. It is often what people feel they need if they are in the process of being led, or driven, protesting, from a highly cellular environment to a more open-plan one. Another effect is that it is far harder to modify, so that a level of visual and spatial organization is introduced that is less easily destroyed when numbers and functions change.

The furniture criticized in the quote at the start of the chapter had instant appeal because of its color and finish, but the user, not a specialist in furniture choice, readily identified the main causes of problems that recur in some ranges. The joints are poorly designed and not robust; the locks are badly made; and the cheerful glossy finishes do not make up for the structural deficiencies. One organization believed it was getting a good deal when it bought 1,000 desk pedestals at a bargain price from a furniture company that was going out of business. This was twice as many as needed, but the facility manager felt that if there were a few duds in the batch, the low price would more than make up for the inconvenience of storing the surplus and redeploying it as required. However, the furniture manufacturer was going out of business for a reason. The pedestals were badly made, and at the rate at which they were literally falling apart, the whole stock looked as though it would need replacement within two years. So considering the initial cost, the problem of finding storage space for the surplus until it was used up, the irritation of those whose pedestals fell apart once, twice, and yet again, this was a very bad bargain indeed.

Standards for strength and safety with which manufacturers are expected to comply have been drafted by government bodies. Certificates can be requested of suppliers to prove that their products meet the necessary levels. In addition, simple common-sense checks can test most aspects of the suitability and sturdiness of furniture. If you sit heavily on the edge of the desk, does it feel as if it will collapse? Are the edges smooth, with neatly finished corners? Do desks placed side by side line up at the same level? Is it easy to pull off pieces that are supposed to be demountable—the covers of cable runs, fabric panels, and edge trims? Is it easy to put them back again? Do the drawers open smoothly, and do their fittings feel robust? Do the file sizes that you use fit into them easily, with minimum wasted space? Do keys protrude so far that a passer-by will be snagged? The furniture supplier also needs to be checked. A guarantee that parts will be available for up to 10 years is important. The turn-around time for additional orders needs to be agreed. The quality of the installation service must be checked against references. If special finishes have been offered, then continued availability without a penalty price must be established. Before a big order is placed, a factory visit may be warranted to see the quality of the supplier on home ground rather than in a showroom, where problems can more easily be disguised.

The Process of Choice

There is huge range to choose from. To review and choose suitable workstations, the process can be broken down into stages:

- Create a general policy covering desired performance levels for different tasks. Consider size, storage, screening, cabling, meeting needs, finish, and quality. Also specify expected churn, furniture lifespan, servicing, maintenance, and budget (Fig. 5.3).

- Identify planning concepts for layouts and a detailed performance program related to work styles.

- Select a short list, using criteria that have been tested, refined, and agreed.

- Meet prospective suppliers, select specials, and coordinate different suppliers as part of the buying process.

It is possible to decide whether a particular furniture option meets your needs only when the clear statement of requirements has been made, by identifying the work styles and their requirements and taking the character of the organization and the building into account. If the various types can be dimensionally and aesthetically coordinated, with interchangeable parts, the work of the facilities manager

Desk based, heavily dependent on paper

Size	Large, 5-ft (1500 mm) or greater width, 2 ft 6 in (750 or 800 mm) depth
Storage	Local filing—desk pedestal and perhaps shelves over or beside the desk
Screening	Concentration likely to be required; at least mid-height [4 ft 6 in (1400 mm) from floor] screening to avoid distraction
Cables	Average provision; locally controlled lighting may be important.
Meeting area	Not desirable in open plan
Finish and quality	Standard

Desk based, dependent on computer

Size	Large, 5 ft (1500 mm) or greater width, 2 ft 6 in (750 or 800 mm) (more for deep screen) to fit screen, keyboard, and processor; L shaped is ideal. A floor-based processor requires adequate leg room.
Storage	Minimum for personal possessions and desk stationery, unless also paper dependent
Screening	Orientation with respect to glare may require screening or window blinds.
Cables	Extensive and easy to change; screen and keyboard may still be needed even when docking port for laptop is provided.
Meeting area	Not desirable in open plan
Finish and quality	Standard

Telecenter

Size	Small; minimum of 4-ft (1200-mm) width, 2-ft 6-in (750-mm) depth
Storage	Minimal, may not require any at all
Screening	Low (say, 3 ft 6 in [1300 mm] from floor) as telecenter staff often wish to talk to each other
Cables	Standard
Local meeting	Not required
Finish and quality	Standard

Figure 5.3 Workstations to suit different job types.

Hot desks	
Size	Small for short use touchdown [3- to 4-ft (900- to 1200 mm) width] larger for all-day or longer booking. Can be, e.g., a large library table or work bench for a hot team.
Storage	None at the desk; personal and group storage conveniently local
Screening	None or low
Cables	Extensive and easy to change; screen and keyboard may still be needed even when docking port for laptop is provided.
Local meeting	None
Finish and quality	Standard
Managerial	
Size	Large, 5-ft (1500 mm) or greater width, 2-ft 6-in (750 or 800 mm) depth
Storage	Local filing—desk pedestal and perhaps shelves; may need some with special locks for confidential material.
Screening	Some privacy may be required, midheight [4 ft 6 in (1400 mm) from floor] or higher.
Cables	Average provision; possibly local lighting
Local meeting	Will be required; locate in positions least likely to distract others.
Finish and quality	Only vary from standard if company culture stresses hierarchy.

Figure 5.3 Workstations to suit different job types. (*Continued*)

will be eased and the efficiency of the organization will be enhanced. These characteristics will help the process of adaptation to the inevitable changes that come about as equipment sizes change, work styles alter, and groups and numbers fluctuate (Fig. 5.4).

Storage

> *People are like bloody squirrels—they keep everything they ever come across.*
>
> **—TRAINING MANAGER OF A LARGE CORPORATION**

Storage is possibly the most important aspect of office furniture. There are rapid changes in what is being stored throughout the office and what is needed at the desk. Electronic storage is in its infancy but will certainly increase over the next decade. Meanwhile the storage of physical items con-

Capital cost	Note that price negotiations and "deals" are standard when purchasing workstation furniture.
Cost in use	Durability and quality of the design engineering and the cost of adaptability and need to reconfigure workstations.
Extent of enclosure	For example, free-standing in the open, low screens on the desk, tall screens that surround the workplace area
Desk construction type	For example, screen hung, beam based, supported on C frames—these affect how workstations come together or fit to the edges of a space.
Cable handling	Capacity for cables, ease of access for changes, number and location of outlets
Range available	Number of types and how well they match your requirement
Standard of service	Suppliers' delivery, installation, and repair including availability of spare parts over a 10-year period
Dimensions	Desk sizes—e.g., small, 4 ft by 2 ft 6 in (1200 mm × 750 to 800 mm) rectangle, to large, 6ft 6in × 6ft 6in (2000 mm × 2000 mm) by 2,000 mm L shaped
Storage	Variety, whether commonly stored items fit economically
Finishes, aesthetics	Color, appearance, surface finishes—are they suitable in quality and image?
Ergonomic, comfort, health and safety, green issues	Are your company requirements, as well as all statutory regulations, properly met?
Mobility and flexibility	Increasingly available but needs careful matching with real needs

Figure 5.4 Issues on which to base furniture choice.

Partnerships—Furniture Fitting the Organization

The partnering approach is frequently used when off-the-shelf furniture does not seem ideal for a particular project. It is often the user community that provides insights for the furniture designers to turn into the real requirements. New lines are designed to capture new and emerging markets and meet new needs. Sometimes user panels are invited to comment on designs as they are developed before full-scale marketing. Alternatively, a company may feel a need for custom-designed items. Partnering can help to meet a very tight timetable or budget or to fit into an awkward building, which nothing on the market can adequately serve. It can also help to meet new working habits if furniture design is based on a good understanding of the actual way in which people will work. If the solution is specific to an organization's particular situation, it may go no further than a single installation. However, when a large manufacturer—such as Steelcase—cooperates with an acknowledged leader in the field of alternative officing—such as TBWA/Chiat/Day, a new product that can be generally marketed—such as the Nest—may be the result.

tinues to expand. People keep far more than they need and need what they have not got (Fig. 5.5). Policies for storage must be worked out. How much paper is it reasonable for each member of staff to keep personally? Does your organization generate so many administrative forms, from staff-appraisal documentation to time-and-expense sheets, that the company is paying time and again for creating, copying, and filing such records? Should each person be offered space for spare shoes, handbags, personal mugs, and coffee jars? Should people keep their own mini-stationery store at the desk? Whatever the policy is, you must seek out the right containers.

The most desirable desk may come from a manufacturer who has not given sufficient thought to storage requirements. Maximizing the use that can be made of the internal dimensions of an under-desk pedestal or a free-standing cabinet unit requires detailed attention to height and width. Finding the right storage furniture for different purposes is *never* simple. If many different requirements must be met, it can be almost impossible to find the perfect solution that allows

	Linear feet	Linear meters
Academic in own office with bookshelves on the walls	40–50	12–15
Desk-based worker with unrestricted accumulation	20–50	6–15
Allowance where space efficiency is encouraged	10–12	3–4
Mobile workers, or IT efficient or space-conscious groups	2–6	0.5–2

Figure 5.5 Average amounts of personal storage.

some coordination of the items selected. As always, compromise may well be required. Books, files and folders, computer printouts, and computer tapes and disks all need different body movement to pull them off the shelf, come in different sizes, and are referred to in different ways. Consider the simple file. In the United States both *foolscap* and *quarto* are in common use. In Europe the occasional foolscap file coexists with those for A4. A drawer designed for foolscap is too wide for A4 (or quarto), and the hanging frame in the drawer needs to be adjusted. This may mean that A4 files hang parallel to the sides, not the front of the drawer. Why should anyone complain about this? Because it is unfamiliar and, if it is also unexpected, it may be the straw that breaks the camel's back during a period of change. Storage systems are normally built of either timber or steel. Timber filing units cannot compete with metal ones, which are often better designed, more space efficient, and more robust.

The capacity of different units varies considerably in relation to the space they occupy. A four-drawer filing cabinet, a common item of furniture, takes up more floor space for the volume of storage that it contains than a cabinet containing lateral files. The difference is partly in the different way the files are accessed. If a person is to pull out a drawer before leaning over to extract a file, the floor space needed must accommodate the cabinet, the open drawer, and the user standing in front of the drawer. With a lateral filing unit, the user stands in front of the cabinet to extract the file from a hanging pocket. Doors either stick out in the same depth of space that the person occupies, or they may be the tambour type that roll down the side and behind or up at the top. The space used is about two-thirds that of the drawer unit. A further advantage of lateral files is that they can be in a taller unit than filing cabinets without toppling over and thus save even more floor area for the amount of material stored. To see which file to extract, it is not possible to look into a drawer whose top is above eye level; hence usual heights are two-, three-, and four-drawer cabinets but not five- and six-drawer ones. Lateral frames can go higher, typically to five, six, or seven levels, because it is possible to reach up to a shelf above your head to pull down a file as long as the label can be read.

The capacity of different storage units is shown in Figure 5.6. High-density storage units are suitable if large volumes of files need to be frequently accessed. The larger and heavier the equipment being installed, the more care must be taken to ensure that its location will not need to be changed in the future. It should be easily accessed from as many parts of the office as possible but should not break up space into arbitrary chunks based merely on the user groups identified at the planning stage.

An ingenious revolving storage unit, *times two,* doubles the amount of storage in each cabinet by placing a second row of shelves back to back with the first. If what you want is not on the open shelf, simply spin the shelf around, and it will appear from the other side. Another system is rolling or sliding shelves, common in many libraries and increasingly used to control the growing mounds of paper in offices. Its efficiency comes from the fact that only one access aisle is required for many shelf units. The most up-market versions of these have a digipad on which you dial up the file you need, and the shelves open electronically, revealing the file. The power filing *paternoster* units similarly allow a

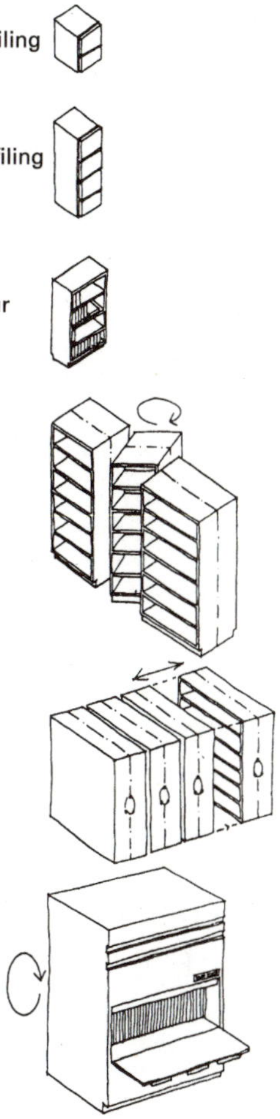

	Linear capacity, feet	Footprint area used including access	Linear feet per square foot	Linear capacity, meters	Footprint area used including access	Linear meters per square meter
Two-drawer filing						
	4	8	0.5	1.	0.8	2
Four-drawer filing						
	8	8	1	2	0.8	3
Cupboard four rows high	12	10	1	4	1	1
Revolving						
	34	19	2	11	1.8	6
Moving aisle						
	18	9	2	5.5	0.9	6
Power filing						
	170	35	5	50	3	16

Figure 5.6 Approximate capacity of different storage units.

(AMA Alexi Marmot Associates.)

specific location to be called up by a keypad entry system; then the machine, electronically guided, moves around its belt system until the desired shelf is in front of the open slot so that items can be accessed. Manufacturers of these systems stress savings in staff costs because file retrieval is so efficient. Whether or not such claims are justified, space efficiency is certainly achieved.

Just because a unit is capable of high-density storage does not always mean that it will automatically benefit your organization. The essential issue with storage is that heights and widths, both of the furniture and the material to be stored, must be measured precisely and carefully related to each other. A specific area to house, for example, a reference archive may be occupied by tall shelf units nearly reaching the ceiling. Installing a mobile racking system could mean that, although additional runs of shelf units would fit in the space, the height of each unit would be reduced because of the height of the rails supporting the racks at floor level. The difference might mean that the whole top shelf has to be reduced, making it useless for the material in the archive. The lost shelf on each unit might well not be compensated for by the additional number of units. Poorly installed or badly balanced mobile units of any kind are prone to problems that never arise with fixed, static units. The new British Library in London, used to dealing with book storage, had to combat difficulties with the mobile racking ordered for the stacks in its new building. The original shelves had to be redesigned resulting in time and cost overruns. That items may drop off mobile units always has to be taken into account. With the revolving units, for example, if a file falls to the floor at the back of a unit, there must be some space behind, and a way to access the space, if the file is to be retrieved. Some companies are offering mobility of another sort. They are providing units with specially adapted plinths, or new plinths to existing units, to enable miniforklifts to be used to move large cabinets without emptying them. The more sophisticated and complex the storage system, the higher the cost and the more that can go wrong. These are the penalties that must be paid for the very real advantages such units can offer. Another point to remember is that to change from one type of unit to another takes time and effort. Converting from file drawers to lateral frames requires new file pockets and days spent relabeling everything, which is, in short, a clerical nightmare.

What to Look For in Storage Furniture

- Dimensions that suit what is to be stored, that fit with other furniture and the building. Test these dimension by trying out typical items in your normal storage when viewing samples or visiting showrooms.

- Strong construction that meets regulations and will not fall apart.

- Smooth finishes, especially where people will come in contact with edges and corners.

- Doors and drawers that move easily, do not take up unnecessary space or restrict access when open, and return firmly to the closed position.

- Good locks, with suited keys available, where locking is needed.

- Easily interchangeable inserts for cabinets that may perform many tasks.

- A slot for a label to allow a person's name or the contents to be shown.

- Variety in sizes available to enable coordination of different areas and needs.

- Robust casters on any mobile items with strong locking mechanisms.

- Materials or colors that can be easily coordinated with other furniture.

- Potential to adapt, for example, from fixed to mobile, or from open shelves and rails to lockable inserts.

A Storage Policy

Selecting storage furniture is greatly helped by having a storage or records management policy. Many organizations already have one, at least as far as document storage is concerned. It may be that they are being driven or led toward electronic storage so that the approach to storage must be compatible with all other decisions about computer technology for the business. Electronic storage must be borne in mind as it becomes more familiar, efficient, cost effective, and therefore more prevalent. Other ways in which a storage policy will be shaped include the pattern of work and the consequent patterns of requirements for access to papers, or legal and accounting time limits that must be respected.

Storage Policy

Objectives:

- To ensure that what is needed can be accessed efficiently and promptly
- To reduce unnecessary duplication and waste
- To keep secure as required by law and business needs
- To control intrusion on the environment and erosion of work space quality

Content:

- What should be kept in the working area
- How long should each type of item be retained there
- How much should be allowed per person
- What amount is needed for shared group access
- What should be gathered for centralized access
- What can be archived on site or remotely
- Timing and process of regular culling of local and central storage
- Furniture and space for specialized or bulky items—for example, artwork and samples
- Access for heavy items

Once the decisions about each aspect of the policy have been shaped, it becomes easier to choose between different methods of storage and different types of furniture and to plan their locations in the office building.

The Mobile Worker's Unit

A new storage unit has emerged in response to the needs of mobile workforce. It provides for the storage requirements the worker who is often not in the office and is accommodated in some form of alternative office provision (see Chapter 1). Without a desk of one's own, there is no personal desk pedestal, no shelf or bulletin board above the desk, nor is there a desktop on which to put photos of the family, a stapler, a pen holder. A furniture solution used when this type of work first attracted attention was to give each worker a standard mobile pedestal and exploit its mobility by storing it in a pedestal "parking lot," allowing its owner to wheel it to a desk when in the office. This has sometimes been found to be unsatisfactory. Most pedestals are not particularly easy to move when loaded full of files—in fact, they are an ergonomic disaster as far as daily mobility is concerned. They are often not large enough, and they take up as much floor space as would a taller unit of greater capacity. They also have a tendency to be left around the office instead of being returned to their parking space, and then they get moved out of the way by an exasperated colleague. When people return to the office, they have to spend time searching for their own units.

Mobile storage solutions and a mobile "place of their own" for mobile workers, have been developing apace to try to solve some of the problems first encountered. Since the early 1990s when, for example, IBM UK developed a special unit locker for the company's first generation of mobile workers, there have been many different offerings in both the office and the home markets for foldaway, pull-along, storage-cum-additional desk surface. Designs have taken time to evolve and cannot yet be considered to be fully mature, though there are many products on the market. The problems that need to be solved for mobile units include the following:

- Wheels and brakes good for rolling about and stopping dead

- Handles for easy pulling and good balance when standing in an upright position, but not in the way

- Labels to identify the owner

- A space-efficient place to keep them when not in use

- A workplace planned so that they can be used alongside if that is intended

- Sufficient internal storage for the personal items and work files likely to be needed

- Ways to connect to power for laptop use or phone recharging as required.

Another approach is to concentrate on fixed but efficient storage, accessible to the mobile workers as they arrive in the building or near the desks they are likely to use. The solutions vary from assigning a unit from the standard storage range to special lockers. These may be designed to create a special visual effect or be tailored to the needs of those who have no other place of their own and therefore will wish to pin up family photos, receive mail, have a place for post-it memos. Portable units for files and for desk accessories such as pencils, staplers, and even the mobile phone recharger, are usefully designed into such units — detachable and easily carried to the desk chosen as work space for the day. It is important to locate the storage carefully. Storage units must not become a solid, unappealing mass of storage at important entry points to working floors. They should instead be attractive, easy to use, and placed in convenient clusters nearby desks.

The most elaborate units are almost complete offices designed to fold away like an interlocking puzzle. Such a unit may appear to be a simple cabinet when closed, but it can provide a desk surface, a full PC set up inside, shelves, and a pedestal unit that allows additional surface when everything is opened up to its fullest extent. Sometimes these units include a letterbox in the door to accept the owner's mail. A unit of this type may be fully mobile and stored at the edge of the work area unless it is in use, when it can be moved to wherever there is space and a suitable power connection. It may alternatively be permanently parked where it will be used but closed up if unoccupied to exploit the empty area around it so that others have a more spacious environment. This form of unit has been developed for the home office as much as for the "office office." New versions are being developed all the time. For some time to come it will be necessary to review carefully different items to see which fulfills your needs.

Health and Safety Law Requires You to Replace the Furniture — Or Does It?

The existence of back pain is not disputed, though its causes and prevention are debated. *Repetitive strain injury* (RSI) is not accepted as a real condition by some, although some sufferers claim to be unable to work as a result of it. Regulations attempt to limit the problems encountered by office workers as a result of the ergonomics of their furniture and equipment. People vary greatly in their physical dimensions. The task of the furniture industry, in attempting to meet the ergonomic needs of all users, is not simple. Health and safety regulations for the workplaces of people who use visual display terminals (VDTs) have been hammered out in the European Community and enacted in the United Kingdom since 1993. They give guidance on the performance of desks, chairs, and the VDTs themselves. When a new project is undertaken, or a new building built, these requirements are liable to be checked. Any new furniture must comply with the new regulations, and noncompliant furniture must be replaced. In contrast, in the United States there are three standards that call for voluntary compliance. New York is the first local area to adopt regulations regarding VDT work. The voluntary codes, each somewhat different in focus, cover issues of light levels, glare controls, vision testing for VDT workers, (NIOSH 1984) display technology, illumination, noise control, workstation design, and seating design (ANSI-HFS 100-1988), and lighting design (IES/RP-24 1989).

Many organizations have replaced their office furniture in order to be sure of complying with the regulations. Often their old desks would not have failed an assessment of compliance (although chairs are more at risk). Main desk surfaces do not have to move up and down on an ingenious crank system. An old-fashioned, unattractive, and otherwise undesirable desk may comply perfectly well with the regulations. Good practice simply demands that desks be large enough so that people working at a computer screen are able to position themselves, and the equipment, in a variety of ways and thereby achieve a comfortable working position. Space to allow a substantial VDT screen and keyboard to be placed together, with space for resting wrists, needs to be at least 2 ft 6 in (760 mm) deep and preferably deeper, 2 ft 7 1/2 in (800 mm) for part of the desk. The possibility of adaptable height should be considered and furniture manufacturers making desks that adjust have tried to imply that this is a legal requirement or, at least, a good way of complying with the law. It may be helpful particularly if someone is certain to sit at the same desk for many months or years. It can often be achieved with panel-hung system furniture, and for keyboard-entry staff many ingenious especially adaptable solutions are also available.

Chairs and VDTs

Q: **Why shouldn't I get the cheapest chair I can find? After all, the efficiency, image, and style of the office is determined by the desk—its shape, size, and storage capabilities—not by the chair. Chairs are all much the same.**

A: **There is great variety so choose carefully—more features cost more, and some may be more for the sake of image than for comfort or healthy posture. Also, be aware important advice to sedentary workers is to move around in the day, to stand and stretch, to get fresh air, to be thoughtful about posture, rather than to assume that a machine for sitting in will sort out comfort, safety, and work effectiveness.**

Desk-height adjustability is less relevant than adjusting the height of a chair, a simpler, cheaper expedient. Concert pianists have long been aware of the need to place their hands at exactly the right height in relation to the keyboard. No one has ever suggested that the adjustable piano stool is a silly solution, that a better one would be to ratchet the piano keyboard up and down. A chair that can be positioned at a comfortable height is what a desk worker needs, particularly when working at an office keyboard. A foot rest should be available to allow a chair to be raised high enough for someone tall without leaving short legs dangling. For someone who is exceptionally tall, it is likely that the height of a desk will need to be adjusted. In these cases people are best served by having either a special desk or a standard one that has been raised up on additional supports that can move whenever the place of work is changed. A chair with a seat height that ranges from 1 ft 4 in to 1 ft 9 in (410 to 530 mm) will suit the majority of people, but this is a wide range, and not all products meet it. When a manufacturer offers a range of adjustability, be sure that the range described is met, as some start well below and may not reach the upper measure. Adjustable chairs have to be strong enough to carry most people. Additional strength may be required for people who are at the extreme end of the weight scale and also for chairs used for 24 hours a day by shift workers, as these are subject to extra stress.

In addition to height adjustability, a chair should satisfy other criteria. It should offer support in the lumbar region of the back, and the seat and back should both adjust in height. A fixed relation of seat and back, such as a "shell," can be height adjustable if the whole can be raised and lowered, despite the fact that it does not provide good back support for people outside the range of the proportions for which the particular shell was devised. Generally independent adjustment of both back and seat will provide better comfort for more people. Chairs should have stable bases and casters; a five-point star base is generally recommended. The features that a good chair should have are sometimes not found in the older furniture that lurks in offices. The replacement of inadequate chairs should be taken in hand. If people do not work more than a few hours a week on a VDT, then they do not have to be provided with a chair designed to meet the needs of a VDT worker. But if they do, even if they are fond of their familiar, substandard seating, the organization should try to provide a fully suitable one. Forcing someone to sit correctly at it is another matter. The arms, if there are any, should give support, for which their height may need to be adjustable. They should not catch on clothes or on the desk. The chair back can provide better lumbar support if it follows the body movement as you lean forward. Despite much research and reams of guidance, chairs do not make everyone comfortable. There is a steady market of special chairs and shops devoted entirely to supplying seating solutions for the suffering masses with back pain.

Back and other musculoskeletal problems are a cause of many lost days of work, not to mention a considerable amount of pain. There are many good reasons, apart from the law, why suitable chairs should be provided for all desk-based staff. Simply complying with the law is not really what it is all about. There are plenty of serious physical problems associated with desk work. Many of these are the result not of bad furniture being provided but of people being unable, or unwilling, to adjust the good furniture that they have been given so that it suits their needs. If the adjustments are poorly designed, the controls are hard to find and hard to use, and the instructions difficult to understand, they will not be used, and the provision of an adjustable chair will have failed in its intention. Try asking the next lucky company that gets your order for 250 chairs to provide full pictorial and verbal instructions about how to adjust the chair and who to telephone if the adjustment does not work. If this can be supplied on a computer disk, compatible with the software and hardware used in your organization, which can run as a screen saver on VDTs in your office, so much the better. Competition in the furniture industry is so acute that you may succeed in getting this prepared for you if it is a condition of your buying the chairs. Good luck.

How many different types of chair are needed in one organization? Variety in chairs, somewhat like space standards, has a history of being used as much to denote status as different work. Few organizations benefit from devoting management time to marshaling the right chair behind the right desk when the chairs wander or the staff numbers change. A visitor chair need not be as complicated as a desk chair since it is only for short-term use. A simple, cheap construction is more than adequate. A standard visitor chair can be used in conference rooms or lounges and at any tables intended for meetings. The desk chair, on the caster base, can be the same for all desk-based staff. There is no need for a high back, or a different construction, or more adjustability, or a leather finish, for senior staff. A chair that can be provided either with or without arms, simply by screwing on or taking off removable ones, can be the way to give the necessary variety to one chair. Variety in color scheme is a good way of introducing color into the office, but beware if allocating certain colors to certain areas will take time and effort to retain in the right location.

Adjustability needed to reduce the strain of working at VDT equipment really does need to be provided. The position of the screen should be adjustable on a swivel or tiptilt base; the relation of the keyboard and the screen must not be fixed; the height of the keyboard must be adjustable. Since equipment changes fast, when it is replaced, these factors should be considered, though it would be unlikely that any modern desktop equipment without these characteristics is available. Some things need to be watched. Companies giving all their staff laptops need to consider the desktop availability of an independent screen. The laptop does not allow the screen and keyboard to change position in relation to each other, except by altering the angle that the screen makes with the keyboard, which is not sufficient.

Cost

Furniture is generally over-designed for cable management. Go for simple solutions and expect the furniture to be in use for fifteen years.

—IBM'S DESIGNER MANAGER IN *ARCHITECT'S JOURNAL,*
OCTOBER 1993

You can pay anything you like for one person's furniture, from a few hundred dollars for the lowliest clerk to many thousands of dollars for the chief executive. As a general rule, you get what you pay for. The issue is: What should you pay? What is worth paying in your situation? The necessary basics—a desk, chair, and local storage—has a price tag reflecting the size, the quality of construction, the details of the surface finishes, the designer's name, the degree of adjustability, the volume purchased, the length of guarantee, the professionalism of after-sales service—and some hard bargaining. The market is highly competitive; there are always bargains to be struck, and the list price is *never* the real one, so discounts quoted must usually be substantial to be attractive. A modest cost workstation may be purchased for, say, $2,000.

A cube with all supporting screens but no chair could cost from $4,000 and upward. You should not expect a long life or any after-sales service from a cheap product, and you may need to assemble some of the furniture yourself. Higher prices cover higher quality, more expensive finishes, and unusual designs. An office chair with all necessary adjustability to meet health and safety needs, pur-

Quality Costs

As features are added to the basic chair, the price may rise. The following indicates optional additions:

- Either a way to adjust the height of the back independently of the seat
- Or a synchronized movement of seat and back in relation to each other
- Fixed arms
- Or adjustable height arms
- Or arms that swivel as well as rise and fall
- A sliding seat to accommodate taller people more easily
- Adjustable lumbar support, for example, air or a separately tensioned structure
- A change to a more expensive fabric
- Stronger gas lift for heavier people
- Wider and deeper seats for heavier people
- A high back for a manager's chair

As new information is uncovered by research, new design approaches may become standard and eventually be recognized in regulations. Designers and users need to have an overall awareness of the principles of good posture and may need to consider not only the chair but accessories such as wrist rests, document holders, foot supports, shaped keyboards, mobile equipment stands, or other aids that help in a particular situation to reduce problems caused by rigidity and awkward positions. A chair alone cannot solve the problem of back pain, and at present the designs we rely on have not distinguished themselves in eliminating it.

chased from suppliers of office stationery and equipment, may cost as little as $60, but $250 buys a far more robust and attractive product. At the high design end are chairs costing over $800. The bulk of the furniture budget goes to individual workstations, but do not forget the cost of furniture in meeting rooms and reception and amenity areas, which could add 25 percent or more to the final furniture bill.

A Beauty Parade

You can have any color you want—as long as it's black.

**—ATTRIBUTED TO HENRY FORD AS A SELLING
POINT FOR THE MODEL T FORD**

Choices have to be made. Should they be democratic? Should the cost decide comfort levels? When an investment is made in new furniture, it makes simple sense to ensure that the majority of the people who will use it find it acceptable. This need not mean letting everyone have a say—representatives can play an active role on behalf of the majority—nor does it mean that views expressed through representatives can all necessarily be acted on, even though they are listened to. Cost must obviously be an important factor. Within any cost range, suited to the budget available, there are always a number of products. Once the short list has been chosen, a "beauty parade" has much to commend it in helping you to reach the final decision.

Ask the selected short list of suppliers to provide a mock-up of a workstation. Mock-ups can be brought in to let people see them or be placed on the office floor and actually used by various members of staff. The mock-ups must be of a typical workstation. Each supplier should provide an identical arrangement as far as their product range allows: a desk of the same size and shape, with the same amount of under-desk storage, and the same types of local free-standing or screen-mounted storage. A chair is needed too. If different suppliers are used for desks, storage, and chairs, record keeping about who has supplied what needs to be meticulous, and possible choices need to be clarified. Chair A can be placed with desk B and cabinet C if they are all from independent suppliers.

The choice of performance requirements should have restricted your inquiries so that only firms making things that you want are inspected. The beauty parade establishes whether the workstation works the way you and the users want it to, whether one works better than another or better fits your image. The choice now comes down to things that matter. Does the edge of the desk snag your clothes when you get up? Is the color, sheen, and feel of the finish acceptable? Are the legs supporting the desk in the way of your own when you sit down? Can you put the cables in and out of the cable tray when you want to change the computer on your desk? (Whether or not there needs to be a cable tray should have been dealt with by the specification for each mock-up in the first place.) Is it easy to slide the chair under the desk? When you get up, do the arms wedge under the desktop? Is the pen tray functional? Can you fit your files into the storage units? Does the desk drawer open fully and smoothly?

Careful labeling of the items being judged is essential. Do not depend on a description of their virtues by the sales representatives vying with each other for business. A simple questionnaire, allowing space for a clear statement of preferences and judgments, needs to be filled in by all who inspect the workstations. Labels on the items may usefully give the cost of each. People need to be credited with enough intelligence to judge value for money. A marginally more alluring finish is unlikely to be credited with sufficient benefit to justify a doubling of the price. An irritating pen tray may not rule out the desk that is demonstrably better value for the money. When users appreciate the real costs, they are less likely to behave childishly about minor problems. Any special features need to be examined by those who are most affected. In an organization where everyone uses VDTs and cable management is vital, the opinion of the IT department must be sought. If there are complex filing requirements, the relevant group needs to be involved. If foot rests are being ordered for some people, ensure that they are tried out in advance by those who will use them.

Having displayed the workstations and received the ratings of the user representatives, the choice remains that of the management. Representatives should not expect that what they say they like will automatically be what they get—public relations and communications have to be better than that for a successful participatory choice. Managers need to be aware of the feelings of the body of people likely to use the workstations and to know that if they choose the least popular one, there had better be good reasons.

Summary

This chapter helps you pick a way through a maze of decisions to be made when choosing furniture and lighting and offers a process whereby this can readily be done.

Furniture is used to convey status and image as well as having function. There is so much to choose from on the

Managing the Beauty Parade

- Decide what you most want to see. It may be just the basic desk and operator chair, it may include several chair types, or the bulk storage furniture as well.

- Give each supplier an identical brief.

- Provide suppliers with a sketch of the way you want the furniture set up — if, for example, you want to see how two desks fit together with a screen between them.

- Arrange a date when they can all be seen together.

- Bring files and equipment that are commonly used in the office to test that they can easily fit with the furniture.

- Arrange for department representatives to spend time trying out all the options.

- Provide users with a questionnaire that allows them to rate different aspects of the furniture. The following are some of the most important considerations:
  - Comfort and convenience
  - Suitability for the task
  - Looks and appropriateness of image
  - Cost
  - Quality of finishes
  - Accessories and options for variation

market that it can be difficult to distinguish priorities. There are two different types of furniture: *systems,* in which all the parts are interdependent, or *separate items,* which can be combined in many different groupings. Systems are more constraining and more orderly. Mix and match can allow for specific needs to be met by all the different elements. Mobility is a new feature of increasing importance.

Storage is one of the most crucial elements in office furniture. Units that allow lateral filing can accommodate more material on a smaller footprint than traditional filing cabinets, especially where additional height is also possible. Specialist storage furniture companies have developed elaborate ranges. The image of furniture made of wood has traditionally been of higher quality than that of metal. Metal, on the other hand, can provide robustness and neatness of design. Expensive, high-density storage units can be extremely useful. However, the costs are high, the limits are not fully understood, and they can introduce inflexibility. The requirement of a mobile worker, who is not always based in the same place, has begun to be considered seriously. New furniture types have come on to the market that will prove very useful for these workers.

Health and safety guidance is exploited by manufacturers who make it sound as if the old furniture you have is unacceptable. The furniture, as opposed to VDT equipment, has some conditions with which it should comply: The desk should be large enough to accommodate a VDT in a variety of positions; a depth of 2 ft 6 in (760 mm) is generally ample. Once flat screens are common, desks will no longer need to be L shaped. A foot rest should be available if requested. The chair should have a seat and back that can be raised and lowered. The back does not need to be independently adjustable although this may be beneficial.

The cost range for furniture is enormous, just as the variety available is mind boggling. There can be a thirtyfold difference in the cost of a chair. If you are planning to spend

$2,000 to $6,000 per workstation, it is vital to get the choice right. A beauty parade at which possible products are reviewed and judged is a good mechanism for involving staff in a decision that affects them all. The choice cannot be wholly democratic, but some items fall easily within the province of a user group. The color of chair fabric, for example, is something that can be chosen by staff representatives.

CHAPTER 6

Buildings in Sickness and in Health

CASE HISTORIES

See Case Histories 15, 16, and 17
on pages 377–392

The maladies that afflict clerks...arise from three causes: first, constant sitting, secondly the incessant movement of the hand and always in the same direction, thirdly, the strain on the mind....What tortures these workers most acutely is the intense and incessant application of the mind, for in such work as this, the whole brain, its nerves and fibers, must be kept constantly on the stretch; hence ensues loss of tonus. From this result headaches, heavy colds, sore throats and fluxes to the eyes from keeping them fixed on the paper.

—BERNARDINO RAMAZZINI
Diseases of workers, 1713,
translated from the Latin text *De Morbis Artificium—Diatriba.*

So Do Buildings Make You Sick?

Is it the building, or your job, or the boss? Every day new health hazards devised by human beings are identified. Coal mining, forestry, and construction work, for example, all seem intrinsically dangerous. By contrast, it seems incongruous to associate ill health with sedentary office work—

so blame the building. The maladies described by Ramazzini, and assumed to be an occupational hazard, are still suffered by "clerks." More than 250 years after Ramazzini's description, an apparently new scourge has emerged, *sick building syndrome,* or SBS for short. This, by the way, is not the same problem as *building-related illness.* Some illnesses are contracted by people as a direct result of some aspect of a particular place. Microorganisms, indisputably identifiable and causing some very nasty illnesses, are sometimes found in, say, the water supply in a building.

Legionnaires' disease, for example, has killed a number of unfortunate people, and buildings are clearly implicated. Serious illness, such as humidifier fever and Legionnaires' disease, must be guarded against. Ways in which these can be transmitted and prevented are clearly understood. Suitable measures to determine whether your building is at risk and, if so, taking appropriate action, need not cost an arm and a leg. For example, monthly testing for the presence of *legionella* bacteria in cooling systems for air-conditioning has become standard practice among efficient building managers, against whom a charge of negligence might be leveled if they fail to organize the tests. In other cases, though health consequences are taken seriously, the action taken is not necessarily effective. Asbestos has been clearly linked to asbestosis, an unpleasant and debilitating lung disease, and a specific type of asbestos to a fatal form of cancer. Millions of dollars' worth of work has been done to eliminate asbestos from buildings, often creating considerable disruption, despite the fact that most asbestosis is linked not to working in a building in which asbestos was incorporated but rather with working on the processes of making or installing the material. Smoking, even passive smoking, is known to damage health (see Chapter 7), yet not all employers ensure that their workforce is protected from passive smoking.

Less fatal and much more difficult to pin down is sick building syndrome. The term describes a group of ailments including headaches, dry throat, sore eyes, lethargy, blocked and stuffy nose, and dry or itchy skin. These symptoms, as a cluster, have come to be causally associated with buildings, especially offices, though it is worth observing that a few of them are also associated with winter coughs and colds. When a significant number of occupants suffer from this group of symptoms and when they say that their symptoms diminish or disappear when they are not in the office, researchers have drawn the conclusion that it is the office building that is causing the problem. This has been eagerly pounced on as an idea by the media, who like a good disaster, and by people marketing services designed to detect and clear up the problem. SBS is said to lead to days off work, so the company suffers loss, staff suffer discomfort and are demotivated, and the cause of the problem cannot be easily identified and cured. Are there really symptoms that people get just because of the building they work in? Should you worry about all this (Fig. 6.1)?

> If they get a bit of a headache, feel a bit sick, their eyes itch, then it is much more difficult to trace the cause. There are about 28,000 things in the built environment that can cause people's eyes to itch. Even then, with a bit of luck you can sort it out. But it's difficult, expensive, and can take a long time. You need a team of about twenty people, and you can spend a third of a million pounds looking at a big building.
>
> PROFESSOR PATRICK O'SULLIVAN,
> INTERVIEWED FOR *UCL UNIVERSE*

What is the chance that your building hosts one or more of those 28,000 itch-inducing substances? With that many possible causes, it seems highly likely. But it will probably be difficult to identify which are actually present and in unacceptable—but measurable—quantities. It may be even harder to link the presence of the substances with the symptoms reported by the staff. Eliminating them or preventing them from affecting the staff may be impossible. No wonder it may cost a third of a million pounds. Sampling and testing for a

Figure 6.1

(*Louis Hellman.*)

known problem in a known location, as is required when controlling Legionnaires' disease, is a manageable proposition. Tracking down unknown agents for an unspecific problem can be frighteningly expensive because the number of possible items to test for is large and the quantities of the offending agents may be small, so that detection equipment and tests are complex and costly and the ways in which they affect people may differ. This is amply demonstrated in the case of allergies. Some individuals can be nearly incapacitated by a substance that others are never aware they are inhaling, ingesting, or touching. Identifying unusual allergenic agents can take a great many tests. These are real difficulties. But if the tests do not produce results, spending the money may not be worthwhile. And will failure be even more expensive? Litigation against companies by their employees is increasingly frequent, particularly in the United States. Successful litigation on account of SBS has not yet been achieved, though it has been attempted. Perhaps the problems associated with SBS will join the list of reasons why employers are taken to court. Then you will really have to worry if the connection between building and sickness can be proved incontrovertibly.

It has come to be accepted, as a result of research projects carried out in a number of different countries, that the syndrome is real—that something about buildings is able to make people unwell, not merely feel uncomfortable. As yet, however, research has not pinned down what it is about buildings that causes the sickness. Various culprits have been named. Air-conditioning, noxious gases, negative ions, and dust mites have all been implicated. An air-conditioned building must be sealed from penetration by outside air, and this has led to SBS being described by some as *tight-building syndrome*. Another group of suspects are volatile gases, such as formaldehyde, which can be found in large quantities in new buildings, as they are used in the manufacture of carpets, furniture, and wall materials. Volatile gases sometimes smell nasty, and it is possible that some people are actually allergic to them. Or dust mites. They inhabit fabric, live off flakes of dead skin, and multiply happily on the warm seat of your office chair. They do not bite, but some people may be badly affected by these microscopic creatures and their byproducts. These are only some of the front runners under consideration in the search for a solution to SBS. All the agents that could be associated, individually or in combination, with the reported symptoms have not yet been clearly identified. Another approach is also receiving increasing attention. It is suggested that when people perceive that they can control their working environment by changing, say, temperature, air movement, or lighting, they avoid the symptoms of illness suffered by those whose perception is that their environment is beyond their personal control.

> *I have experienced sore throats/colds recently. Must be associated with the move of office.*
> —QUESTIONNAIRE RESPONSE FROM STAFF MEMBER
> AFTER AN UNPOPULAR OFFICE MOVE

There is evidence that people who work in office buildings suffer from a range of symptoms embraced by the various descriptions of SBS. What is hard to establish is whether the level experienced in some buildings is above the normal level to be expected in a randomly selected group. Do these symptoms occur anyway, because of people's general health, or are they related to factors such as the type of work people do or their psychosocial situation—the boss or the spouse? If buildings are to blame, is it the office or the home? Could the culprit even be the journey in between? Some sufferers say that the symptoms improve or disappear when they leave the office building. As a skeptical manager, you may wish not to put too much trust in this claim or in answers to the question of whether people have suffered from a particular symptom "in the last year." Recall is not infallible over this length of time—a few weeks is the most that people can remember accurately. Much of the research into SBS is marred by unreliable information gleaned from questionnaires and so far has not demonstrated incontrovertibly that office buildings really "cause" the symptoms.

Nonetheless, so-called sick buildings are newsworthy; occupants are persuaded of the truth of the proposition that some office buildings make you "sick." If a building is suspected of being sick, it attracts attention. When a publicized case turns out to have been a false alarm, it does not prove that no buildings are ever sick. It does suggest, however, that remedial actions and costs may not always provide much

A multistory office tower in the Midlands was featured in a television documentary program on sick-building syndrome. Staff complained eloquently of their difficult working conditions—they were tired, had headaches, sore eyes, and runny noses, experienced difficulty in concentration, and felt generally miserable. Absenteeism was high. The building was blamed for their problems. Following the broadcast of the documentary, studies were commissioned to identify and solve the problems. Specialists crawled over every inch of the building. They could find few problems. The main failing seemed to be poor management of the air-conditioning system—it was not operated according to its design, hence some areas were far too hot, others too cold. A new firm was brought in to operate the air-conditioning, and their work was closely monitored. Complaints from staff working in the building fell dramatically. To the occupants, the building was no longer sick.

A couple of years later the building changed hands. Staff in another organization were informed that they would soon be moving into that building. They remembered the TV program and were sure that it was a "sick building." They generated enormous resistance to the move. Moving there was seen as proof that management did not care about their employees or their working conditions. Unions contributed to the outcry. More studies were commissioned. More specialists crawled over the building. They found very little that was untoward. Staff resistance continued—the label "sick building" clung on tenaciously. Eventually, management and staff agreed to the move but only on the condition that the building would be totally redesigned before they did so. All windows would be replaced, all the air-conditioning would be changed, as would most of the plant that controlled it. The bill was tens of millions of pounds, and there were a couple of years of delay during negotiations and building work, just to remove the damaging "sick building" label.

measurable benefit and should be undertaken with caution. If it is not proven that SBS is a measurable phenomenon against which action can be taken, what other approaches are there to achieving a healthy, happy workforce?

Comfort

Take a step sideways for a moment. Without needing to be committed over the issue of whether your building makes you or your staff sick, consider whether a building can contribute to comfort—or, rather, to discomfort. The general consensus is yes. Most people can identify situations in which they are uncomfortable for which they blame the building. A definition of comfort is not easy to come by, as it varies for different people. Men and women, for example, do not find the same conditions comfortable. This need not surprise anyone. For a start, the clothes that they wear are usually of quite different weight. Physiology also affects comfort. Nonetheless, comfort may be a more manageable topic than SBS, as it is more familiar territory, and it deals with fewer possible variables. Furthermore, most reasonable people are already aware that it is not an absolute measure (Fig. 6.2).

Comfort is generally considered to be related to temperature, relative humidity, air movement, and probably light and noise levels. Generally acceptable standards have been proposed in a variety of guidelines and regulations for building design, but consensus has not been reached. Lighting levels of anywhere between 200 and 2,000 lux are considered appropriate for office work, depending on the exact nature of the work task. The American National Standard Practice for Office Lighting notes that lighting levels should

Figure 6.2

(Louis Hellman.)

be adjusted depending also on the age of the workers and the speed or accuracy demanded in their work task. For those working on computers, glare and the veiling of reflections are as much of concern as absolute lux levels.

Comfortable temperature levels are no more firmly established. Ignoring for a moment the technical difference between "radiant" and "dry-bulb" temperature measures, the range for comfort in sedentary work recommended by the UK Health and Safety Executive, whose mission is the health of people in the workplace, is 70 to 75°F (21 to 24°C) ambient air temperature. An allowance of plus or minus 2°F (1°C) is sometimes included in a statement of a target range. The blurring of the edges of the range need not be taken to indicate sloppiness. After all, the concept is not precise: Temperature changes through the day; measuring instruments may be only approximately calibrated or inefficiently used; and people differ about what they consider comfortable. An example of confused and conflicting advice that can occur in this field is the UK government regulation that buildings that are occupied by civil servants should not be heated to temperatures above 66°F (19°C). This is part of a laudable effort to conserve energy but somewhat misses the comfort target quoted above in regulations prepared by civil servants themselves. Common sense tells you that a howling draft or freezing ankles and a hot head are rarely popular. An acceptable differential of 7 degrees between the temperature at ankle height and that at head height, and a maximum air speed of 5 feet (1.5 meters) per second are also part the same recommended standards for comfort. Indeed, the definition of comfort in these standards, that 90 percent of those exposed to the conditions should find them acceptable, may not be capable of a proof more scientific than common sense. Cultural differences seem detectable in the temperatures that people actually find comfortable, or at any rate acceptable. In Germany, for example, exceptionally high temperatures in summer may mean a building reaches over 86°F (30°C), which would certainly be unacceptable in other countries but is tolerated there because it happens infrequently.

Does the lack of a single, accepted set of guidelines, a single known set of targets, mean that it is impossible to provide a building in which most people feel comfortable? Not at all. Temperature and relative humidity together are more important for comfort than either on their own. In temperate climates such as the United Kingdom and much of Europe, North America, and Australia, these are not often far outside the broad range that would enable most people to be comfortable. No excessive effort is needed to modify them. A well-built building, with windows that do not leak and a good level of insulation, served by a simple radiator-based heating system for winter months, is often perfectly adequate and should offer a comfortable environment. This being so, it is depressing how often buildings are, in fact, not comfortable. Often the problem is related to modification of temperature. In some buildings one side roasts in the sun, while the other is chilled. If the heating system is designed without local controls, this is hard to regulate. In others, the air feels warm and stale, but when windows are opened for ventilation, the traffic noise is deafening, papers are tossed by the wind, and grit is blown into the coffee. (In some you may get a hernia just trying to open the window.) In yet others the radiators belt out heat regardless of the outside temperature in obedience to the calendar: "If it is after October 1, it is cold."

> *Overshoes and topcoats may not be worn in the office, but neck scarves and headgear may be worn in inclement weather....It is recommended that each member of the clerical staff shall bring four pounds of coal each day during cold weather.*
> —COMPANY INSTRUCTIONS TO STAFF, 1852

The clerks described above, able to throw their own fuel on the fire and get up a blaze, may have been happier than you think. Recent research indicates that when

than natural ventilation. Capital costs are 20 to 30 percent higher; the landlord's service charges for an air-conditioned building may be higher; and annual running costs can be three times as much. And in exchange for all that extra expense, you may get more complaints. The extra running cost represents extra energy use, which makes it less environmentally responsible as well. A combination of problems can afflict air-conditioning. In the first place, systems frequently do not work as users expect nor as they were designed to do by engineers. Long periods spent fine-tuning sometimes fail entirely to bring them up to the desired performance level. Sometimes details are badly designed. Delivered temperature levels and speed of air movement are not always acceptable, and the noise of rushing air can be irritating. Smells may be transmitted from one area to another within the system, and more often than seems possible a fresh-air intake is located where it sucks in smells from, say, an adjacent kitchen exhaust. Many systems recirculate some of the extracted, "used" indoor air to reduce the cost of raising or cooling raw outside air to the desired temperature. When filters are not properly cleaned and maintained, the system can transport unwanted pollutants (germs that hover among those with coughs and colds or substances that cause allergic reactions) all over the building with maximum efficiency. This is also a well-known problem in aircraft. Reasons for the wide range of problems experienced with air-conditioning include incorrect commissioning (starting up) so that the system never even starts working the way it was designed; too much complexity in the design so that there are lots of parts to go wrong; poor management and maintenance so that the system progressively deteriorates; and the destruction of the balance of air in/air out by placing partitions in offices where they had not been anticipated when the system was designed.

Developers and real estate agents have put office users and purchasers under pressure to demand air-conditioning as essential in a high-quality building. It is not. It may be essential where outside conditions are extreme, but it is not essential in temperate climate zones. There are situations where even in a mild climate air-conditioning brings benefits. It can be used to exclude dirt and noise generated in central urban areas, especially on traffic arteries. It can make it possible to create internal rooms such as lecture theaters, which do not require windows, or to use very deep spaces where windows cannot supply sufficient ventilation to the central areas. It can keep areas filled with heat-producing equipment, such as computer rooms or reprographic facilities, at suitable temperatures for both people and the equipment itself. Where specific benefits of this type are not required, resist the temptation to believe that air-conditioning makes the office a more prestigious place and impresses clients, sponsors, or staff. If possible, occupy a building that is designed not to need air-conditioning, one where natural ventilation, or at most mechanical ventilation, is used for cooling, with a simple radiator-based heating system. This is not an obvious option in, say, New York, which is noisy and dirty and where summer temperatures and relative humidity rise to extremely uncomfortable levels. Though even when summer outdoor temperatures are high, well-designed openings, which provide sun shading and allow cross ventilation, and night-time cooling can go a long way toward keeping people comfortable. Rarely do staff in naturally ventilated UK office buildings gasp for air on sweltering summer days. It can happen, but an office full of fans whirring is as likely to be the result of high temperatures caused by heat generated inside the building, particularly by lighting and maybe also by computing equipment, as from high outdoor temperatures.

If you need air-conditioning, make sure that the system is sensibly zoned—that is, designed to serve areas that have different requirements using separate controls and appropriate equipment. As an example, zoning a system so that each floor of an office building is separately controlled will be necessary if several organizations occupy each floor independently, as they may have different needs. If areas on a single floor many be separately occupied or have varying needs (say, because the south face of the building gets much hotter than the north), the floors may need to be further subdivided into separate air-conditioning control zones. When a building is advertised as having a flexible system that can be adjusted to suit the needs of any tenant, check that the locations of air intakes and outlets can be placed where *you* will need them and that the overall capacity and control system will suit all the different areas *you* will occupy. Then see that the system is properly used and well maintained. Expert advice will probably be needed for this, but a short visit to the plant room may tell you a lot about quality control in that department.

Let There Be Light

How much light should you have? Does everyone need a desk lamp of their own? There are shifting standards in the amount of light that should be provided. What must also be noted is that if an engineer is asked to specify a lighting system to produce a particular light level, you may well get one that provides a much higher level when the lamp bulbs are new. The engineer has automatically taken account of the fact that the light output of a lamp diminishes as it gets older. If the diffuser on the fitting never gets cleaned, this compounds the light loss. It is not necessary to provide each person with a private desk lamp— or *task light,* as they are called. A well-designed lighting system can deliver suitable light to each desk, as well as different light levels in areas that need them. Not all lighting systems are well designed, so if a separate light is specifically needed, it can still be provided, bearing in mind that it needs its own power outlet and should be securely fixed so that it cannot be dislodged from its position as people brush past.

Many new office buildings are equipped with a basic lighting system that the new occupier instantly wishes to replace or supplement, as it does not provide the amount and type of light that is required. This is, of course, not the case only in new office buildings. Old ones too may suffer from inappropriate lighting. In a new building it seems less excusable, as the right decisions for today's needs are well served by today's technology, and they could surely have been taken at the outset. Common sense tells you that you are looking for light that will not give people headaches, that will not get left on when not needed, that will not reflect off computer screens so that the only thing to be seen on the screen is the pattern of lights on the ceiling. There is a range of issues and choices to be navigated: halogen, tungsten, metal halide, UV radiation, uplighters, energy efficiency, movement-sensor control, daylight-corrected fluorescent fittings—is another specialist needed to sort through all these possibilities? There is a danger that the specialist may be so taken with the special properties of the many available lights that the building manager will end up having to stock 57 varieties of light bulbs, each matched to different situations in the building: the general office floors, the atrium spotlights six stories up in the air, the dining area and the lit-up self-service chilled-food cabinets, the front hall, the chairman's desk lamp, the reading area in the library, not to mention the conference room and its projectors. The lighting specifier should be asked to keep track of the types of fitting, check the bulb types, and, once their number reaches about 10, try to find fittings that use the same bulbs as fittings already chosen. (The office with the 1,000 dud pedestals described in Chapter 5 also has a janitor's store that has to carry an inventory of 35 types of light bulbs. Long-term management of this building had been ignored in more than one area.)

It should not be an opaque problem. People generally like the tungsten—incandescent—lights to which they are accustomed at home, but these are not very bright, give off a lot of heat, and are unsuitable for large areas of general lighting, such as offices. Fluorescent lights suffer from flicker, poor color, and badly designed fittings that are unattractive and hard to clean. The old-fashioned installations still around are enough to give fluorescent lights a bad name with many office workers. This is to some extent unjustified. Today there are many fittings and types of tube that provide glare-free light of a suitable color and give a good quality of light. To replace the fittings in an existing installation may be trickier than creating a new installation, as the existing ceiling has to be suited to the new fittings unless the whole ceiling is replaced.

Brighter halogen lights have been developed in the search for better ways to light large spaces. These give out good, bright light, but they have other problems. The fittings get too hot to touch safely and must not be placed near combustible materials; they require transformers to modify the power input; the light is too bright to look at directly without getting after-images; and, if unprotected by glass, they give out an unacceptably high level of ultraviolet radiation. Despite all these drawbacks, when halogen lights are used as uplighters, they give an attractive general light that is also suitable for office workers seated at VDT screens. Their main benefit is that their light is diffuse, because it is reflected rather than direct, so that there is little likelihood of distracting reflections. A space lit by uplighters must not be too low and must have flat white or very light colored surfaces off which the light can be reflected. A ceiling height of at least 10 to 12 ft (3 to 4 m) is best. The fitting will fry the ceiling if it is closer than about 2 ft 6 in (760 mm), and when the light is bounced off the reflecting surface, it must be able to spread over a considerable distance; otherwise, too many fittings would be needed. The fittings must be well above eye level. Metal halide lights are also used as uplighters. The main disadvantage of these is that they take some time to warm up. They may be switched on at the beginning of the day and left on all day, but as they take about 10 minutes to reach their full intensity, they are quite unsuitable for places where the light can be turned off several times in the course of the day either because the available daylight is strong enough without added artificial light or because there is no one in the space, so that for energy-saving reasons, the light should be turned off.

Stickers by the light switch never saved much money. People are fallible and forget to act on them, especially in large, shared areas where no one feels responsible for the general environment. So automated systems have been developed. There are many complex electronic and mechanical systems for controlling the amount of time that lights are on in offices. They depend on a variety of technologies. Photoelectric cells determine whether there is insufficient natural daylight and, if so, switch on the artificial lights. Movement sensors turn *on* lights if they detect movement. If the occupants of the room are asleep, or hiding under the desk, the lights go out. If they are stock still, thinking profoundly, they will have to flap their arms like a scarecrow from time to time to keep the light on. Other systems operate on a simple time-switch basis. Any light that has been switched on will be switched off at, say, lunchtime, at the end of the average working day, and at chosen times, such as half an hour after the cleaners should have gone home. If people are working in the space at the time or come in subsequently and need light, they must switch it on. This system deals with forgetfulness or flagrant carelessness, and lights being left on potentially forever once they have been switched on. It does not attempt to use sophisticated technology to decide if the light is needed at all. It can be irritating to have a light switched off while you are working, and it is more than irritating if light switches are far away, hard to reach, or badly labeled so it is unclear which you need to use.

In the United States, because of the energy-saving fittings that have been introduced into modern offices, several utility companies have been able to avoid building expensive new power stations, and they actively promote the use of such lighting. This indicates the enormous amount of energy used by lighting, generally thought to be about 25 percent of electricity demand. The Environmental Protection Agency's Green Lights program showed that energy saved in lighting could significantly reduce emissions of carbon dioxide, nitrous oxides, and sulphur dioxide. To reduce the heat output of the lights by means of energy-efficient fittings is frequently the most effective way of saving energy. The energy used by the lights themselves is reduced, as is any energy needed for cooling to compensate for the heat generated by the lights. The extent of such saving varies in different climates and building orientations, but even in temperate climates the heat given off by lights and electronic equipment together can make it hard to create a comfortable working environment on a hot summer's day (see Chapter 8).

Where is the switch? How many lights does it control? And who gets to use it? These are vital questions in determining the way lights are used, how much energy they mop up, and how satisfied people are with their working environment. Individual control is much prized by staff. Those without control feel that their working environment has become hostile and inhuman. The pull switch dangling overhead may look ridiculous, and it is certainly a problem if the only way to switch off rows of fittings when people have gone home is to stroll down the aisles pulling each switch. But it gives people a sense of control over their immediate needs. In the next chapter research is discussed that considers how far the ability to change and retain some control of one's workplace is crucial to satisfaction.

Windows

Windows are a brilliant invention. They let in light, keep out heat, cold, dirt, and noise, and provide a view. They are also a point of weakness, through which unwanted people can get in or cause damage. The most common image of an office building today is one where on all façades, at all heights above the ground, the windows are identically designed. This makes it harder for them to do the jobs they are there for, as conditions change with the orientation of the sun, the height above a noise source, the view, or the potential intruder.

Well-designed windows are needed to create comfortable conditions. Size and shape are important, but they are not all that window design is about. There are many other decisions to be made. On a south-facing façade, where heat gain in summer needs to be controlled, double glazing, special heat-reflecting glass or low-emissivity glass, film, external screening, and deep reveals and blinds are all useful devices. The benefits are purchased at additional capital cost, but all these devices should be considered. They also help in controlling glare. Blinds that can be used variably to shut out glare as the sun changes position are usually needed where people use VDTs. The amount of light coming in changes from the top to the bottom of a window, especially if sky shows at the top and land below. Thus, in cutting down glare, horizontal slatted blinds, or full screening types, perform more efficiently than blinds with vertical slats. For any blind the controls must be easily reached. It is sobering to discover how often controls are inaccessible—too high, behind screens, across wide pieces of furniture. This is a design failing that also frequently applies to levers and locks for opening the windows themselves and must be avoided.

The Carpet Debate

It has become standard to carpet office buildings. Carpets bring sound absorption, color, and individuality to a room; weaving in new patterns and customized designs is not difficult. Carpets have replaced wooden floors or substances like linoleum, making a warmer, and—of significance in open plan—a quieter environment. Much research has been done to create fibers and weaves that suit every budget, are hard-wearing, and are easy to clean and resist the build-up of static electricity. The results have been reasonably successful, and suppliers, consultants, and cleaning companies will give advice about the products that are succeeding best at any particular time.

Problems with computers spurred the development of antistatic fibers, but static may affect some individuals badly too. Another problem is that the off-gasing of the glues used in carpet construction when they are newly installed, and the release of fibers into the air as they are abraded, could contribute to the poor air quality that is associated with SBS. There is little proof of this, though the Scandinavians are returning to wooden floors, ostensibly for this reason. Of course, they do grow a lot of trees in Scandinavia, which may be influencing this fashion. On the other side of the world, the Japanese are only gradually moving to carpeted offices from linoleum or other hard finishes. The carpet debate has not yet been resolved.

Cleanliness Is Next to Healthiness

Thorough cleaning is often the key to providing an environment that is healthy. This does not just mean having doormats that extend far enough to capture most of the outside dirt from shoes, powerful vacuum cleaners efficiently and frequently used, and a contract with a specialist firm to bring sparkle to the WCs. It is about cleaning the parts other cleaners do not reach, the ones that cannot be seen—the ductwork and filters for an air-conditioning or ventilation system. These are in a position to deliver dirty air as easily as clean. The first point at which cleanliness must be demanded is during installation. A clean building site reduces the chance of the wrong things getting left behind in the duct in the first place. Once installed, a maintenance schedule that acknowledges the need for cleanliness can keep air-handling systems working more efficiently. Voids under raised floors can also provide a home for dirt, and occasionally pests, if not kept clean during and after construction.

Watch out for water. Water supplies can harbor potentially harmful bacteria. Tests are easy to carry out and occasionally reveal unwanted coliforms in taps in kitchens or teapoints. Usually the bacteria found in these tests are themselves intrinsically harmless but are an indication that more harmful ones may be present. Water coolers and vending machines are more frequently found to be contaminated. They need conscientious maintenance and cleaning.

Know Your Environment; Monitor It

Buildings do not always deliver an environment that falls within acceptable ranges. The first requirement is, as always, to know what is going on. Knowledge—of temperature patterns by time and place, whether carbon dioxide levels are high enough to make people feel sleepy, how much light is reaching the desks, how noisy the rooms are, whether the water supply is breeding bacteria—is important management information. This type of information should be collected regularly and systematically, especially if there are complaints. Some checks can be done by anyone with very simple equipment, such as thermometers and light or sound meters. Others require more sophisticated equipment, which may need special calibration or expertise. With good information it is possible to anticipate problems rather than being forced to react to them. It may also help to ensure that comfortable conditions are achieved and maintained and thus reduce the likelihood that your building will be found to be sick.

Responsible, Sustainable, Green

Promoting planetary health, watching expense, preventing profligate waste, promoting occupant health—all have become more important concerns as we have started to realize how many unwanted consequences may accompany our activities. Staff increasingly demand an office organization that demonstrates that it cares about the environment. Governments can also put pressure on organizations, through taxes, fines, or financial incentives, to behave in a more environmentally responsible way. They can affect location very powerfully in this way. Other changes that can be implemented to make an office more environmentally friendly involve building design or internal management. From surveys it seems that even these, closer to home, are not very likely to come from within. Managers have until now shown a limited commitment to energy-saving policies and, sadly, an even more limited one to the green agenda. This stance is influenced by the fact that there are few, if any, major cost savings in going green except those associated with energy saving. The basic principles are to avoid waste, to reuse and recycle wherever possible, not to deplete irreplaceable or slowly replenished natural resources such as tropical hardwood, and to minimize the production of pollutants and the exposure of staff to them. In numerous areas of building management, this type of responsible approach may be no more difficult or costly than the standard practice. There is scope in the office for the collection of used paper and the purchase of recycled stationery. Furniture and cleaning products can be purchased in a responsible way. Equipment such as photocopiers, printers, and computers can be chosen and sited with good practice in mind and care taken to avoid toxic materials and to promote the safe handling of any chemicals used. In the catering field, the provision of a balanced diet, safe waste disposal, including composting of appropriate food wastes, the recycling of glass and tin, washable rather than disposable utensils, and the avoidance of styrofoam blown with CFCs are all to be recommended.

"The Environmental Protection Agency (EPA) has—very appropriately—sought to be as "green" as possible within current available technologies in its new headquarters in Washington, D.C. The EPA occupies 200,000 ft^2 of a larger project—2.3 million ft^2—that has involved reconstruction of a number of buildings in the Federal Triangle district of Washington, as well as a new building. In line with what many users would like, though not with the approach hitherto considered standard in federal buildings, there are openable windows allowing users to influence the air quality by their actions. As well as low-emission building products where new materials have been used, the opportunity for reuse of materials offered by reconstruction of existing buildings has been exploited and calculated. Land-fill sites have been deprived of the following materials:

- 75,000 tons of concrete

- 6,000 tons of steel

- 100,000 ft^2 of glass

- 3,000 tons of masonry

(Continued)

(Continued)

Energy-efficient services including low-flush WCs and advanced lighting systems designed to reduce eye-strain as well as conserve energy have been installed. Other organizations are following similar policies—improved air quality, energy conservation, and sustainable use of resources. Prince Street Technologies, for example, has a new headquarters in Carterville, Georgia, where antimicrobial additives to most interior products have been specified to improve air quality, low VOCs were sought by using low-formaldehyde particle board and carpet adhesives as well as natural materials such as cork and linoleum. In addition, chairs were made of renewable or recycled material in the interests of sustainability.

All these are small contributions to the solution of a big problem. This does not invalidate them, but a bigger impact can be made in other ways. When new buildings or large renovation projects are undertaken, there is an opportunity to make environmentally sound decisions in a number of areas. Reusing rather than replacing buildings and furniture is less wasteful in many situations. Adopting a sane attitude to location, allied to a suitable national policy on transport, is vital. Saving energy by care in building design can make its contribution. Savings in lighting, heating, and cooling can be achieved by good window design, adequate insulation, external sun shading, and tree planting (to avoid excessive heat gain), well-planned ventilation, and sensible, energy-efficient lighting installations. There are a few clients, and some developers are active in using and spreading as many of these ideas as possible. But not yet enough. To be responsible, you must use every opportunity to make green improvements whenever you alter buildings.

Summary

This chapter puts the problem of "sick" buildings into perspective and helps to return the focus of attention to measures that can be taken to optimize conditions for people working in offices.

Office workers have suffered "sickness" for centuries. Infectious diseases, such as Legionnaires' disease, in the transmission of which building services and systems play a role, are in a different category and need stringent measures by which to guard against them. The symptoms, including headaches, lethargy, stuffed or runny nose, and itchy eyes, referred to as "SBS," are much less certainly connected to buildings. Possible causes, such as air-conditioning, dust mites, and volatile gases, have been suggested. There are a very large number of possible agents for some symptoms, and identifying and dealing with them can be extremely expensive. There is no proof that specific attributes of buildings cause the symptoms in question, and seeking to eliminate the problem by getting rid of a specific cause may not be cost effective.

Comfort is an important goal. Temperature, relative humidity, air-flow rate, light, and noise contribute to comfort. A building modifies these conditions, and if acceptable levels are not achieved, the building can be said to affect comfort. Generally agreed upon levels of comfort are difficult to establish, as standards vary. The modification of temperature is often a crucial area in which success or failure resides.

Air-conditioning is frequently implicated when people are uncomfortable. It is not essential in temperate climates and should be avoided where possible. The costs are not justified if the results are complaints. The complexity of systems, the low levels of maintenance and management, the constraints on people's ability to modify their immediate environment or, in the longer run, replan its layout, all contribute to its patchy reputation.

Lighting has many possible solutions. The much-maligned fluorescent tube has been greatly improved and can provide a satisfactory solution. Other approaches, in particular uplighting, have benefits. Energy-saving devices need to be considered early on in the building design. A control system can be incorporated as an element of the lighting installation. Relying on individuals to switch off lights is unlikely to make savings, but, if possible, people should be allowed the freedom to switch lights on and off for themselves if they feel the need.

The design of windows must ensure that they perform in all the ways that they should. They have often been treated solely as a visual feature of the elevation, with no variation in design as different conditions demand. Window manufacturers provide a wide range of ways to increase comfort: double or triple glazing, special glass, and internal and external shading.

Carpets, taken for granted in high-quality offices in many countries, are a relatively new introduction. They offer a domestic feel, an opportunity for color, and noise absorption. They have disadvantages in the form of static build-up, off-gasing when new, and increased fluff is released in the air, which may be inhaled. Some organizations in Scandinavia have deemed it better to provide hard-floor finishes in offices for these reasons.

Monitoring environmental conditions and gathering accurate information, as with all issues, is essential. It can help you to create comfort and to anticipate rather than react to problems.

Green agendas have been shown by researchers to be of little interest to today's managers. They have been a major media issue, but collecting paper for recycling is about as far as most offices go. All consumables could be more rigorously treated; work and management practices could be tailored to a green agenda as well as immediate business requirements. This may come about in significant amounts only when pressure is brought to bear through centrally imposed incentives and penalties.

Amenities: Sharing and Caring Spaces

CASE
HISTORIES

See Case Histories 18, 19, and 20
on pages 393–415

Rising staff expectations in the developed world mean that many office buildings now offer far more than a basic working environment. This is in complete contrast to other developments that are making the office building less central to the lives of some people, who spend less time there and have freedom to work wherever it suits them. Large offices and headquarters buildings have grown so complex that they have become small communities, with places to learn, to eat, to shop, to exercise, to be entertained.

A prestigious office in Helsinki is likely to have a well-appointed sauna in the building, available to staff for their leisure and used as part of the paraphernalia surrounding an elegantly conducted meeting with important clients or colleagues. Buildings with many Muslim staff may have a small mosque for daily prayers. In Britain new government offices in Leeds are equipped with generous sports facilities, catering, and a day care suite. One of the first postwar office buildings to be considered for historic listing in England, the

Note: Some of the material in this chapter first appeared in *Space Management,* 1997–1998, Eclipse.

office of Willis Faber Dumas in Ipswich, was built with a swimming pool inside the building as well as a turfed roof garden for the leisure needs of the staff. Why? Surely people go to the office to work. You'd think the last place they would want to spend their leisure time was at the office. If they go to the gym during office hours, can you be sure they are giving the right amount of time to their work? An orderly world has a place for everything and everything in its place, and the office is the place for work.

Amenities: Lots of Them? For Whom?

Additions to the office building cost money to provide and maintain. Can you afford to provide them? Can you afford *not* to provide them? The range of provision varies from country to country, company to company, building to building. Space is provided for many different activities in addition to the individual work areas. These were referred to in Chapter 2, when mention was made of support space. Some facilities appear to be so much part of the work requirements of the organization that they are taken for granted as part of the office. Others offer support for personal needs— that may have to be met to fulfill expectations of the workforce. They are not always used as part of the job but rather in private time (Fig. 7.1).

The specific details of the provision of work-based amenities need careful consideration. What should they be? How many should there be? Where should they be located? How should they be equipped and furnished? How should they be managed?

The extent to which amenities are needed, and on what scale, varies. In a small building for, say, 50 people or fewer, the most that can be expected is a meeting room and kitchenette for making tea and coffee. In a large office building with, say, 2,000 people, many amenities are often provided. On a large office campus in an out-of-town location, most facilities are found. A sauna may never become

Work-related amenities commonly include:

Reception areas	Front door and waiting area for visitors and a back door for deliveries and waste
Reprographics	Centralized photocopying and printing—almost a separate business
Conference suite	Many variations, from a room with a folding wall to provision for several hundred delegates, with theater, catering, exhibition, breakout, and demonstration areas
Training suites	Lecture and syndicate rooms, sometimes with sophisticated audiovisual aids, computer training rooms, breakout areas
Library	Active archives; also daily papers, trade magazines, and reference material, with comfortable seating, and no disturbance from telephones

`Personal' amenities commonly include:

Catering	Cafeterias and restaurants, kitchenettes, coffee and vending areas, catering for meetings and bars, cybercafés
Sports	Facilities range from a gym, swimming pool, sauna, and game rooms inside the building, with associated showers and changing, to outdoor sports fields and club huts
Social support	First-aid room, day care room, branch of bank, travel agency particularly to assist with corporate travel arrangements, staff shops, hairdressing, medical or dental clinics (especially on isolated sites)
Smoking room	A facility where staff who need to smoke can do so and may be able to work at the same time for short periods
Transport	Car parking is much in demand; some people need bus services connecting them with town centers or linking corporate buildings
Quality of environment	Enhanced by works of art, water features, and plants, as well as the overall quality, color, and finish of the work areas

Figure 7.1 Amenities in offices.

standard outside Scandinavia; a day care suite may attract little custom in the heart of a big city, a long way from home; but a good cafeteria on a suburban industrial estate may make the difference between attracting and keeping staff or not attracting them at all.

A Perk or a Tool of the Trade?

An office building exists to facilitate the transactions that must take place between people—the agreements, the promises, the decisions, the information exchanges. The most important transactions are not necessarily conducted in formal meetings or even on the office floor at all. It has been recognized in the design of other building types that useful exchanges between people may take place, for example, in circulation routes. The "corridors of power" are a reality. Lobbying does take place in lobbies, as well as elsewhere. Important exchanges between members of the legal profession take place in the corridors around the courts in a justice building. Even if a corridor is noncommittal and informal, how much nicer to conduct business in a leisure or health spa type of environment. In Helsinki it is appropriate to conduct business in a sauna. Golf club memberships are often given to executives in the knowledge that the club offers suitable entertainment possibilities for business colleagues that can help to lubricate business deals, with the added bonus that playing golf is a better way to keep fit, healthy, and useful than performing a similar service for the company while sitting drinking in a bar. Boxes at the opera, tickets to major horse racing or tennis competitions, seats in the local theater are all ways of offering business hospitality, and with the hospitality, it is assumed, some business will be transacted or at least eased.

Providing decent facilities for customers in the office building is an obvious extension. Is this sensible? What are the costs and the benefits? Extra touches—well-appointed elevator lobbies that help to orient the user, an attractive reception area that does not mingle important clients with helmeted couriers or van drivers in coveralls—attract tenants. In new buildings these are taken for granted, and they have become a new standard rather than additional amenities. They may not exist in older buildings and may be hard to introduce. Amenities that contribute to the organization's real activities may be viewed slightly differently to the plush, the lavish ostentation in the form of ultraexpensive materials, space to impress rather than to use. Much can be understood about an organization's culture and attitude to its employees by reviewing the amenities considered necessary. After the recession of the mid-nineties, *The New York Times* reported that "others simply emerged from the recession weaned of the need for frills. They will pay top dollar for efficient space; they will let others pay a premium for glitz" (February 1996). A large telemarketing center for British Telecom in northern England exemplifies this approach. It provides a canteen and the use of free telephones for private calls, but it has no day care suite, no sofas or breakout areas, and no plants or exercise areas for its many staff who are arrayed in rank upon rank of desks in a huge open warehouse-like area. After all, the Willis Faber Dumas building in Ipswich, referred to earlier, has covered over the swimming pool in order to make more space for the expansion of staff that has inexorably taken place over the last thirty years. So what and how much do you need to provide?

Attracting and Keeping Staff

Amenities may be offered as a way of attracting and retaining staff. If there is nowhere to buy a meal in the vicinity, a cafeteria may be needed or at least a good kitchen in which people can prepare their own midday meal. A subsidized cafeteria may be provided, even if there are other local options, as a way of offering staff a special benefit for working with the organization. Child care facilities fall into a similar category, being offered as a way of retaining expensively trained staff when they have young children. Another reason behind the provision of amenities may be to compensate for other losses. Staff who have recently been placed in open-plan offices or, more radical still, moved from allocated to pooled desks, may be offered a staff gymnasium or game room. A decentralization policy that involves many staff in moving homes and following the employer to a new city, where people will take time to become integrated into the local scene, may be eased by providing leisure facilities on office premises that all the family can use. A large office in a remote location, or perhaps in a hostile neighborhood, may provide some of the shops and services that are often visited in lunch hours, thus making the location more acceptable. The cost to the organization of these amenities may merely be the opportunity cost of not being able to use the space for other purposes. A commercial enterprise operating the amenity will pay rent and all its own management costs. Alternatively, the host organization may choose to incur some higher costs because it subsidizes the use of the available service—say, hairdressing or a day care suite—as a way of increasing the rewards offered to staff.

The provision of office-based amenities, rather than higher pay or a shorter working week, may be beneficial to the organization. Consider catering, for example. This can be very expensive—as much as $2,000 per person per year in all. But it need not be. Providing a subsidized canteen can cost less than a general pay raise, and it is easier to reverse later. A pay cut is more damaging to morale than agreeing that the canteen is losing money because no one uses it (it can be done away with) or because the prices are too low (they can be inched up). It may even be possible to dissociate the organization from the problems, as it is the catering organization that must rectify them. Intangible benefits are also assumed to flow from this type of in-house provision. Staff may take a shorter break if lunch is available on the premises. It is possible to help form a healthy workforce, or at least support those trying to eat a balanced diet, by providing a range of healthy foods. As a last resort, the space given to the cafeteria may be reclaimed for meetings outside peak meal times if more space is required, adding a little flexibility to the building.

What about a gym or sports facility? The cost of a 300-ft^2 (30 m^2) gym, suitable for a few people to work out in the lunch hour or before or after work, may not be high. It could serve perhaps 150 people. Not everyone would wish to use it, but they would all get the feeling that the management took them and their well-being seriously and believed that they were worthy of such an investment.

The Office *Is* the Amenities

As more people work away from the office more often and for longer periods, their reasons for coming into the office have changed. Charles Handy, in the *Harvard Business Review,* commented, "Paradoxically, the more virtual the organization, the more its people need to meet in person." They come to the office to be part of larger groups and teams, and they need spaces and places for this to happen. They come in for stimulus and companionship and need spaces and places for this too. Many of these places fall into the category of amenities. They include coffee bars, sandwich stands, conference and meeting rooms, breakout areas, fitness rooms, sports and games opportunities, and shops.

Silicon Valley is widely known to have buildings equipped not only with lounges and gourmet cafeterias but also the corporate behavior to go with it, that organizes sports tournaments, concerts, and parties. The young but intense professionals may work as semirecluses, but they need to meet their fellows in relaxed surroundings. Charles Dilworth of STUDIOS is quoted as saying, "It's like fish who live in a coral reef and come out every so often to swim in a school."[1]

[1]Charles Dilworth, *Architectural Review,* June 1998, p. 157.

The amenities serve those who are able and encouraged to work elsewhere much of the time, and they also act as an attraction should the organization wish to counter the effect of the opportunities for remote work and encourage staff to work more in the office. If the culture of the organization is suffering from fragmentation and lack of focus because few people meet as they are all elsewhere, then decent amenities may help them interact and bond.

Management Burdens

Amenities require both space and management. The host organization incurs responsibilities when it provides amenities. Every country has laws and guidelines relating to the safe design and use of specialized facilities. Even if a canteen is not aiming to promote healthy eating habits, it must not spread salmonella. A gym has to be managed so that the equipment is suitably checked for safety and stability, people are properly instructed in its use to avoid injury, and appropriate action is taken if there are accidents. Child care facilities have to comply with many stringent requirements.

Is it worth the hassle for an organization whose business is not pre-school child care, or catering, or fitness and leisure management, to embark on the minefield that amenities can create? Complying with the health and safety requirements associated with office work can seem onerous enough. Can you avoid making a rod for your own back?

Outsourcing to Reduce the Burden

To DIY or not to DIY, that is the question. The answer has changed over the last decade. In fact, the meaning of the question has changed. It used to be a question about whether or not to provide a particular amenity. It is now more likely to be about whether the amenity should be run and managed by the organization itself or run by an outside specialist or even by a person, team, or company whose sole role is to provide essential building services for other companies, a facilities management specialist.

Back to catering as an example. It is less common for companies to hire their own kitchen staff, and manage them directly, than it was 10 years ago. Company tea ladies were made redundant decades ago, replaced by itinerant sandwich sellers and vending machines. Specialists run the kitchens and restaurants; outside suppliers have the responsibility of checking, filling, and servicing the vending machines. But there can be disadvantages as well as advantages to outsourcing, whether in providing bijou executive dining, a mass-production, subsidized self-service cafeteria, or phalanxes of leased coffee-making machines. In the first place, there must be a contract with the outside company. This has to be written by, or at least read and managed by, someone inside the firm to be sure that it really does serve the organization's interests. To allow the outsourced caterers to write their own rules, police themselves to see that they keep them, as well as set the price for their services, would not be consistent with good management practice. As the catering firm becomes well established, serving the company from year to year, it is increasingly difficult for someone within the office organization to be fully aware of what the service could and should be like. The further away managers are from knowing what the business of catering is about, the harder it is to do anything other than accept what they are told by the specialist is the "best" way to do things. Some specialist providers learn to take advantage of the unsuspecting organization. If catering staff are on the company payroll but managed by the catering specialist, the contractors may not do their utmost to ensure that efficient staff are hired, that overtime is paid only when it is essential, and that staff costs are minimized while efficiency is maximized. Similar problems can arise with the purchase of raw materials. There is little incentive to ensure that the best quality is bought for the lowest price if the bill is paid by the office organization, with a percentage handling fee for the caterers. This sort of problem can arise in connection with any contract with an outside service. Keeping up to date and staying on top of the cost consequences have become more necessary and more difficult. To combat the problem needs continual monitoring and updating. As an example, Volvo in Sweden obtains office stationery through an outside provider who runs a "shop" within the office as an alternative to a company-run stationery cupboard. The contract demands a regular reduction in supply costs, which gives an incentive to the provider to bring best-value opportunities to the notice of the company.

Catering

Even in an imperfect situation, the problem of managing an out-of-house catering company, which takes full responsibility for the kitchen and its output, may still be less burdensome than dealing with the proliferation of DIY coffee clubs that may be the alternative. A high electrical bill, trailing kettle leads, desk drawers full of coffee jars and biscuit crumbs, interdepartmental fights over which cupboard in the kitchen belongs to whom, whose milk is off in the fridge and why the sink is never wiped clean, and the drifting aroma of fries and tacos as microwave cookers hum into action on every floor, may disappear like snow on a warm spring day when an imaginative company runs vending and catering for the whole building. Or it may not. So what should you do?

Catering takes a bewildering number of forms, reflecting eating habits, fashion, social structures, and food technology. The traditional triptych of an executive dining room, a management dining room, and a staff canteen, reflecting the industrial origins of on-site catering, has been replaced in most organizations by a single cafeteria. This attempt at equality and social mixing, which is supposed to bring with it the benefits of communication, camaraderie, and company loyalty, is often side-stepped by the provision of visitor dining facilities that are used by senior staff for eating-meetings—that is, when they don't arrange to wine and dine an important visitor at the best local restaurant. An advantage of city locations is that they offer people a wide range of possibilities for lunches, from cheap take-out sandwiches to exotic foreign cuisine or bar and pub food. When a staff restaurant is provided, the feel of the place should be carefully considered. A complete change in lighting, color scheme, and general atmosphere is relaxing and provides more of a break from office routine than dining under the same lights and looking at the same interior design package as on the office floor.

If you are feeling peckish when in a large hotel, you have the choice of making a cup of tea or using the minibar in your room, munching a quick snack from the functional cafeteria, or dining lavishly in one of several different restaurants with varied cuisine and decor before retiring to the lounge for coffee. In some office buildings the range is almost as extensive. In the SAS headquarters outside Stockholm, staff may relax with a sandwich in their own group lounge, enjoy an *espresso* coffee and snack in the café on the main covered "street," sit under a large garden umbrella on an informal balcony overlooking the street, or go to one of two restaurants, with different menus, overlooking the lake. In the main restaurant they can choose to settle down by the fire in the warmed room or sit under the ivy in the conservatory. Are any of these choices available in your office building? Should they be?

How much to provide, what is essential, what impact an amenity has on staff, to what extent coffee is free to all staff—all are questions specific to each organization, to be answered in the context of its history and location. The HR team is likely to have opinions and knowledge about these matters. Questionnaires can be used to tap staff opinion. The implications of making different sorts of provision that should be taken into account in an office building include the following:

- Different space requirements for different types of catering, ranging between about 10 and 45 ft^2 per seat, including kitchen and serving areas

- Overall space needed to cater for different numbers of staff—area per seat in serving area only, multiplied by the number of people per sitting

- Possibility of several sittings over a longer lunch period, which requires a smaller area

- Space-saving possibility of cashless transactions via smart cards or similar gadgets, reducing queues at the till

- Dual use of cafeteria area for informal meetings and "cybercafé"

- Hygiene rules for preparation and waste

- Control of water contamination in kitchen areas, vending machine areas, and water-cooling machines

- Finishes and cleaning in catering areas—relative costs, suitable specifications

- Increase in average space per person if catering facilities are installed

- Impact on energy costs and the advisability of separate metering

- Suitable location of kitchen extract, away from windows and ventilation air intakes

- Goods access for daily supplies and waste disposal

- Provision of extensive plumbing and drainage

The Disabled: Amenity Becomes the Standard

The needs of the disabled are many. There is a tendency to equate "disabled" with "in a wheelchair." Without suitable ramps and door widths, a person in a wheelchair cannot even get inside a building. The blind and partially sighted, those with reduced mobility or reach, the deaf and those with hearing difficulties, epileptics—may all be able to climb stairs and use ordinary doors. But their needs are not served if they cannot see the numbers on the elevator buttons, or use a normal telephone, or enter a lavatory cubicle and use it unaided. These and other failures of provision mean that their ability to use office buildings can be seriously impeded.

Provision for the disabled in buildings is no longer simply a refinement provided by the philanthropically minded. In most countries it is now a requirement that new buildings meet some, though by no means all, of the needs of disabled people. In the first instance, access has to be suitable, with level changes accommodated by ramps and elevators and doors sufficiently wide and easy to negotiate to enable people in wheelchairs to enter and to move around the building. A large lavatory cubicle is not a discretionary luxury. There must be at least one, with suitable support rails, in any new office building. This bears no relation to the likelihood of there being a disabled employee who needs this particular form of assistance, as statistically this is comparatively unlikely. Minimum provision is not enough if it blocks equality of opportunity, and what was once considered an amenity has become a standard. While the new concern is an important step forward, the measures adopted must be assessed in relation to the benefits achieved. New provision must meet the standards, but upgrading substandard buildings is sometimes a poor use of resources. If necessary, an escort could help a disabled user confronting an inadequate elevator, but front doors are another matter. If a person cannot get into the building at all, then changes must be made.

The significant issue in providing for the disabled is to appreciate that their needs must be met in a precise way. The greatest challenge for people with some level of disability is the difficulty in adapting to a wide range of physical circumstances. A comparatively small variation from the ideal (say, in the height of a door handle) may not be noticed by a person who is able to bend, stretch, and twist, whereas it can make things impossible for someone without full mobility.

Common mistakes in the design of office buildings that make access difficult and must be avoided include the following:

- Doors that are too heavy
- Ramps with slippery surfaces, no handrails, and inadequate landings
- Reception counters that are too high for wheelchair users to be seen or that have no induction loops for the hard of hearing
- Lobbies and landings where door swings interfere with maneuvering a wheelchair
- WC cubicles with some or many details incorrect
- Light switches that are inaccessible or not in intuitively sensible places
- Elevators without a voice indicator or Braille buttons
- Fire alarms with no visual signal
- Vending areas and kitchens with controls that are too high
- No suitable furniture or spaces in waiting or meeting rooms

Smoking Rooms

Medicine's best-publicized research has established the dangers to health caused by smoking. Passive smoking has put the final nail into the coffin of equality of opportunity for those who feel they need to smoke or have a right to smoke wherever or whenever they wish. Smoking is a subject that arouses passions. Smokers feel that restrictions on their freedom to smoke where and when they like is an infringement of their civil liberties. Nonsmokers behave as if they were narrowly escaping premature death by enforcing restrictions rigorously (Fig. 7.2).

The employer's duty to provide staff with a healthy environment is now often interpreted to mean that it is essential to have a smoking room or a no-smoking policy. Many organizations, public and private, already have a "smoking policy" (the usual name for a nonsmoking policy). In fewer and fewer buildings is smoking freely permitted. Elevators

Figure 7.2 The Smoker's room. (Darius.)

and corridors, canteens and coffee lounges have all gradually become out of bounds to the cigarette. So have individual offices in many organizations, to avoid setting an example that managers prefer not to endorse. Controlling smoke in places shared by smokers and nonsmokers is harder than confining the problem to a few locations used only by smokers. This means that a room for people to retire to for a smoke must be provided in convenient locations, unless the company decides not to allow any smoking except outside the building. The consequences of that decision are not always acceptable as most companies do not care for the first view of their entrance to be a group of smokers and the ground littered with stubs.

The ventilation and decor of smoking rooms have not been given adequate attention. The surfaces rapidly become dingy, impregnated and discolored by smoke. Yet without these rooms, however miserable the environment that they offer, some smokers are convinced that they could not do an effective day's work. How far this is true is not at issue. The decision on how to provide for smokers' needs may be the result of the fact that the chief executive smokes, the international policy of the organization, the need to set a health-conscious example, or fashion. In a few more years new forms of employment contracts may make the need for smokers' rooms unnecessary. Today what is needed is to be sure, if there are smokers' rooms, that they are properly located, designed, and cleaned. Floors and wall finishes should be easily cleanable and need to have a more stringent cleaning regime than the rest of the office. Ashtrays should be large and emptied frequently. Soft furniture should have removable covers that are regularly cleaned. It is a poor solution to provide vinyl chairs so that they can be wiped clean. They create an impression of a "poor-relation" environment and are often difficult to keep looking good.

Smoking rooms must also be carefully ventilated. By their nature, they smell like a noxious kipper factory, and the smell percolates rapidly into adjacent circulation routes and beyond. A lobby can help to solve this problem to a certain extent, but it is important to reduce the concentration of smoke in the room. A window that can be opened is inadequate to ensure that used smoke is dissipated. Ventilation requirements are high, so use sufficiently powerful and adequately sized extract systems. Smokers are no keener than anyone else to freeze on a winter day. The recommended rate of fresh-air change in an office needs to be doubled if smoking is allowed, and for heavy smoking, as in a smoking room, it has to be doubled again. A high fresh-air change rate leads, of course, to higher costs in heating (or cooling) the air. On top of this, a high rate produces a noticeable draught and a noise. Research suggests even these levels are inadequate to reduce the likelihood of death from passive smoking to an acceptable minimum. To ensure that not more than one death occurs per 100,000 nonsmokers over a 40-year working life would require 300 times the normal rate of air change or prohibitively expensive air filtration. A ventilation system is not an unmixed blessing. Without vigilance it sends the smoke, by indirect but effective routes, to the smoke-free zones in the rest of the office. Poor plant and duct maintenance, inappropriate locations for air outlets and intakes, and incorrectly balanced systems can create this sort of problem, pleasing no one at all.

Car Parking

Q: **What are the main problems that you have with this building?**

A: **The biggest issue right now is car parking.**

—DISCUSSION BETWEEN USERS AND CONSULTANT PRIOR TO REPLANNING THEIR BUILDING

The managing director gets a car parking space whenever he wants, but we workers do not have the right to one even if we need it.

—COMMENT BY A CITY CENTER OFFICE WORKER

Car parking is one of the most emotive issues in office management. As internal space within the office is gradually being made more equal, parking is a lingering area where status is still made absolutely clear. In the choice of a new office location, senior management is more likely to reject one with insufficient car spaces for its perceived need than one with poorly designed internal spaces or low specification. In some organizations parking spaces are provided only for key workers whose jobs require the use of a car. But if offices are located at a distance from public transport, many people cannot get to work without the use of a car, even if their private transport then spends all day sitting in the car park. If spaces are allocated to specific individuals, others grow frustrated by seeing empty spaces while they are unable to park. The outcry when spaces are reduced is loud, the deprivation heartfelt. Car parking takes up a great deal of space, so it is not surprising that status helps to decide who gets it. Each car requires about 250 ft^2 (25 m^2) for its bay and its share of the space to maneuver into and around the car park, which puts it on a level with the average lettable area per person in a typical office. To provide this space is costly, whether in a basement area or outside the building. It needs lighting and security, and if it is outside, it should have some planting to mitigate the impression of a sea of asphalt.

It is hard to satisfy everyone. Car parking may be needed for staff, for visitors, and for deliveries. At some times of the year there is more pressure on this scarce resource than at others. In early winter there are usually more people in the office than at other times—few people are away on holiday, as it is too late for autumn breaks and too early for skiing. The size of marked bays never match the size of cars. If the car park is underground, the columns, designed to suit the spaces above, never fit the circulation and parking requirements. If it is outside, spaces are often generous enough for the directors' limousines, so cars at the economical end of the range are swimming in space. Office users tend to want as many spaces as there are people. In urban areas, planning officials may prevent them having any at all as part of a strategy to prevent traffic congestion and pollution. Public transport needs to be excellent for this strategy to contain the spread of cars without generating apoplexy among commuters. It rarely is. Even in suburban areas users may not be allowed as many spaces as they would wish, although in suburban office developments a larger area of ground is covered by car parking than by buildings, an unattractive sight without landscaping. In a more environmentally conscious world it is important to consider forfeiting a few car spaces for bicycle parking, ideally under cover, designed to permit secure locking, and near to showers and lockers.

WCs and Lockers

Necessities, not discretional amenities, the quality of washrooms says much about an organization and its landlord. Washrooms can be sumptuous or dirty and unloved, poorly designed or a pleasure to use. Their design should acknowledge the social role such spaces may play—for example, during the informal chat at meeting breaks. International research by a multinational company providing washroom services found high levels of user dissatisfaction with washrooms, particularly with their lack of cleanliness. In many organizations, to the great annoyance of staff, visitors' washrooms were better than those for staff. The environment matters: Toilet areas must be clean, should smell pleasant, yet not too strong, and they should be well ventilated. In some office buildings, management has chosen to add pleasing little touches more common in luxury hotels—boxes of disposable tissues, a clothes brush for grooming, a small vase of flowers, a comfortable easy chair.

Fashion, culture, and budget dictate the details. In Scandinavia each cubicle is a complete room with solid, soundproof walls, its own light switch, basin, mirror, and lavatory. In the United States and United Kingdom, it is more usual to find cheap and flimsy partitions between cubicles and an open-plan basin area. Partitions that reach neither the floor nor the ceiling are cheap to install, allow simple floor cleaning, and make it easy to rescue someone who is locked in. They are less private than full-height ones and unattractive to many users. There has been a succession of ideas about the most hygienic type of hand-washing and drying devices. "No-touch" is now believed to be cleanest—electronic beams that start the water spray or the hot air when broken by your hands. They may be preferable to taps left permanently dribbling, or drifts of scrunched-up buff paper towels that run out when you need them, or continuous rolls of laundered fabric toweling, but they may also end up as yet more pieces of equipment to break down and require repair. The design of washrooms needs to have their management in mind. If an outside specialist cleaner cares for them and maintains all systems in sparkling order, then elaborate equipment may help to keep standards high. If not, simpler things may be preferable. Wash basins integrated into completely flat surfaces, beloved by architects, allow unattractive pools of water to collect. Elegant design and expensive materials do not compensate for this.

WC areas are usually designed differently for men and for women, which means estimating the likely sex balance of the occupant population or building in an excess to allow for any mix from all males to all females. Equal opportunity of employment has its effect here. To avoid overprovision, some companies now specify identical areas, with no urinals, so that they can be used for either group depending on the numbers of staff involved. Unisex WCs for the disabled are considered appropriate, so there is no reason why the same principle should not be applied for all.

In some companies, lockers are needed for people who have to wear uniforms, such as receptionists, bank tellers, airline staff, or security teams. People grow very attached to their lockers, and they like them to be as large as possible, with generous space for changing near by. This can be at odds with efficient space use, and there is a trend, abetted by increased commuting by car, toward encouraging people to travel to work in their uniforms. Where lockers are needed, they can be provided in one unisex space with individual changing cubicles or separate changing space for men and women. With areas for physical fitness creeping into office buildings, more rather than fewer lockers are needed.

Gyms and Fitness Rooms

The health of the workforce has always been a concern of employers. First-aid rooms for people who are injured or feeling ill and occupational health suites, where medical checks are carried out, have not completely disappeared. They are, however, being replaced by spaces for active physical exercise, now widely recognized as important for promoting health. Gyms and fitness rooms are often provided in larger buildings; even a small area can accommodate an extensive range of equipment. There are indications, from some companies' experience, that the overall health of staff can thereby be improved, and the space devoted to a facility amply repays its cost. Some companies have allowed public use of the gym when the staff do not use it, or they have been paid by people outside the company for its use.

The design of a gym is a subject for a specialist, who should also be asked to advise on the legal requirements and the best management practices. Safety issues must be taken into account. For example, it is good practice to insist that fitness checks on prospective users are carried out by a qualified doctor and that a minimum of two people use the facility at any time in case of injury to one of them.

There is a need for additional ventilation in gyms, showers, and changing areas. If the office population is small, there need be no objection to showers that can be used by anyone, although privacy of changing within the cubicle must then be provided. Even if no gym or fitness room is included in a building, the provision of showers, mandatory in some countries, should be considered. They will be well received by those who bicycle to work and by joggers and will be used if general sessions of keep-fit, aerobics, or self-defense are held on occasion in spaces such as the canteen or restaurant.

Color-Conscious, "Feel-Good" Offices

Facilities that are additional to the spaces required for purely work purposes are one aspect of a high-quality, attractive environment. Environmental psychologists find that the small, cheap, changeable items close to people are often the things that matter most—an elegant letter tray, pen holder, or waste basket, used many times daily, is appreciated. Details, such as locks and hooks on WC doors, door handles and window catches, signs and labels are all part of the quality of the place. Finishing touches are often provided by green plants, flowers, and by artwork. A small percentage of the project budget can work miracles in this respect—"1 percent art" is a goal of the artistic community, but even half of this can go a long way.

Two significant areas that have received much attention and have a considerable effect on office design are use of color and the ideas embodied in *feng shui*. Color often plays a role in the small details as well as in the larger elements of walls, floors, and ceilings, and furniture and other finishes.

Light and color make up our visual world. It is not surprising that people have strong reactions to color. The evolution of color vision is related to the need to perceive colors for survival. Different living creatures perceive colors in species-specific ways. Humans are no exception, and are thought to have universal, cross-cultural reactions to colors.

Research into psychological reactions to color has been influenced from two directions. The first seeks to underpin color forecasting and the advice given by an army of consultants and advisors, relating to the cycles of preference, fashion, and the consumer culture. The second looks at the use of color for therapeutic reasons in health, and especially mental health environments. Both strands provide real evidence for a degree of consistency in human reactions to different colors, which should be of assistance in making decisions for the office.

> Red energises, leads to increased blood pressure and affects the muscular system. Yellow stimulates the nervous system, changes pessimism to optimism. Green touches deep seated emotions and induces peace and harmony. Blue calms and heals the mind, reduces blood pressure and gives one greater awareness. *(Marie Louise Lacey, The Power of Color to Heal the Environment, 1996.)*

There are many references in the literature to the appropriate colors to be used in offices—though which you believe will depend on your overall approach (Fig. 7.3).

> Earth colors are reassuring in an office environment and greens are calming. But yellow is known to improve work attentiveness and create a cheerful atmosphere. White gives too much glare in the workspace. Blue though calming can also make employees feel cold and distant. Maroon or deep green used as accents are associated with dignity and power, especially in reception or executive areas. *(Robert F. Ladau, et al., Color in Interior Design and Architecture, 1989.)*

Minimalist

Credo	Offices are for serious work by serious people. Color has no place.
General design	Keep everything neutral.

Styles

High-tech minimalism	Keep everything in pale gray, white, some black, stainless steel, and glass.
Natural minimalism	Keep floors, desks, tables, and chairs in pale timber (oak, ash, maple, beech), perhaps wheat colored carpets of sisal or wool.

Highlighter

Credo	Offices are for serious work by serious people, but a little color is good for variety.
General design	Neutral colors predominate—accents of bright color in special areas.

Styles

Special area highlights	Bright, even riotous, colors in reception, bright chair fabrics or screens between desks, colors in kitchens and cafeterias, meeting rooms, metal storage units.
Art highlights	Keep all walls white, all surfaces neutral, but bring color through well-displayed and well-lit artworks.

Colorist

Credo	Color helps office work, but it must be carefully used.
General design	White, gray, and black are out. Color can be bought at no extra cost on most products—and it makes people feel good. So do it. Use color on carpets, work surfaces, or screens, chairs, meeting furniture, furniture, window and door frames, blinds, wastebins, and desktop accessories.

Styles

Color for wayfinding	Different color themes for different floors or building wings or departments.
Mood colors	Control color for different purposes—cool colors for reflection in library and solo offices; warm colors for meeting rooms, green for training.
Exterior colors	Turn the building inside and out into a memorable color statement, e.g., Disney Studio offices.

Figure 7.3   Three philosophies on color in offices.

First come those colors that should not be used as dominant wall colors: no purple, violet, vivid yellow, yellow-green, bright red, and please—no white or gray. In general office areas soft yellow, sandstone, pale gold, pale orange, pale green and blue-green are always appropriate. (*Frank H. Mahnke, Color, Environment and Human Response, 1996.*)

Implementing Color Strategies

Colorist

At Lawrence and Mayo, an advertising firm in Newport Beach, a bold decision was made with color. An old banking hall was converted by Gensler to accommodate this lively and energetic client. Low walls in the office, inset doors, and columns are finished in kiwi green and deep purple. Soft furniture, chairs, and sofas with extravagant curling back panels pick up the same colors. Elsewhere in the breakout room is a different pair of bright colors, cherry red and yellow, the colors of one of the agency's clients. Contrasted with the bright white interior walls and brushed aluminum metal coil drapery, the strong colors set off the geometric forms and well suit this extrovert group.

Minimalist

At British Airways' new HQ in Waterside, Niels Torp from Norway, by contrast, follows devotedly the minimalist naturalist approach. Only the colors of natural material appear in the shared areas: mixed granite colors on the street surface, wicker café chairs, wooden floors on the office landings, green plants (no garish flowers). Stainless-steel handrails on the stair and etched glass for the signage complete the picture. Office walls are painted white, desks are wood topped, tall storage cupboards are white with some wood tops, the carpet is a neutral gray. The effect is cool, harmonious, and in very "good taste." But there are also delightful touches of color, tiny and jewel like. The most noticeable are the small glass lampshades over the coffee counters and meeting tables, color-coordinated to match a leading wall at the entrance to each floor plate—red, blue, green, yellow, possibly helping in direction finding but also breaking the "natural" look just a tiny bit. This is a building, however, where people provide the color.

Color strategies should be chosen in relation to the culture of the organization expected to occupy the space. But they cannot be left to chance. When not managed skillfully, pitfalls abound. Consider lawyers who may use color to impress clients (and each other) of their reliability and their worth. While creating a generally controlled and sober environment for the office as a whole, if the partners are left to exercise personal preferences in their own offices, chaos can result. In one example (understandably nameless), a budget was allocated to all partners to arrange individual decorative schemes for their private offices. The offices all had glazed front walls, to allow those in the heart of the building a small share of the natural daylight. After all the different color schemes had been implemented in these offices, the effect of the varied and incompatible schemes in each room was, as you could have predicted, wildly discordant, conveying disorganization rather than the clear headedness that clients might expect from their lawyers. All the different carpets had to be removed, all the walls repainted, and the furniture upholstery coordinated. This sort of experience would turn any one into a minimalist.

All the Colors of the Rainbow

If accents are your strategy, be careful to choose the right bits to accent and in the right way. Consider, for example, the furniture. Chairs are often chosen as a good opportunity to introduce a spot of bright or unusual color. They can be covered in the full range of colors, or in a patterned fabric. Fine—this can work very well—especially as it tends to be a muted effect when the chairs are either in use, or pushed in to the desk at the end of the day, as then only the back shows, often not even upholstered, so the impact is not too extreme. But be sure that the colors are well coordinated or related to each other

Chairs with different functions—say, operator chairs, visitor chairs, or dining chairs—are usually different shapes. Distinguishing them by color as well emphasizes the different functions, maintaining one color stresses unity. Colors that contrast with wall and floor dramatically alter spaces. Differentiating the chair colors for different floors of a building, or departments, or functional areas, may seem to be a simple way of giving each area its own character—but beware: The housekeeping problem can escalate out of control, and herding the pink ones back to the pink floor and weeding out the blue from among the green can be a frustrating consequence of moves and inevitable changes in group sizes and locations. Before the designer and the last furniture installer are out of the door, everything is already on the move, chairs first of all with their smooth rolling casters making it so easy.

Another color candidate is the desk. Work surfaces of lime green, mauve, even passion pink appear in furniture showrooms as an echo—about two years later—of fashion colors in the retail and garment world. Think carefully before leaping in this direction. As with wandering chairs, the users instantly change an environment. Once they are released into the newly furnished, sparkling, designer-crafted office, they start spreading papers around, leaving files open, creating a mess. This, of course, is mostly on the desk surfaces—at least until everything overflows onto the floor. So if the brightest, most arresting color is the desk, your eye is immediately drawn to the messiest aspect of the office. This is generally not the objective of bringing in lively colors. Unfortunately, a similar effect is often seen with storage furniture. This may explain why, although metal cabinets lend themselves well to color, and some companies offer *any* color of your choice with no cost premium, it is not taken up as much as one might suppose.

Accent colors are often chosen for areas that are slightly apart from the work areas, the fashionable breakout areas, the canteen, the reception areas, or the client dining room. Here you can afford to be bold, make strong statements, do things with color that people would quickly tire of. People are in a coffee area for only 10 minutes at a time, so you can use red—a "noisy" color that "makes a statement." A glaring color, allied to a strong shape such as a square, can be even more powerful. A calm color such as green, juxtaposed to patterned glass screening, can evoke water, with its soothing qualities and universal appeal—making it suitable, for example, for a client dining area.

Leafy Offices

Plants in buildings, a source of soothing green, have been in fashion since *Bürolandschaft* days. They are sometimes attributed with a beneficial role in removing pollutants through absorption, or in humidifying otherwise dry office air. There are different management strategies for providing plants. None is intrinsically more "right" than another, but they all demand different things of the building, different provision of floor space and ledges on which to put the plants, shorter or longer routes to fetch water, different hazards for the plants to encounter as they grow. One approach seeks a dramatic impact in central and public areas: the tall bamboo grove in the atrium, the 40-year-old palm tree brushing the receptionist's collar. In some buildings this is taken further to encompass a landscaped area with waterfalls, Japanese pebble gardens or cascades of creepers inside atria, on top of roofs and clinging to façades, with special lighting to help them grow and show them off to good effect. A different approach provides smaller plants around the entire office, so that everyone, wherever they are sitting, has some greenery to look at. This may be less impressive for the visitor, but it is more fun for the staff, who can observe the emerging new shoot, the unfurling leaf of "their" plant. At the DIY end of the scale is the encouragement, or at least passive acceptance, of anyone and everyone bringing their own pots from home. The resulting jungle of variegated greenery can be charming or messy. It needs care—plants wither over the summer holidays, floods from overfilled saucers may stain the carpet, tendrils twine themselves where they are not wanted. It has the merit that the plants belong to, and are tended by, people who care, and consequently they receive pleasure from the plants. The first two strategies require the services of a plant-maintenance company to select and tend the plants on a regular basis, feed them, shower and shine their leaves, and retire them to more hospitable climes when the office environment causes droop, replacing them with bright young things. Such services can be excellent but come with a hefty price tag. Surely, says the finance controller, greenery can be bought for less money? Enter plastic and silk. The myth is that artificial plants have the same appeal but are maintenance free. They do not, and they are not. They collect dust, look grimy, and never attract the same allegiance from staff.

Outside spaces—courtyards, ornamental ponds or lakes, and roof terraces—should be made accessible to all staff to offer the benefits of fresh air and opportunities for meeting or sitting outside on fine days. To plan them behind locked doors to prevent access is foolish and unnecessary. The best locations are adjacent to the staff lounges or cafeterias or the reception and waiting areas.

Artwork, paintings, wall hangings, banners, and sculpture are an easier source of quality and of color than plants. They do not have the same maintenance cost; they are not killed off by unexpected downdraughts, or blighted by an unchecked attack of red spider mite. They can also be modestly priced. There is every reason to seek the quality and interest that they can bring to a building. In some organizations artworks are viewed as an important corporate investment that will appreciate in capital value, that can be shown off to visitors in reception areas, that may grace the lavish conference facility to impress customers or be hung on the executive floor. Your organization needs to be clear about whether its strategy is art for the bosses, art for the investors, or art for the workers. Building design and layout must take account of the positions such items will occupy, and in some instances particular items may be commissioned to occupy especially prominent places. Business galleries rent out pictures and other artworks so that they can be changed from time to time if you prefer not to commit your offices to a particular style over a long period. Remember that extra security and insurance may be needed for special items.

Light provides the other half of the color story. It is how we see color, and the color of light affects mood and behavior too and causes colors to create different effects. The blue light—daylight tones—that is used for office areas is particularly suitable for reading papers. However, it casts a cooler tone, clean but clinical, and accents the brightness of whites. These are often modified to warmer colors such as magnolia, buttermilk, and all the other off whites. The range of soft yellows and sand tones are popular, to bring the feeling of warmth, and, if not too strong, they can be used for whole walls without appearing radical. Often there is a white ceiling, part of the impression of corporate sobriety as well as for the reflection of uplighting. This too can be modified. There is a "metal-friendly" paint that can be sprayed onto acoustic ceiling tiles, apparently without clogging the holes, to change the glaring white to a soft cream color. This still allows reflected light but eliminates the shine and glare, so that people cease to "see" the ceiling. Light of different tones is used to give an added warmth. A golden light in a dining area always makes the food look better.

Health, Wealth, and Happiness

Feng shui (pronounced "fung shwey" and signifying Wind Water) is said to have been cavalierly characterized by a

Chinese tour guide, not wishing to be drawn into a long discussion, as "Chinese building regulations." It is more seriously described as "the ancient art of spatial design for business and home enhancement." It is a set of principles by which spatial aspects of location, orientation, and interior arrangement are decided. The principles have been formulated to promote the well-being of individuals, and, in the case of offices, also of the business itself, by seeking harmony of the building with natural forces. It has a growing number of adherents in Western countries, and also many skeptics. Some large international corporations have seen fit to consult *feng shui* experts about their buildings while others see it as irrational.

The fundamental *feng shui* forces considered are fire, earth, air, and water and the flows of energy along straight lines. Some aspects of the natural environment with which relationships should be sought are clear and obvious, such as a mountain view or flowing water; others are less so, such as the dangerous influence of a sharp cutting edge—a poison arrow—which may be symbolized by a corner, or the pages of a book inside a building, or a straight road, or a pylon outside a building. Anything of this sort, with a threatening appearance, can send dangerous shafts in straight lines, so a doorway, or a desk in the office (or a bed at home) must not be aligned with them. There are symbols too of good fortune. Gold and clear rippling water are two important ones, as well as a variety of living things, such as the elephant, bamboo, pine tree, and crane, which may be used in a variety of ways to bring benefit.

When these principles are to be applied, it is necessary to use an acknowledged expert as they cannot be understood at a superficial level and effectively applied. Many organizations have come to appreciate the value of such an approach, and experts are now available in the United States and elsewhere who can advise on the design of a building from this point of view. The habit of incorporating some of these ideas is a result of the increased globalization of business and the exchange of ideas. Western architects have built in Hong Kong and elsewhere where this approach is a standard part of the building process, and Chinese-based companies are increasingly present in the West. If *feng shui* is to be used, it is important to do so from the outset as some of the very first decisions with respect to location and orientation could be considered inauspicious and may be hard to rectify further into a project.

When applied to offices, in a city rather than the countryside, some of the original concepts have been gradually re-interpreted to enable the artificial environment to be considered as easily as the natural world, on which the approach was originally developed. The nature of the business is also relevant and will cause a change of emphasis in some concepts. Some of the more important *feng shui* principles are the following:

- Orientation

- Relationship to other buildings

- Location of main entrances

- Characteristics of roads and local traffic directions and speeds

- What protection is at the "back" of the building

- Vertical location in a high building (if only on some floors)

- Shape of floor plates

- Pattern of internal circulation in relation to workplace location and orientation

- Location of toilets, especially with relation to doorways, and above or below

- Shape and interior arrangement of offices and work areas

- Placement of desks including reception desk
- Arrangement of boardrooms
- Positioning of good luck symbols—flowing water, for example
- Color of decor

Summary

This chapter will help you to decide if your organization should provide special facilities beyond the working areas, which ones and to what quality. Office buildings offer a variety of facilities that are not designed directly to enable the work of the office to be carried out. These may be considered perks, additional amenities, making the office a better place to work, or they may be thought of as essentials for the support of the office staff. Special leisure areas, cafeterias, or a day care room can seem like a luxury, but for sites where local services are hard to access or when change is introducing added stress or when staff are hard to attract, they may become vital. Some facilities are a legal requirement.

There are disadvantages as well as advantages for management. The responsibilities that go with amenities must be taken into account. Kitchens have to be run according to strict food hygiene legislation; sports facilities have to follow safety procedures. These responsibilities can be placed on someone else's shoulders. An amenity such as catering can be outsourced—that is, given to a specialist company to run under contract. A disadvantage of outsourcing is that, once you shed the burden, you may lose the in-house expertise to evaluate services provided by others.

The requirement to provide for disabled access and use of buildings is an example of how what in the past may have been a luxury provision, offered only by the richest companies, has become a necessity—a legal one as well as the response of a generation of caring companies. There is considerable emphasis on the requirements imposed by wheelchair access, but other forms of provision, for the large group of deaf, blind, or partially sighted and partially mobile office workers and visitors, are no less important. Very heavy doors, highly polished floors, exclusively audible fire warnings, and written instructions for safety or elevator operation may present problems for disabled people who are non-wheelchair users.

Colors evoke different emotions, and each person reacts differently to them. There is plenty of scope to think actively about the use of color in the office environment, and no one approach is the "right" one. There is virtue in keeping things simple, only allowing fashion to take hold if you are prepared to continually change with the times, and in understanding the cultural context of the organization for which the colors are being chosen. Plants and art have a role to play in creating attractive work environments. *Feng shui,* increasingly fashionable as a discipline, needs to be taken into account early if maximum benefit is to be obtained.

The overall quality of the environment is an important amenity. All the options suggested in this chapter are positive, whether included in the building as requirements for legal or work reasons or supplied in the spirit of providing an excellent workplace. Even if only small areas can be devoted to special facilities, they can be planned so that a range of activities can take place in them. Conference suites can accommodate classes after work; cafeterias can be equipped with stacking furniture so that they can be cleared for exercise groups or the Christmas party. These areas are more cost effective if they can be well used throughout the day and the year.

Technology in Office Buildings

CASE HISTORIES

See Case Histories 21, 22, and 23
on pages 417–435

Q: What price the paperless office?

A: More paper.

The paperless office, the office of the future, is a promise to be realized by the huge changes that information technology—IT—makes. E-commerce and E-business are transforming the way we communicate and transact business. New and glamorous ways to record, retrieve, and transmit information are predicted. The office will come into its own, efficient as never before. Rapidly falling prices of electronic equipment have had a serious impact since the early 1980s, but at a price. As the cost of equipment plummeted, the cost of buildings rose with higher capital as well as maintenance and running costs. Office buildings are filled with wires and heat-producing equipment. Everyone, or almost everyone, now has a computer on their desk, some people have more than one, and other equipment like printers, faxes, scanners, and copiers are cheap enough to scatter throughout the office for convenient access. More space at the desk, more wires to be hidden, more air-conditioning means that low-specification buildings, particularly those built in the 1960s and 1970s, have become unfit and cannot cope with this relentless march of progress.

The speed and extent of the impact of computers was not understood until it happened. Office work can no longer be conceived independent of electronic equipment. There is some form of equipment to carry out any task you can imagine, and some organizations are moving toward reduced paper processes that almost merit the term *paperless*. Everyone is dependent to some degree on computerized systems, as witnessed by the serious effort put into ensuring that the transition into the year 2000 would be free of computer-driven disasters. There are organizations with more computers than people, and though others still lag behind, the impact is not dependent on simple quantity. The speed with which the World Wide Web has been accepted, now that the Internet has reached beyond the world of the military and academia into business and personal spheres, foreshadows continued and ever-astonishing, exciting, and productive change in this area. E-commerce will continue to change the office world, eventually perhaps out of recognition.

Proliferating Equipment

Many people have the creation and handling of knowledge as the core of their work. Some of this may not take place in offices, but increasingly the "knowledge-based industries" have a large office-based component. Throughout their history, office work and offices have been transformed by access to key pieces of equipment at different stages, especially the telegraph, the typewriter, and the telephone. Consider the typewriter. In 1873 Remington was looking for an outlet for precision instruments because firearms, his specialty, were no longer in high demand. In 1879 fewer than 200 typewriters were sold, but by 1890 annual sales had reached 65,000. The development of office buildings at this time was influenced by the need to house the large, low-paid, largely female labor force employed to use this equipment. The telephone too started as a specialized piece of equipment, and there were maybe one or two in an organization. Tales of the days when there was only one in the entire British Foreign Office, located in a basement corridor, are still current. They may be apocryphal, but they are a reminder of how rapidly the telephone has spread. In such organizations many desks have had several telephones for decades now. In most office buildings most people have access to one, normally on their own desk. They may also have a company mobile plus one of their own. The telephone has changed the speed with which things are done; it has changed the distances over which business can be performed; it has transformed business life. Introducing telephones into offices was slightly more complicated than placing a typewriter on a desk, but not much more so, as the wires required are tiny, flexible, and easily routed to almost anywhere. The equipment has shrunk a bit, but it was never very large. Miniature, cordless, and mobile telephones have extended the situations in which they can be used, and M-commerce further stretches their utility beyond voice; but the major impact on office work came about by making them available to everyone on their desks.

With such precedents it is hardly surprising that information technology generated great changes as it entered the office in the 1970s and 1980s. As the office workforce had grown so dramatically, a great many people were going to be affected by the monumental changes. The spinning jenny appears to have had nothing on the computer in its capacity to cause vast and permanent changes in the working lives of millions. The first mainframe computers were very large, very expensive, and could be used only by experts who understood them. They did not become common in office buildings until they had shrunk a little, and even then they still needed special rooms with air-conditioning and special people to look after them. What a few people had on their desks then were "dumb" terminals, able to perform only when connected to the mainframe. Minicomputers, no bigger than a family fridge and not requiring nearly as much space or such special conditions, were miniaturized versions of mainframes. They spread the computing habit to a wider range of users. The quantum leap occurred, however, when technical advances and further miniaturization led to a powerful computer, cheap enough to buy for individual members of staff, in a piece of equipment small enough to fit on a desktop. The most influential was IBM's PC (personal computer), introduced in 1980. That opened the floodgates of opportunity for the equipment to proliferate. The increase in computers, Internet users, and telephones shown in Figures 8.1, 8.2, and 8.3 are an indication of the extent to which organizational work patterns have been transformed.

Getting IT into the Building

Major changes to be accommodated are still in the pipeline. The effects of miniaturization, and the organizational and social transformations it engenders, have not yet had their full impact on building design or use. It may happen in a series of tiny waves and jerks, just as the impact of the IT we use in offices today has infiltrated. Many of the changes to which the buildings of the 1960s and 1970s have been subjected have resulted from the increased use of information technology. To start with, there were more extensive telephone networks and telex machines—whole rooms of them in some organizations. Then centralized photocopying

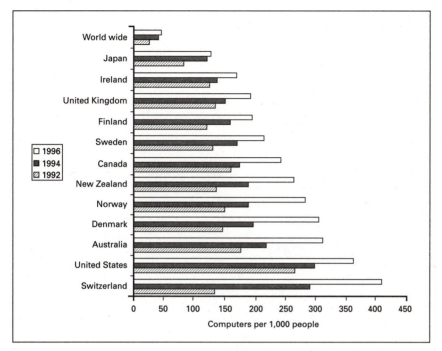

Figure 8.1   The number of computers per 1,000 people, 1992 through 1996.

(International Telecommunication Union (ITU), World Telecommunication Report; Information Infrastructures; World Telecommunication Indicators, 1995 and 1998 editions, Geneva; Also Karen P. and Egil Juliussen, The 6th Annual Computer Industry 1993 Almanac.)

and the electric typewriter pool needed rooms, power supplies, and heat extracts. Central computers required new risers for the huge bundles of cables, followed by a spread of desktop equipment necessitating the introduction of cable routes cut into solid floors, cable routes through raised floors, or cable trays in the ceilings.

Buildings have been ripped apart and threaded with wires and equipment intended to control the building. Fire-alarm systems, electronically controlled boilers to deliver monitored temperatures, security systems, updated lighting with electronic control devices—all require routes for the wires, new equipment such as lights, boilers, and thermostats, not to mention a space for a computer workstation for the security guard. As one system replaces the next, the remnants of the old are often left behind. Extra wires have been added with-

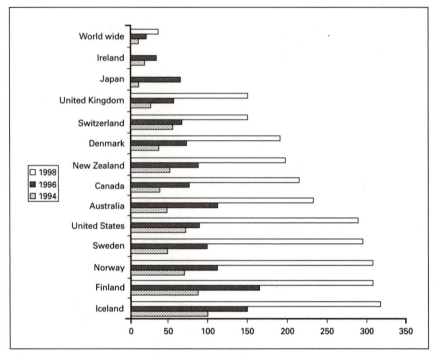

Figure 8.2   Internet users per 1,000 people, 1994 through 1998.

[International Telecommunication Union (ITU), World Telecommunication Report; Information Infrastructures; World Telecommunication Indicators, 1995 and 1998 editions, Geneva. Also press release from the 1998 Computer Industry Almanac Web page www.c-i-a.com/199907ciau.htm]

out removing old ones, as they could not be easily reached, which makes it hard to know whether the old ones are connected to a vital piece of equipment, and gradually ducts have become clogged. It is surprising, after this treatment, that any of the buildings that were predicted to fail under the strain of the introduction of IT survived the experience at all. Some have found the strain too great. They stand unloved and empty or have been pulled down and replaced.

Space and Furniture

As IT entered the office, the workforce felt invaded. Space was being given to machines at the expense of people. Temperatures shot up because of the heat output of computers,

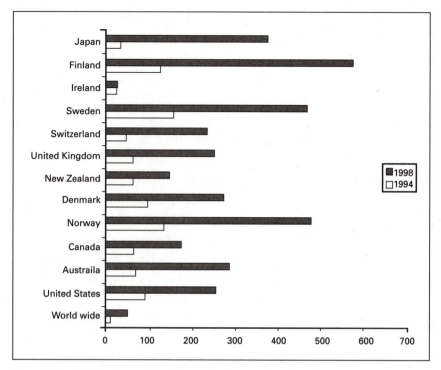

Figure 8.3   Mobile phone subscribers per 1,000 people, 1994 and 1998.

[International Telecommunication Union (ITU),World Telecommunication Report; Information Infrastructures; World Telecommunication Indicators, 1995 and 1998 editions, Geneva.]

but only the computer rooms get special air-conditioning, not the people. Amenity areas were taken over by computer rooms. Desks were too crowded to work at comfortably. Unions representing office employees affected by these changes were distressed. Luddism prevailed. Afraid that people themselves might be put out of work, employees were often hostile to any introduction of equipment. The white-collar workforce continued to grow, despite union fears, and the struggle concentrated on ensuring that a good working environment would be maintained. The early equipment was, indeed, large and cumbersome, intrusive and space hungry. The desks that had suited an earlier work style did become crowded, with little room for anything except the video display terminal, and they were rapidly buried in a tangle of cables. Breakthroughs came only as the equipment began to shrink. Other equipment has also proliferated: fax machines, answering machines, desktop copiers, printers, and scanners. The extra desks required for the IT are a factor to be taken into account when deciding how many desks are needed for a group of staff. Though equipment is small enough to fit on a desk, shared items need a place of their own, so that a procession of users does not disturb anyone too much. In an open-plan arrangement there is often a convenient corner to place them. If the organization uses a series of small, enclosed offices, the equipment may end up in the corridor, unsupervised and abused, or someone has to share their office with it and it becomes a burden for them to be disturbed constantly and a bore for others who wish to access it.

Changes in technology have taken place so fast that the furniture industry seems to have been left one step behind. To a complex problem a specific solution has been offered, but the problem has changed. Desk-based cable-management systems, created to hide and contain wires safely, are often more complicated than they need be. A basic, roomy basket hooked under the desk may do a better job than cable routes needing fancy threading, cover strips, and a built-in channel with an elaborate lid that turns out not to fit the socket extensions. Individual air-conditioning at the desks to cope with local heat gain has been made redundant by small equipment producing less heat. Special desks that accommodate clumsy keyboards at the best level for VDT users but do not suit tasks using pen and paper, have been displaced by thinner keyboards. The universal desk takes into consideration the new reality that anyone, anywhere may have a VDT but every desk must also work for people who do not. Mobile computer trolleys were useful where only a few computers were available to a large group, but increasingly organizations provide at least one on every desk, so the trolleys have become redundant. Desks with deep corners accommodate large monitors, but the flat screen has arrived, and it can use a smaller and simpler desk. Special multi-level printer tables with slots for continuously fed paper have been replaced by small desktop laser or inkjet printers. There are organizations, such as the financial brokerage houses, where up to six VDT screens appear on each desk. Special furniture has been created, like something out of *Star Trek,* so that everything can fit and be reached without causing an accident or missing a deal. Elsewhere advances in technology have reduced the six VDTs to a few with a "split screen," a single screen functioning as several independent ones, with software that allows a single piece of equipment on a standard desk to carry out functions that previously needed several separate screens in a special console. Generally the simpler furniture solutions have fared better over time.

The terminal, VDT, and keyboard have been joined on the desktop by so many gadgets that it is now essential to supply six or more power outlets and data to every desk. Communication is fast and furious between the office and many other locations (Figs. 8.4 and 8.5). The flexibility offered by ensuring that anything could, if necessary, be placed anywhere in the office is very valuable. There are the desktop printers—far too many of them in some places because cables to connect them in networks to a whole group of computers have not been used. Sometimes this is the result of using many different and incompatible pieces of equipment. Initially different machines were marketed to do different tasks, and as the software was not interchangeable, there seemed to be as many makes and models as tasks. These different machines could not "talk" to each other, so, among other problems, they could not share printers. This type of confusion has subsided; more of the bits of kit are now interchangeable or compatible. There is little excuse for a printer for each machine, one on every desk. Where this still occurs, steps should be taken to link several to a single conveniently located printer.

Larger equipment in special rooms has not disappeared

Technology	Function
E-mail plus fast plus wide bandwidth	Document transmission
Cordless (e.g., DECT) phones	Move about all over the office
Cordless-to-mobile phones	Move about anywhere in or out of the office
Phone hookups	Dispersed meetings
Video conferencing	Dispersed and personalized meetings
Desktop video	See remote colleagues, share remote documents
Palm tops	Work remotely without back strain
Voice recognition	Document generation on the move
Voice to screen and vice versa	Mobile interaction, multiple systems
Wireless local area networks	Laptop use all over the office
Data conferencing	Dispersed project sessions
Voice mail	Personalized messages
Integrated voice, fax, and e-mail	Single source for messages
Digital imaging	On-the-spot documents wherever you are

Figure 8.4   Newer technologies supporting office work.

just because there is more equipment all over the office. Mainframe and larger-computer suites are still needed by some organizations, and these still need raised floors, temperature and humidity controls, a dust-free environment, and special security control points. Some smaller organizations have computer rooms, maybe with air-conditioning and a raised floor, but they are not the laboratory type of environment staffed by high-level specialists of the early mainframe days. They are often more like warehouses-cum-workshops. New equipment delivered in boxes sits in piles on the floor, waiting to be checked and then installed on someone's desk; shelves are crowded with repair kits, broken modems, manuals, and miscellaneous cables; and the file server hums and growls under the workbench. The most complicated copiers, printers, or mailing machines—now electronically controlled, less noisy than in the past, and smaller—are generally used only if they can serve the whole office, so they still get a separate room accessible to every

Figure 8.5

(*Louis Hellman.*)

department.

As far as everyone is aware, the paperless office is the bit of the science-fiction scenario that has not quite come about. Bearing in mind that it takes 10 years for a tried and proven technological development to be turned into usable and affordable machines, the spread of desktop and general office electronic equipment has been as rapid as intelligent predictions of the early 1980s suggested. The range of tasks, the ingenuity with which these have been combined into multifunction machines, the speed and power that can be afforded in desk-based equipment have all come up to expectation. At the same time the manufacturers of paper filing systems have expanded their ranges, streamlined their products, and moved in for the kill. The Swedish paper industry has doubled its production in the last decade. The new machines have made it possible to generate vastly more paper ever more rapidly; multiple drafts are so easy to create and meeting minutes can be easily photocopied and automatically stapled straight from the word processor, and e-mails can be printed out for easy reading. If the new equipment has permitted some reduction in paper—"hard copy"—this has merely served to keep things in roughly the same place. At the same time computers have raised expectations about speed of retrieval. No wonder high-density filing, described in detail in Chapter 5, is creeping (or rather, lumbering, as it is bulky stuff) into more and more offices.

Electronic filing is getting closer to becoming an affordable technology. There have been a number of attempts to miniaturize paper records. Microfilm and microfiche systems have been adopted by some organizations. These involve expensive photographic sessions and the use of bulky microfiche readers that are too specialized to perform any function other than to provide a hard-to-read version of a document that cannot be taken back to the desk. Methods to capture documents on computers are now affordable. Optical character reading, advances in equipment that can read varieties of handwriting, and electronic storage on laser disks with fast retrieval systems are all coming together to make it possible that far more files will soon be kept in purely electronic form. Large insurance companies, banks, and car and home loan organizations are the type of businesses that have invested in such electronic storage and have reaped enormous gains from it. The potential market for electronic document storage is vast and will be exploited in the next decade as electronic storage grows cheaper. Then some of the rotary filing units described in Chapter 5 may not be wanted after all. If people can be prevented from overworking the printer, some of the stationery cupboards can go as well. The in-tray, fax machine, and a good part of the mailroom are starting to become redundant as the use of e-mail spreads and memos and messages are sent around the office, or around the world, at the press of a computer key.

Cables, Heat, and Noise

No one anticipated that the price of the paperless office would be more paper storage equipment. It was going to be cables and heat. Well, that prediction has come true, though not always in the way that was imagined. The first companies to invest in desktop equipment for large numbers of staff were swamped in tangles of wires. Cables were seen lying on the floor, sometimes taped down to ensure passive behavior, wandering down corridors and disappearing into holes in the walls, crawling over desks and leaping gaps between wall sockets and computers. A serious danger to safety, the cables had to be controlled. At this point the furniture manufacturers homed in on a potential selling point and invented "cable management." They rapidly developed desks that take care of all the cables, and, if you pay enough, they do other things like provide local air-conditioning.

Even if the desk can subdue the cables once they reach it, there is still the problem of getting the cables there. Providing socket outlets near the desk is thus a priority. Creating routes around office buildings for cables is a major preoccupation. The question is how to get traditional cables around the building and equally important, how to alter them as people move or their requirements change. Small buildings or highly cellularized ones have managed perfectly well with cables buried in walls, partitions, or columns or running round the edge of the building. If a great deal of equipment is needed, the cable-route problem can be solved by trunking, into which socket outlets can be fitted as often as required. Prairie farming has created huge fields—great for tractors but with no hedgerows for wildlife habitats and hiding places. Deep or medium open-plan offices have stripped away walls, the normal hiding places for socket outlets near each desk. Many 1960s buildings were built with small cable trays in their concrete floor screeds to bring socket outlets to the middle of open office floors. Some of these could take only two sorts of cable and only in small amounts. Drilling out extra or bigger routes took place time after time as equipment poured into these buildings. Electrical track with almost no thickness, cunningly laid under carpets, was tried but did not provide the ultimate solution. The need to handle two kinds of wire, one for power, the other for data and telecoms, means that crossover points and times when there are changes in one but not the other are more easily dealt with using more traditional wiring technologies. A raised floor—that is, a second floor that is supported on a series of short legs to provide a surface to walk on above a structural floor—had been a feature of mainframe computer rooms, where they could be up to 3 ft (1 m) above the structural floor. These are now commonplace in ordinary office areas, though very much shallower. Some designers use the ceilings as a distribution plane and to bring cables down from above. In some cases they use large plastic-coated colored coiled cables and make a feature out of them. Others have adopted similar but more discrete systems as used in factories, where the cable is a spring that retracts out of the way when not needed. Power poles, fixed from floor to ceiling, offer another solution and may be independently provided or can be found as part of some furniture ranges.

To get cables under the floors or above the ceilings in the first place means that big bundles of them have to be carried up vertical ducts from the main switches. Sometimes the bundle is as thick as the torso of a body-building fanatic. New ducts have had to be cut into the concrete floors of old buildings, as the original ducts were too small. These are some of the reasons why the offices of the 1960s and 1970s did not measure up to the demands of the IT revolution. There is not enough floor-to-ceiling height in many of them to insert raised floors and no efficient way of adding the vertical ducts to carry the cables around. Buildings were, and often still are, built with low ceilings, partly in an attempt to cram as many floors as possible into them, within imposed height restrictions, and partly because heating tall rooms is an extravagance office occupiers are keen to avoid. Older buildings have often fared better, as they started with more generous dimensions.

Cables have not gone away. Some of them will stay for a very long time, perhaps forever. But fiber-optic cable and cordless radios are now being used more widely Fiber-optic cable may be useful where large capacity on a simple route is required, but it is far from being a panacea. It suffers from high cost, jointing problems, a requirement for a wide bending curve, and it needs protection throughout. Cordless systems using radio and microwave bands or infrared light are also expensive and so far support only slower transmissions, so they are less appealing for transmitting large volumes of data. Nonetheless, these technologies are well suited to specific tasks. Cordless telephones using radio transmitters are gaining value within office floors, as people work in different "settings" and move from place to place. Infrared beams, which are used in most homes with a television or stereo set in the form of a remote-control unit, can easily be put to use in switching lights on and off. For example, a system designed to control electricity costs, which switches all the lights off in an open-plan office by means of a simple time switch, can also be equipped with an infrared remote-control system allowing individuals to switch "their" lights on if they need to.

More important is the fact that people have become familiar with the problem—the proliferation of cables, the reluctance to pull out obsolete cables when alterations are made, the number that people need and where they want them. So places to put them and sensible patterns in which to lay them are being devised. *Structured cabling* is one

High Bandwidths are the Key to Good Electronic Communication

1 to 4 Mbps cordless phones

100 Mbps Cat 5 cable

350 Mbps copper

example: A tree type of distribution is used with a main trunk to all floors, big branches to convenient switching points, and twigs that can be removed and reattached at these points to connect specific outlets to the tree. Structured cabling reduces the need for miles of cable and allows for cost-effective rerouting, so it is a sensible expedient for many reasons. Data transmission by twisted copper wires like those of telephone technology but of a heavier variety is now possible. Without the phenomenal capacity of fiber-optic cable, it has a number of substantial advantages. It is far cheaper to install, is less temperamental, and has no need for special devices at the ends to connect it to the rest of the system. Short lengths work best, so it relies on the continued development of structured cabling. Other problems have not yet been solved. The provision of both raised floors and suspended ceilings in a building can represent overspecification. Funding institutions still expect raised floors, and cheap lighting systems popular with developers are often integrated into suspended ceilings, so many overspecified properties are around or still being built. It is also common now to find fully exposed ceilings where all the services including the lighting are on public view.

Smaller equipment has reduced heat loads. The typical equipment ratings on the manufacturers' metal plate at the back, where only the technical team ever look, are cautious and tend to give a higher rate of expected heat output than is found in reality if the equipment is tested. Naturally the manufacturers' figures are believed, as they are usually the only ones available, but the actual load is often smaller than planned for—about a third the amount is typical. The discrepancy went unnoticed at first, as the rate at which the use of equipment would expand was underestimated. There was a lot more equipment than had been predicted, so the overall heat output was more or less as expected, or at least not noticeably lower. The internal climate is extremely uncomfortable in some types of office (dealing rooms are an obvious example) if there is no extra ventilation or air-conditioning. Heat from small equipment is less of a problem than it used to be, but it must be taken into account when planning how to design and run an office building. For example, rather than being an unwanted burden, the heat from both equipment and lights should be regarded as part of the heating system and used positively.

Noise has crept in alongside some of the equipment. Advances in technology tend at first to produce noisy intrusion, which has vanished as further improvements have been made. Typewriter pools used to be pretty noisy places; modern keyboards produce a gentler sound. Early dot-matrix printers clattered loudly, even under those ugly hoods, whereas inkjets and lasers merely swish. Developments in telephone systems have silenced the incessant rings. You can be found by your mobile telephone or cordless phone, voice mail, or a follow-me system, or a message can be radioed to your pocket bleeper, so your neighbors next to your empty desk are no longer obliged to block their ears to shut out the bell. The next noise frontier of concern is voice-activated computers, which are already entering the office.

Energy Efficiency

If they are not economical to operate, office buildings as we know them, even properly filled with the right equipment and activities, could disappear. One of the costs that can be reduced is expenditure on fuel. Buildings use a large proportion of the fuel we burn. In fact, 50 percent of our energy consumption can be attributed to buildings. A large part of that is used in houses, hospitals, and factories, but offices use enough to make a very sizeable impact on the consumption of finite resources and the generation of pollution. A great deal of work has been done to demonstrate how energy is used in office buildings and how it can be reduced. Very little real effect has yet been seen in changed management decisions, although the design professions are trying hard to incorporate some of the research insights into buildings and systems. Despite all manner of publicity programs, saving energy is still low on the business agenda. It should not be. Saving costs means higher profits; efficiently designed and managed systems are the best defense against rising costs for the future. Saving energy and reducing pollution are vital, in the longer term, for the whole population of the world. Even if the total effect on a nation's energy consumption can be affected only marginally by energy saving in all existing offices, this is no justification for ignoring the issue.

The UK Energy Efficiency Office, with the help of the Building Research Establishment, has published a series of best-practice guides that explain the most efficient approaches to energy use in offices through a series of real case studies. They identify four general types of office building. For each type the guide gives an average and a target for energy consumption and contrasts these with what can be achieved by good practice. There are some clear messages. Good-practice levels of consumption can save between 30 and 40 percent of the cost per square foot of treated building (that is, excluding places like plant rooms and car parking lots). This is true whatever the type of building, whether naturally ventilated or air-conditioned. It is an amount well worth saving. The larger problem is more often electricity consumption than heating. Mainframe computer rooms use large amounts of electricity, of which some can be recouped if heat gains are recycled to where heating is required elsewhere in the building. If the building is air-conditioned, it is not the refrigeration that uses the most energy, but fans and pumps, so it is not the amount of cooling but the time it is in operation that most influences the cost.

It all sounds straightforward. Why are the improvements fewer than they should be? Because managers do not know how easy it can be. To save energy, you need good information. You must know about quantities of fuel used, areas in which systems operate, and hours of operation for the different systems. Meters to check the amount and pattern of energy use are needed to collect this information, such as a meter for kitchens and computer suites or a meter to separate lighting costs from those of other power used. Even if meters have to be retrofitted, their cost can be recouped in energy saved. Lights are often the largest individual item among electrical costs, so work out what to do about them. It may be a simple matter of replacing those that are on for longest with up-to-date bulbs, reflectors, and controls. If a totally new system is required to reduce consumption, there is an opportunity to create a more congenial working atmosphere. Bear in mind, though, that the total energy costs, including those of energy used in production of new equipment, are not really incorporated in the calculation of the payback period. What is good for your organization may not be good for the global use of energy.

Focus the management of energy on matching performance standards to real needs. In other words, do not run things when you do not need them. See that office equipment is not left on unnecessarily, especially overnight. Ask your purchasing and IT departments to select only equipment with automatic power savers to switch it off after a period of inactivity. Make sure that air-conditioning does not run longer than needed to keep the building at an acceptable temperature where and when people are actually working and that the plant is sized to accommodate this. If you have an air-conditioned computer suite, make sure that you keep separate records of the power running the computers and the power needed for the air-conditioning. If the air-conditioning is using more than 60 percent of the amount of power needed to run the computers, it can probably be made more efficient.

Intelligent Buildings or Intelligent Technicians?

How can a building possibly be described as "intelligent"? If it is, is it a willful Frankenstein monster? Is it something the average office owner, renter, or user wants to have, or should you fend it off with a barge pole? Our cut-throat culture prizes intelligence, so intelligent must be "good."

Intelligence, knowledge, and feedback have all been muddled up in this handy portmanteau term. The Citroën car in the 1950s was one of the first consumer products to make use of the concept of feedback and response in machines. The relationship of the suspension to speed and to steering around corners was interactive. What was happening as a result of one had an effect on the behavior of the others, and the driver could benefit from the feedback. Generally it is the possibilities inherent in the feedback of information, rather than any concepts of knowledge or intelligence, that are of importance in buildings. And the feedback is only as good as the information it has to work on. An example of the way such feedback can be used is in ensuring that safety regulations are not breached. For a building where flexitime or hot-desking is used, or where large meetings take place, maybe you need "eyes" in the door frames to count people in and out, so that the security system "knows" if exceptional attendance means that the occupancy of the building as a whole is approaching its limit for fire evacuation purposes. This information could trigger a ban on additional people entering, just like a parking-garage system that says "Full" at the entry gate. Few office buildings really have a need for this, so to provide it as an "intelligent" feature would not make a lot of sense. This sort of gadgetry is not intrinsically desirable or intelligent. It is useful in specific, rather limited circumstances, but the problems must be framed by people, and the solutions must serve them.

The massive developments in electronic equipment over the last 30 years have attacked office buildings from two directions. The huge expansion in the use of computers in offices has been discussed above. From the other direction, electronics have been deployed in the systems that control different aspects of buildings—the heating and cooling systems, the elevators, the security and fire-alarm systems. As these have become more sophisticated, they have been able to make a building behave a bit like that famous Citroën, to respond more sensitively to needs, to work with feedback from the effects of the last thing that happened. Each of the systems in the building has been enhanced in different ways. Heating and ventilating systems can calculate optimum running patterns to achieve desired temperatures and air movement under different external and internal conditions. Elevators can do more than just respond to the first demand made on them; they can work out the optimum route for the calls demanded. Electronic security systems can report who has been past the most sensitive barriers, which is invaluable for an organization concerned to protect itself against industrial espionage. Fire-alarm systems can carry information about how many people are in a particular part of the building or which sprinklers have been activated, and they can flash instructions about evacuation during an emergency. Choosing a system that will offer the organization benefits that it needs, based on equipment that it can manage, is a specialist skill.

The controls of all these systems can be linked together through a single piece of equipment, so that what one is doing can be taken into account by the others. These are known as *building management systems* (BMS), or, if intended particularly to handle energy and fuel use, *building energy management systems* (BEMS). They enable effective fire-safety systems, complicated and specific security needs, and elaborate heating and ventilation systems to be installed and run in large and complicated buildings. They are an important element in the energy-saving approaches discussed above. A BEMS can send information and accept instructions about the systems under its control via a remote computer, even one in the chief engineer's home on the weekend, and can permit more cost effective and efficient monitoring and adjustment of the heating. In organizations with many buildings, these systems can be especially helpful, as the remote reporting can lead to immediate action to reduce costs while delivering a comfortable environment.

Building management systems are frequently described as if they were an unalloyed benefit. They are if they have been designed to meet your needs and until they go wrong. They can also cost a lot to buy, and if they do not fulfill your organization's needs, the irritation that they can cause may not be worth the potential savings. Even a simple system may be too complicated for the job it is doing. A security system that cannot be explained to members of staff who work late has disadvantages that a simpler one would avoid. A CCTV in the car parking lot and at the back door may be all that is needed. The significant issue is that many of these systems rely on cables. The routes that cables take through the building need to be simple, accessible for maintenance, and able to accept additions and changes. Introducing such cables has challenged older buildings, while it is becoming more standard in newer ones. Nonetheless, if you need a security barrier at the parking lot gate, which is to be opened by the receptionist pressing a button when someone authorized wishes to enter, a conduit is needed from the reception desk to the gate. Do not leave it until the granite has been laid in the entrance hall and the parking lot has been surfaced before deciding that this is an important part of the receptionist's role. Otherwise, you may have to settle for an expensive wireless control system.

The idea of an intelligent building could have developed into a monster dreamed up by science-fiction writers exploring the limits of computer intelligence, a building so complex that humans would not be clever enough to disentangle all the interconnected parts and would have to rely on computers. Before it did, the idea mutated into something much more amorphous. It is currently couched in terms of responsiveness to user needs, able to service cables or heating systems or change partition layouts—whatever people decide they want. The human choice and instructions come first. The building is intelligent if it is possible to carry out the instructions without tearing it apart, if the layout, construction, and servicing systems have taken into account how different needs may play themselves out over time. This begs the question of what changes an intelligent building can be expected to cope with. It is not possible to replan a long, thin building to work like a big, wide, open-plan one or vice versa. Does that preclude buildings with definite shapes, better able to accommodate one type of layout than another, from ever being intelligent?

Do the people running systems within a building really know enough to manage the more sophisticated products of engineering ingenuity? A bigger danger than an unintelligent, unresponsive building holding back your business is likely to be the difficulty or cost of employing technical staff able to understand and get the best out of even fairly simple systems. Better a familiar set of controls that anyone can understand and that needs regular but easy adjustment than something capable of making its own sequence of adjustments but demanding an engineering degree to understand the manual and maintain the system at peak efficiency. If such a system is working inefficiently, the consequences may be unexpectedly expensive and frustrating.

Future Technology

Technology is moving fast. It is important to stay alert for developments, as there will undoubtedly be useful as well as hopeless new equipment. "Microchips with everything" is not intrinsically good, but it is a reality to be taken seriously. The specialists are not always easy to communicate with. The field does move fast, so it is tempting to believe—or hard to deny—

someone who says, "I must have this," as it is not easy to really know what "this" is. Some developments will be just gadgets; others will represent major changes, leaps forward. Each jump in technology in the past—the typewriter, the telephone, the desktop computer, and now the Internet—has been allied to a change in the way knowledge-based work has been done. The costs of the technology are still in free fall, to which there is as yet no apparent end. Technology changes have been reflected in the buildings. Further changes will alter how people work and what they need and expect of their buildings.

Summary

This chapter helps you to understand the impact on office buildings of the rapid changes in information technology used for office work. It alerts you to changes still to come.

As IT has continued to develop and spread, many claims have been made on its behalf. One, that computers heralded an era in which the office could function with less or even no paper, has manifestly been shown to be untrue. The effects that IT has had—to multiply manyfold the cables that need to be accommodated and to create heat—have, on the other hand, bulked large in people's minds, partly because they were not expected. Cables are now less of a problem. Structured cabling greatly simplifies rerouting, without the necessity to run new links. Radio or microwave transmission of voice or data eliminates the cables entirely. The amount of heat is not so extreme as was thought either. Smaller equipment and more realistic assessments of actual output are cutting the problem down to size. But cabling still needs to be taken into account when ventilation systems and office layouts are planned.

Energy efficiency has been championed by governments for a long time. The cost savings that are the prime incentive to management are proportionately too low to be of great interest. Energy saving needs to concentrate on well-designed lighting, no unnecessary air-conditioning, well-insulated buildings, and excellent plant management and maintenance.

Intelligent buildings are a new focus for interest. These are not simple buildings with well-planned and efficiently managed services using a BEMS or with a computer on every desk. If the term is usefully applied, it indicates that the full powers of computing technology can be used to help create a building in which the users' needs trigger suitable responses.

It is vital that suitable people are available to run the systems installed in a building, whether computer controlled or not. A simple system with little responsiveness and few subtleties, which can be run by the janitor on a part-time basis, may be preferable to one that never works as intended because no one understands how to make that happen.

Providing for the IT needs of a company is always challenging and will, for the foreseeable future, require a high degree of alertness.

CHAPTER 9

Office Moves and Change Management

CASE HISTORIES

See Case Histories 24 and 25
on pages 437–451

So where has all this been leading? What can you do with all these ideas? Do they really apply to your organization and your office building? The organization in which you work may be a bank, a university department, a "clerical factory" back office, a manufacturing head office, a legal firm, a government department, or the administration arm of a museum, hospital, or factory. Each one is different, with specific requirements, experiences, and opportunities. Yet they are all offices. The material in this book covers a range of information about offices couched in general terms. The intention has been to equip managers—you—with the type of information that will enable you to look critically at your present office building or a proposed new one, at your specialist advisers, designers, and your internal building management procedures so that you can uncover ways to create a pleasant environment, promote your business, and increase staff morale and productivity, as well as save money, make better use of your building, and avoid unnecessary or inappropriate actions and pitfalls.

The moment when all the questions about buildings urgently need answers is when major changes are planned, such as the relocation to new premises or the renovation of existing buildings. This is the ideal opportunity to reap the benefits of understanding your office space.

Should You Move?

A manager may be less aware of the impact of inadequate space than are others in the organization. Managers, after all, usually manage the business, not the building. They are often kept remote from the worst effects of spatial problems: by efficient secretaries who shield them, by enclosed rooms that shut them away from day-to-day irritation, by being on the side of the building where the air-conditioning works best, by being so senior that their complaints are dealt with. However, having absorbed the ideas in this book, you know the sort of building you should be in, and you are not, and you can judge whether you are making the best use of the one that you have, and you are not. So if you are planning to move or radically alter your building, now is the time that you probably need help.

As organizations develop, whether they grow or shrink, their needs change. Buildings are rarely exactly right for an organization for very long, if at all. Growth often involves piecemeal additions, in nearby buildings or on other floors of a larger building. This has the effect of fragmenting the organization, often just at the moment when it most needs to feel coherent. As organizations age, they change their composition and way of working. Specialist skills that were initially bought in may be needed in house on a constant basis. Sometimes activities need special facilities, like research departments. Mergers and acquisitions create new companies, and usually these need new homes. Growth may mean that administration and communications departments become larger. Organizations also shrink and wish to surrender unnecessary space. They spin off functions into autonomous businesses with their own small premises. They may buy in services from other organizations rather than retain them in house. They may have a bad year and simply lay off staff. Outside influences are also important: Leases expire, market structures change, or buildings become obsolete and cease to meet requirements or are damaged in some disaster. There are many scenarios.

Organizational changes are unlikely to fit the ad hoc building changes that are made in response to new pressures. The time comes when a radical restructuring of space is also needed. Does this mean a move? Would renovation do? Or would a simple scenery shift, in which partitions are moved, special rooms are refitted, and new furniture is bought, be enough?

Only those responsible for implementing the mission of the company can really answer these questions because strategy and its implications are their business. They must weigh the costs and the benefits. This applies at the top, where changes affect a whole organization and its buildings, and also at the level of a department or group, where the specific changes under consideration are on a smaller scale. That is why it is vital for managers to understand some of the fundamentals about what buildings are and how office space, interior fittings and furniture, and the business interrelate. Their knowledge will help them to ask the key questions, those that will allow them to judge how far the organization's needs can, or cannot, be met in an existing building, and to assess whether proposed new layouts or buildings will perform better. A move or a renovation project is likely to be costly and disruptive, so the reasons for embarking on it must be good.

There are many examples of organizations who have misread the implications of change within and outside them and have become involved in change to their buildings that has sapped their strength just when they needed it to weather the changes around them. Many professional firms—lawyers, accountants, architects—have plunged into expensive premises in times of boom only to be forced out in subsequent recessions. Recent research has found that firms that relocate at the same time as they are undergoing major restructuring are very likely to regret their move. Yet properly selected buildings are a great busines aid. They can serve businesses, provide support for them to meet their objectives, help rather than hinder, and introduce the right signals of organizational changes. Planning carefully for anticipated needs can be the best investment you will make.

Relocation, Renovation, or Rearrangement?

If it is agreed that something must be done about the building, decisions are needed about precise objectives. The basic decision may be simple. For example, a merger has created a group of 600 people who must work together. They are currently housed too far apart for this to happen and are in several buildings, none of which has a capacity for more than 250 people. A move is essential. The choice is between a move to an existing building that will require renovation, to a newly built office that will merely need minor adaptation or to a greenfield or city site and a custom-designed building. Decisions need to be made about location in relation to image, convenience for customers and staff, and costs such as rent and rates. The relative costs of the different strategies may vary because the financial deals will depend on many factors, such as the size of the space required, the state of the property market, and the location and the requirements of the organization that is moving. Each of the possible strategies has advantages and disadvantages (Fig. 9.1).

A new, custom-designed building may give the opportunity to have precisely what you need. The process will take longer than choosing an existing building almost ready for

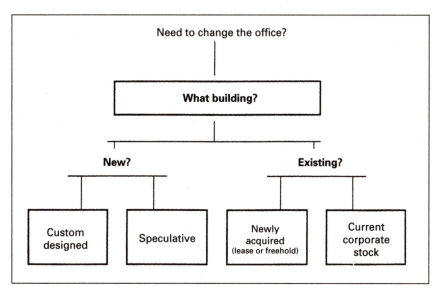

Figure 9.1 Need to change the office? Choosing the building.

(*AMA Alexi Marmot Associates.*)

occupation, so there must be enough time before you need to move. It has the advantage that staff have somewhere to work undisturbed until moving day. The opportunity may also tempt you to commission a building that you will love but that has peculiarities other organizations will not relish. Your gain as an occupier may be your loss as a property owner if your needs change in the future and new users need to be found for the building. A reality check, looking carefully at the property market and at buildings occupied by other organizations, will help you to assess whether your requirements are unjustifiably unusual. This involves comparing hard facts like average lettable area per person, or space standards, proportion of enclosed space, or the amount of space given to amenities, rather than merely whether the color scheme is attractive or the reception area has comfortable chairs, although these details are also important. There are a great many unknowns at the start of a new building project. You need an in-house person or a team that is experienced in writing programs, briefing and controlling designers, interpreting drawings, and balancing conflicting requirements or is able to learn these skills in a hurry and is given the time to do so. Otherwise you must either rely on specialist advisers or take longer making decisions.

There are shades in the definition of *custom design*. If you commit to a speculative office development at a sufficiently early stage, it is possible to influence some aspects of the building design, such as size and number of floors or position and size of cores and entrances. It is likely that the quality and design of elements like windows, insulation, and interior finishes can be specified to meet your requirements. The developers may be reluctant to go to the trouble of making changes or deviating from the normal specification used in the buildings they market. This reluctance should not deter you from insisting at least on being told if changes are possible and what the extra cost will be, so that you can be a party to the decisions. If changes prove impossible, you may be able to negotiate a better financial deal on the grounds that you are being offered a standard different from the one you require.

An existing building has the advantage that you can see what you are getting. However, the more there is to see when you make your choice, the less scope there is for fundamental change. This makes it all the more important to check the basic information, reviewed in Chapter 2, about sizes and efficiencies. See that it really is the size you have been told and that the design provides a high level of efficiency for the user. Consider how you will be able to make staff and clients feel welcome. Check the quality as well as the location of the cores. Will they allow for appropriate spaces on the office floors for your needs and sensible circulation routes without unnecessary kinks? If there are elevators, are there enough, large enough, fast enough, with large enough lobbies? Are the WCs adequate, and are those for the disabled sufficient, well-located, and designed in compliance with guidance? Are the service ducts accessible from the core rather than from usable space, where their opening requirements can get horribly in the way? Are there well-fitted cleaners' cupboards? Is there a sensible place for you to install additional ventilation for computer rooms or kitchens?

A new developer-built building that is on the market may already be outfitted with suspended ceilings, lighting, electrical floor boxes, and carpets. Real estate agents often advise that this is necessary, as they believe that seeing what it is like when finished will encourage tenants to lease the building. Yet everyone knows that occupiers will change precisely these things to suit their needs and tastes. A vicious circle has been created, as this practice means that these items are rarely installed to a high specification, so even if you would have been happy to keep them in principle, they may simply not be good enough. A way out of this trap is provided by the concept of "shell and core." A developer provides the basic building, the shell with its cores, but no finishes or fittings and no partitions. The occupiers can then specify the required partition quality and layout and the finishes, such as carpets and ceiling tiles, and install the lighting and wiring systems that they require. In this situation there is still the need to check the sizes, efficiencies, and cores and not to be so carried away by the ease of implementing your fit-out and finishes that you ignore the basic qualities, or lack of them, of the shell.

Renovation is left as the final option. This is what you do to a "used" building, one that has been fitted out and occupied. In some cases the building may be very old; in others it may have been occupied for only a few years. The building may have been used by another organization, but renovation is also undertaken by existing occupiers because the building is deteriorating or because of new requirements. The difficulties of decanting the occupants are then added to the project. The extent of the work that is required depends on the building's age and condition and how far it matches your needs. It may be necessary to strip out everything back to the "shell and core" and start again. In some cases all that is left is the structure; the exterior "skin" or cladding is replaced, windows are redesigned, and new service cores are constructed with bigger and better elevators and ducts for air-conditioning and cable routes. Total renovation can be more expensive than a new building, so the costs must be investigated very carefully in advance. The extra may be worth paying if renovation offers things that a new building would not. For example, its location may be one in which no new buildings can be built, or it may be a historic building with unique design features. Less expense is involved in less radical renovations. A building may merely have worn-out finishes, or its services, such as boilers, wiring, and pipework, may need replacing, or it may need a scenery shift, or it may simply require repainting throughout. Each of these is progressively less expensive, and thus, assuming that the building is suitably located, with a long enough lease on the right financial terms, that it provides enough space and that it is efficient and well designed for office uses, each is progressively more desirable (Fig. 9.2).

Managing the Process

Early decisions about which route to take—whether a new building, renovation, or just some new furniture—are made within the organization, possibly with some help and advice from outside experts. As the project progresses, you need specific design and implementation skills provided either by internal staff or, more often, by independent specialists. The cast of characters in such a project can be extensive. Good management is vital and is sometimes entrusted to a project management specialist. It is important to define carefully the roles and responsibilities of team members, including that of the project manager, and to be sure that there are

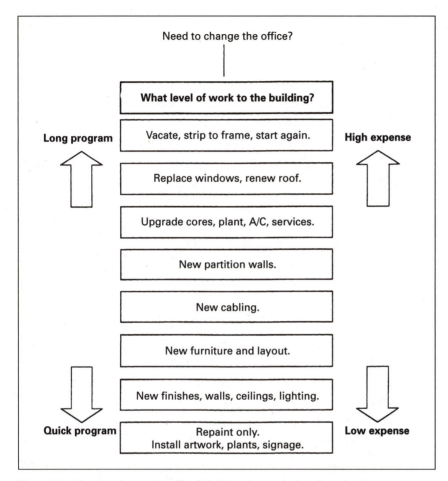

Figure 9.2 Need to change the office? Defining the level of works to be done.

(AMA Alexi Marmot Associates.)

no cracks through which important tasks may slip. Cost control is essential whether carried out with the help of a separate specialist such as a quantity surveyor in the United Kingdom, or incorporated in the designer's role as in the United States and other countries. Design may be done by a single person for a small project or by a team of design specialists with different skills for larger ones—architects for the building design, space planners who specialize in the layout of rooms and desks, interior designers for color schemes and furniture choices, furniture designers for special products.

Engineers advise on, and design, the building's structure, electrical equipment, lighting, heating, ventilation, and other mechanical systems. Specialists for other requirements, from IT to landscape, from catering to audiovisual installations, can be called in. They are usually needed only if an important part of the project lies in their area of expertise. A group of users may be a formal part of the project team, with a role to play at certain points in the process. There is also a considerable number of outside organizations with which the team will interact. These include city planning departments, building regulations inspectors, the utility suppliers, fire safety specialists, insurance and security companies, all of whom will have to be consulted and their requirements met. There are numerous health and safety regulations for different activities and standards for most products used in a building. The project team should be responsible for ensuring that regulations are adhered to and standards met. Local trade-union groups may be included in the process.

Within an organization responsibility often falls to people with little previous experience of building projects. It is important that the process is managed internally by someone who understands the business of the organization as their major contribution should be to ensure that the building is designed or modified to serve the users' needs properly. This internal project manager is, in effect, the "client" for the building and must be someone who has no fear of asking awkward questions at any point in the process. A great deal of jargon is used in any specialized field, and team members must be prepared to explain, in lay terms, the decisions they are making. Ignorance is not a sign of stupidity, though failing to fill the gaps in your ignorance may be. There is a significant learning curve for people who have not familiarized themselves with how buildings behave, what happens to them over time, and what users really do in them. Visits to other office buildings, talking to users about what they would have done differently if they could do it again, discussions with people who manage buildings for others, explanations by the design team of plans for other buildings with which they have been involved, are all useful. Time must be allowed early on in the process to permit the learning to start, and it needs to continue throughout. The project manager must be someone who cannot be easily brushed off with "It's always done this way." The reasons for doing it "this way" must be clarified. They may be obsolete, wrong-headed, unsuitable, or nonexistent. Support for the internal project manager must be given by senior management. Problems during a building project need rapid solution; otherwise deadlines are missed as critical connections in the complex pattern of events fail to be made. A director of a large organization cannot manage the process, but someone, responsible to the board, must be available if required, at least on the telephone or by e-mail, even from halfway around the world.

Decisions have to be made about the extent to which users, the staff in general, will be consulted, how to ensure that the practical knowledge that they have is tapped, how to handle their requests, how to inform them of decisions that have been made, and whether any decisions can be made democratically, and, if so, which. This will determine how a user group functions, how often it meets, and for what purposes. Much of the success of a major building project depends on how well communication is maintained between the project team and the staff. There are several useful devices by which information can be shared even when decision making is not. One device is an intranet site for the project with regular bulletins to inform all staff of the state of the project or to publicize an important decision. Presentations to all staff can be arranged to show them designs or color schemes or to explain a critical stage that the project has reached. Information about how individuals will be affected must be supplied to them in good time, particularly the implications of decanting during the process or how the moving day will be handled. If the move is to a new location, site visits must be arranged so that people are all familiar with it before they move.

Creating the Brief or Program

The brief or program is the basis for decisions about what is to be built. This includes the initial decision about the available budget. In deciding performance requirements, nothing should be taken for granted. A building for even 50 people should not be planned without a cleaner's closet. The architect who uses as his excuse "You did not ask for one" should feel ashamed, but a full brief will help guard against obvious omissions. It may be tempting not to spend too much time on setting down the details, but unless you do, things will be forgotten. A detailed brief should include user consultation with managers and others. Those responsible for the future running and maintaining of the building should also be included in the consultation if they are not members of the main project team. The ways in which detailed user needs and work patterns can be investigated are looked at in Chapter 2. Focus groups, surveys, observations, diaries, and interview techniques are as valuable for briefing as they are for evaluating effects afterward and are important ongoing management tools. It is necessary to understand the possible changes that may occur in the organization once a move is made. Trends in staff numbers and in the extent of IT use should be related to required links between groups, and a judgment should be made about how similar these will remain in the future. Knowledge of the implications of transport and the ways in which the local amenities of the area are used may affect decisions about the provisions of facilities within a new building.

Organizational policies must be considered. These concern large issues basic to the working patterns in the organization and small issues that further describe its character and aspi-

rations. Important decisions about space standards and cellularization should not merely be taken for granted. Policies
and standards may have already been formulated. As often
as not, they are absent, incomplete, or out of date, so they
need to be reconsidered.

Art or plants may seem to be more trivial issues. There may
be no formal policies about them. Now is the time to formulate them. Perhaps they are to be incorporated in the scheme
to impress clients or provide pleasant surroundings for staff,
or perhaps the policy is to have none. Each approach will indicate something about the organizational culture, as will a failure to have considered the issue, which will mean they are
absent by default or haphazardly organized.

Storage is of particular importance. Do not assume that in
new premises, wonderfully organized on the most modern
principles, the need for odd bits of storage will vanish.
Although new approaches to deliveries may be adopted—
"just in time" being a system as well suited to office consumables as to a manufacturing plant—these will not lead to
a no-storeroom scenario. Apart from storing work-associated
files, an office of 1,000 people uses 60 cases of WC rolls in
four weeks, which need to be stored somewhere. Spare parts
for furniture need to be stored, as do unwanted or broken
items, spare equipment, and the Christmas decorations.
There must be a janitor's storeroom able to accommodate
housekeeping supplies and general storerooms for other
items. Basements and attics may not exist or may not be
designed to accommodate such things.

The staff "user group" can continue to provide useful
ongoing input for the professional design team as the design
develops. Its members should have an opportunity to examine and comment on designs at several stages. These stages
should be set out early on so that everyone is clear about
the proposed pattern of consultation and no false expectations are raised. Many decisions cannot be left to this
group. The precise scope of staff decisions needs to be made

clear. The focus may be more on details than on major decisions about purchases. A furniture range, for example, may be agreed on by the main project team while allowing the staff group to select the color and fabrics for carpets and chairs, or one of a narrow range of furniture options may be selected through user input, while the color scheme is fixed whatever the range selected. Where possible, a mockup of the proposed furniture or an opportunity for representatives of the users to visit an office using that furniture should be arranged so that details of comfort and function can be checked. Users are a valuable resource, and their opinions should be used to achieve the best possible arrangement of furniture and equipment. One point at which the user group can make a valuable contribution is at an early stage in the layout planning, since they are familiar with the details of work patterns and processes. Even when radical, possibly unpopular changes may be suggested, what staff say about the existing system has relevance and is of use to the design

A Program for All Seasons

The right building program depends on knowing what you want and being able to communicate it. John Duvivier, of Bottom Duvivier in San Francisco, describes himself as a frustrated mathematician and statistician. He has focused for over a decade on how to help corporate clients define their needs. Starting with a healthy understanding of how to get the most out of computers, he participated in developing Steelcase's Workplace Envisioning tool. He subsequently refined this further into a computer tool called *3t* (*Task, Time, Tools*) used to study, through 3- to 5-person workshops, where and how different types of work are done. The results are used to help organizations to establish their workplace requirements—to develop a brief from information provided by representatives of an organization. To establish three alternate options for Sun Microsystems for a facility for over 800 people in their Operations Division took 32 of these highly interactive, computer-based workshops. He describes this system as more accurate than questionnaire surveys where the sample may be meaninglessly small, and "follow-around observation," which while accurate quantitatively may not provide enough qualitative information. He is confident of the accuracy of the information provided by the 3t approach.

team. In these circumstances users must not be led to believe that the new processes will be abandoned just because they believe the old ones are better.

Too Many Changes Rock the Ark

The office is too far out of town. It is isolated, making lunchtime a bore.
Now too far away from town for personal activities, re bank, etc.
Location is very inconvenient—no shops, banks, facilities nearby. A poor choice of site for a major organization. Right on the very edge of the city, one is totally dependent on a car.

—QUESTIONNAIRE RESPONSES FROM CLERICAL WORKERS AFTER AN OFFICE MOVE TO TOWN FRINGE

The disruptions caused to staff by a move are well explored in management literature. Relocation and the effects on human resources have long been a subject of concern. The problems are real and need to be taken seriously. When a journey to work is lengthened or the transportation mode shifts or a new location involves staff moving house, the web of family life patterns, developed and adapted to fit the old situation, has to be changed. Help may be needed by some people; sympathy is required all round. There are other ways in which a move may cause disruption. People react to their office with strong feelings. If they have other reasons for discontent, then the building may have enough imperfections to act as a focus for their feelings of frustration or dislocation.

A new or renovated building is a new opportunity. If the need for a change in premises results from organizational restructuring, everyone needs to adapt and create new working relationships. This takes time. While moving to a new building may seem an ideal opportunity to replace out-of-date systems, such as telephone exchanges or computer networks, beware of undertaking too many changes simultaneously. Systems that do not perform as expected, in a new place, with a new group of people striving to fulfill a restructured mission, can be crippling. Planning a new office automation system is worthwhile; providing the necessary cable networks and locations for central equipment in the new building so that the change can take place smoothly at a later date is prudent. Funds for the purchase can be allocated and incorporated in the planned budget for the new building. A new system, with its inevitable teething troubles, may be best introduced several months in advance of the move or left for a few months until the organization feels like a working entity rather than an amalgam of disparate parts. Whether this is an appropriate stance depends on a number of factors. How bad is the existing system? How incompatible are systems that must be brought together? How radical are the organizational changes that are taking place? Will it save serious future disruption to make the changes immediately? These are all questions that must be considered.

Whatever decision is made, one objective of a project should be, as argued throughout this book, to ensure that future changes can be made. The building that you move into on hand-over day is not a fixed, perfect solution. Easily accessible and adaptable routes for cables will ensure that any system can be replaced with minimum disruption as it becomes out of date. Careful choice of locations for installations that will be hard to move later will ensure that the building can adapt and provide a good home for a changing business over a long lifetime.

Moving Day

The move itself must be carefully orchestrated. Moving 2,000 people is far more complicated than moving 20, but, whatever the scale of the task, the same principles apply. They apply to the decant-and-reoccupy scenario as much as to a wholesale move. The overriding requirement is that a move should not disrupt the work of the organization. To this end, careful, systematic planning of the actual move must be undertaken. Someone must be responsible for the process and see that all play their parts. One person's time (or a team's time for a monster move) spent in advance is better value than everyone's frustration on the day. Some points to watch:

- Plan ahead and work to a written plan, with as much help as you need. You can hire firms that specialize in move planning if you have insufficient in-house resources to cope.

- Provide clear labels for people to use on their boxes and belongings and full instructions on what they are expected to do in advance and on move day.

- If the move has to take place in stages (for example, over several weekends), set up a rhythm so that a fixed sequence of activities takes place regularly each week for each group as it prepares to move.

- Concentrate on storage, and do so well in advance. Destroy anything redundant. Archive anything not actively needed. Offer incentives to people to get rid of as much as possible. See to it that new workplaces are equipped with suitable, sufficient storage but not over-provided.

- Saving overtime costs by removal teams working only on weekdays may be a false economy as it usually means the loss of several working days.

- On move days, provide sandwiches at lunch for the removal teams so they don't disappear off site for hours.

- Aim to keep the piles of crates and boxes in the new space stacked well below eye level. There's nothing more depressing than moving into a new office, aiming to start work promptly and efficiently, and feeling you are struggling through a confusing and impenetrable maze of rubbish.

- Give everyone in the new building a "welcome pack" of information about how the building works and what to do if it doesn't, what shops and services are available nearby, and where groups are located within the building. A loose-leaf version, which can take additional pages as new issues come to the fore, is a good idea, incorporated in a binder with other useful material, like diary pages or a year planner. A message saying "Welcome" on everyone's computer screen helps establish the positive aspects of the move.

Facilities Management

The facilities management role is another story. It starts functioning at this point, and, well executed, it will contribute to the benefits you reap from your building. The appearance of the office can have a powerful effect on the morale of staff and the opinion of visitors. It depends on how the office is designed in the first place and on the entire approach to its management during use. *Facilities management* is the term used to describe the amalgam of roles involved in ensuring that a building operates at its best in relation to the needs of the users. It covers a wide range of tasks: space management, building and services maintenance and repair, furniture and equipment repair or disposal, the preparation of telephone directories, cleaning, office supplies, maintaining a tidy office, the management of energy, security and other policies, booking routines for facilities, catering, looking after plants.

Each task should have targets. The effectiveness of the activities carried out should be monitored so that remedial action can be taken if standards are not met. This may be carried out by internal or outside teams. To carry it out effectively requires the systematic collection and use of a considerable range of information. First and foremost, the completion of a move is the ideal moment to update all information. The project team can be asked, as part of their role, to provide this service at the end of the job. Necessary information includes:

- Up-to-date plans of building and plant installations, desk and services layouts
- A furniture and equipment inventory
- Operating manuals
- Maintenance information
- Addresses of suppliers and regulatory bodies
- Certificates of compliance
- Directory of staff locations, telephone extensions, and e-mail addresses

This information must be regularly updated and safely stored. Other information resides within the organization and must be accumulated over time. This includes a current organizational chart, data on space allocation, cost information about services, maintenance, cleaning and other contracts, a planned maintenance schedule, and the state of play at any time. The challenge of keeping the building tuned and responsive has begun.

Postoccupancy Evaluation

As with all management decisions, you cannot be sure your offices do what they should unless you find out. After the moving dust has settled, you need to discover what works and what does not. You can do this by informal walkabouts, looking for untoward changes that people have made, chatting with them, specifically asking departments for feedback, or by commissioning full surveys from specialists. Just as your new car has its first inspection after the first few thousand miles, so your new building needs an initial inspection and another after several months. Regular servicing checks are also needed. Knowing what the niggles are means that adjustments can be made. Rearrangements will start almost before everyone has settled down. Your organization may need to make another office move soon. Make sure that feedback helps to refine every aspect of the next move, wherever it takes place.

Now Enjoy Your Building

You have worked hard to get to this point. Despite any setbacks and imperfections, you have a better building than before. The move should be an occasion to celebrate. You have worked out what you need, and, with a few compromises, you have succeeded in getting it. The building can continue to be a pleasure to use, a productive environment for staff and the business, as well as being serviceable and cost effective, for many years. Your ark is ready to sail, with all aboard, toward a productive future.

Summary

This chapter gives you guidance in deciding whether you need to make a major move and, if so, how to go about it (Fig. 9.3).

Organizational needs change for many reasons, and some demand a change in the office building. A choice between relocation, renovation, and rearrangement is the first step in the process. Each has advantages and disadvantages. The most radical is relocation to another building. It may be new, custom built, or speculative. A new custom-designed building can exactly fit your needs but may take a long time to construct and equip and is hard to visualize before you start. An existing one can be cheaper and quicker to occupy but may not meet your requirements as well. If a great deal has to be renovated, it can cost more than a new building. Sometimes an appropriate scenery shift may be all you need.

The process involves teamwork by management, staff, and outside experts. There is an important role for the internal project manager, who must be determined, patient, and persistent. Learning by visiting other buildings is important, particularly if the manager has little previous experience of relocation projects.

The program or brief contains the instructions from the client to all the team. It is a reference point and should be written down. It may go into considerable detail. It should be based on organizational policies and can offer an opportunity to clarify these if they have not hitherto been formalized. There is a role for staff input, but how extensive must be made clear at the outset. There may not be many decisions that can be taken democratically, other than the finishing touches of local colors, choice of art, or placing of plants, but users' experience is needed to design work layouts that will function well.

Figure 9.3 It's your move: Whether going virtal or building new, plan carefully—enjoy the change.

A move is a disruptive period. It is inadvisable to use this time for the complete reorganization of multiple aspects of the business. Some additional alterations may have to take place after occupation. This underlines one of the important arguments in this book, that changes will continue to happen throughout the life of any building. Changes in the plan, layout, and services, to accommodate new needs and replace aging elements, must be allowed for so that they are easy to make.

A well-planned move is one that is planned in advance. A systematic approach that takes care of details is vital. Storage must be sorted out rigorously. Staff will feel good if the environment is kept tidy during the move and information that they need is available. After the move the management of the building will be greatly helped by having clear information, some of which should be obtained from the design team.

A good project is an occasion to celebrate. Whether new or refurbished, a new office environment should be enjoyed by staff, transmit the right signals to customers and staff, and help your company to be more productive.

Case History 1. Only Connect

Organization	British Airways, Combined Business Center
Location	Waterside, London, Heathrow
Completed	July 1998
Area	400,000 ft² (37,000 m²) net internal offices
No. people	2,800
Designers	Niels Torp Architects, Oslo; RHWL, London
Briefing	AMA Alexi Marmot Associates; Building Use Studies; Tilney Shane

A major international airline, British Airways is in the communication business, bringing business and private individuals together across the world. Changing the organizational culture was CEO Bob Ayling's aim in moving to Waterside, the company's new headquarters office building designed by Norwegian architect Niels Torp. Communication between people running the company was difficult in the scattered old buildings, creating a brake on business development. Executives were hidden behind their closed private offices along soulless corridors, protected by outer offices personal assistants who controlled access and ruled the appointment diaries—not the best way to make rapid corporate decisions in today's competitive international airline business.

Waterside is designed for people to interact, to meet casually as well as formally. A grand covered street is the axis along which the six office buildings open, filled with coffee shops, bank, grocery store, and florist (Figs. CH. 1.1 and 1.4). All occupants and more can be assembled here for major company events. The training center, management development suite, theater, corporate library, Internet café, and medical center bring a constant flow of people from all parts of the airline to Waterside, the corporate heart. Services for the whole person—a gym, hairdresser, and grocery order and delivery service—help staff to feel valued and loyal to the company. The $300 million (£200 million) capital cost is fully justified by saving on travel time between different

Figure CH.1.1   Waterside is designed for people to interact, with its grand covered street along which the six office buildings open, filled with coffee shops, bank, grocery store, and florist.

(Photograph: Studio 2, Graham Price.)

Figure CH.1.2 Light and airy team spaces of 6 to 10 desks, grouped into neighborhoods within six office buildings on four floors.

(*Photograph: QFT.*)

buildings, quicker response time, no longer having to hire hotel conference suites, and the creation of flexible workspaces for economical organizational change. The exit strategy, should British Airways ever wish to vacate, has been considered—each building can be separately leased or sold.

Office floors are light, airy, and open (Fig. CH.1.2). Carefully selected workstations are grouped into team spaces of 6 to 10 people, and several teams form a neighborhood sharing local services. Nobody in the organization has a private office though there are plenty of enclosed rooms and open spaces for meetings or quiet work. Some groups who are often away working elsewhere volunteered to give up personal desks and work flexibly from a pool of hot desks and touchdowns. Storage was radically culled before the

Figure CH.1.3   Open areas can be used for solo work. Wireless networks and cordless telephones allow people to work anywhere.

(*Photograph: QFT.*)

move, and new record management policies were introduced. With enhanced technology, people can work from any desk, thus simplifying future moves within the building. Wireless local area networks allow people to use their laptops anywhere in the street or parkland, as do walkabout cordless telephones (Fig. CH.1.3). Before migrating to the new building, everyone needed a passport stamped to certify that they had been trained in the new technology, new work patterns, and paper management.

Postoccupancy evaluation confirms that Waterside does indeed enhance communication and is greatly appreciated, as are the new, flexible work patterns. In the words of one senior manager, "I enjoy the ambience of the building, and I find I know more about what is going on in the company than before. You walk around more and bump into people....It's more sociable now, and I feel better for it. I think the team is happier, and you work better if you are happy."

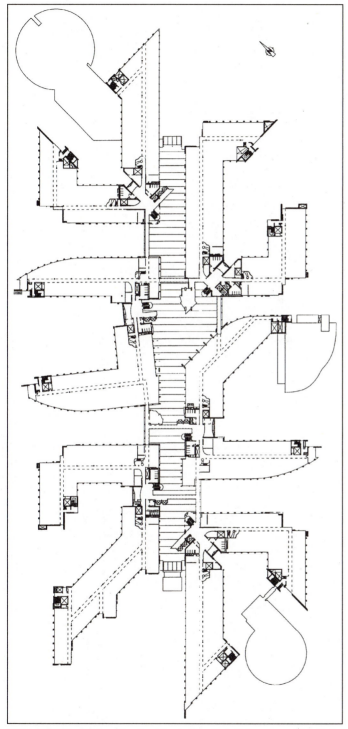

Figure CH.1.4 Waterside plan shows the six buildings opening off the grand street. Natural light penetrates into all workspaces that are never more than 25 ft (8 m) from windows.

(*Neils Torp Architects.*)

Case History 2. Building for Corporate Needs

Organization   First Data Investment Services Group
Location   Westborough, Massachusetts
Completed   1996
Area   300,000 ft^2 (28,000 m^2)
No. people   1,600
Designers   ADD, Inc., Cambridge, Massachusetts

First Data Investment Services Group (FDISG) wanted to consolidate several regional offices into one state-of-the-art facility, a progressive workplace that addressed goals from the corporate mission and vision statements to accomplish the following:

- Maximize efficiency, flexibility, and access to information.

- Enhance corporate culture and client perception of FDISG.

- Make efficient use of construction dollars.

Excellent customer service required a motivated, interactive workforce trained to respond promptly and accurately to client needs. The new workplace had to energize and support employees while easily welcoming numerous visitors. The trick was to turn the goals into a layout that worked in a vast building, the size of three football fields, with deep floor plates and little natural light. This was achieved by several design features:

- Forming an "exuberant parade" down the middle of the building (Fig. CH.2.1)

- Collecting all the shared facilities along it—demonstration spaces, conference center, cafeteria, computer and copy center

- Giving all those spaces shape, color, and vibrance

Figure CH.2.1   The main circulation axis is brilliantly colored, lending exuberance to the work environment.

(Photograph: Peter Vanderwarker.)

- Creating a "corporate wall" displaying the services, history, and future of the company and an "employee wall" for the display of awards, achievements, events, and committees (Fig. CH.2.2)

- Logically and efficiently grouping together all the facilities needed to support work into a "server" space for copier, mail, coats, kitchen, vending, recycling point, and bulletin board (Fig. CH.2.3)

- Putting a light wash and colors over internal walls

- Signaling entry into different departments by a banner and bulletin board so that visitors can enter without disturbing the workflow

- Giving special names to each shared space—"web," "server," and "portal"

Figure CH.2.2   The "corporate wall" and "employee wall" display information on the company's history, services, and staff attainments.

(Photograph: Peter Vanderwarker.)

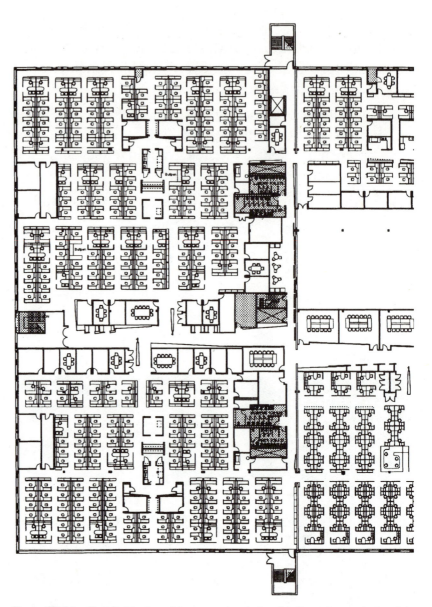

Figure CH.2.3   First Data, plan of the upper level showing the entrance to the right and the circulation web crossing through the floor. All the shared spaces are grouped along the web.

(*Add, Inc.*)

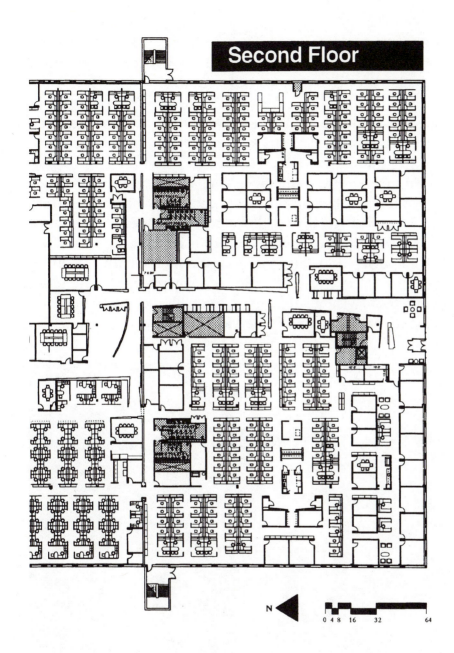

Second Floor

N

0 4 8   16   32   64

The workstations come in four sizes: 6 by 6 ft (1.8 × 1.8 m) for a call center, 6 by 8 ft (1.8 × 2.4 m) for most financial services people, 8 by 8 ft (2.4 × 2.4 m) for administrative staff, and 8 by 12 ft (2.4 × 3.7 m) for managers around the perimeter. Most have screens between workstations to give visual privacy when seated (Figs. CH.2.3 and CH.2.4).

Throughout the building is the belief that workflow is important and having the right technology nearby is essential. By giving employees all the tools they need, where they are needed, signaled and celebrated in bright colors, they will feel empowered to carry out their work efficiently. By giving visitors a clear view of the work environment and ready access to all visitor areas, they too will appreciate the company, its products, and its services.

Figure CH.2.4 Workstations are standard cubicles in one of four footprints, with low screens to permit visual communication.

(Photograph: Peter Vanderwarker.)

The office building that emerged was so successful it became a selling point for the company, with people arriving simply to view the facility. Anecdotal feedback from users shows that they find the workspace uplifting, particularly because of the bright colors and shapes. The fact that the building was economical to lease and the budget for the fit out was very modest helped achieve the third corporate goal.

Case History 3.
Nortel Networks

Organization	Nortel Networks
Location	Brampton, Ontario, Canada
Completed	Phase 1, 1998; Phase 2, September 1999
Area	Phase 1, 1,000,000 ft^2 (93,000 m^2)
	Phase 2, 185,000 ft^2 (17,200 m^2)
No. people	Phase 1, 3,000; Phase 2, 700
Designers	HOK Canada

New-wave officing transformed Nortel's single-story digital switching factory into its new corporate headquarters (Fig. CH.3.1). Fifty million dollars was invested, but it is estimated to have saved the company $100 million over a new building. Architecture is said to have helped reinvent the company, reworked how they work, cut costs, and boosted productivity—an irresistible formula that earned HOK Canada and their client the *Business Week/Architectural Record* Award.

Employees and customers who visit the building can see tangible evidence of Nortel's state-of-the-art technology and state-of-the-art working. There is a centrally located cyber-shop displaying the latest products. "Homebase" is a house within the building demonstrating home office solutions.

Figure CH.3.1   A single-story city of 3,000 with urban gathering points like the People Place and Forum for conferences has been created from a redundant Nortel factory.

(*Image HOK Canada.*)

Virtual-reality headsets can be donned for an interactive ride through the company's intranet. The "City" has many landmarks designed to make the place so attractive that people don't want to leave it. Companies increasingly believe that staff accept a job in the first place partly on the basis of the design of the physical environment. Nortel has seen a rise in job applications since the building opened.

The aim was to stimulate the senses in the course of a day's work as people move away from their workstations into the urban facilities. People appreciate that communication and interaction are far easier here than in most offices. The City map bears names like Main Street and Memory Lane and highlights services from the travel shop, Internet café, restaurant and sandwich outlets, a vast chess board, plazas, artwork, conference area, gym, and a general store (Fig. CH.3.2).

Figure CH.3.2 Main Street and Memory Lane connect people and places—Nortel Networks HQ is made for interaction.

(*Image HOK Canada.*)

Hypercommunication during the planning process informed people of the ideas behind the new workplaces, and several hundred participated in focus groups to invent the details. Many managers were coaxed out of their offices into the open plan. Alternate officing packages of hoteling and homework were made available, with a business center in the HQ. In this building, business units can readily arrange, then rearrange their layouts to meet work demands, as long as they obey the planning rules that govern the building zones (Fig. CH.3.3 and 3.4). And each unit has its own "town hall" of meeting rooms, and a distinctive color scheme.

Nortel and its executives see the facility as a brilliant vehicle for changing the company, promoting its values and products, attracting new recruits, and keeping staff happy. All this and significant cost savings is a winning package for communication and collegiality.

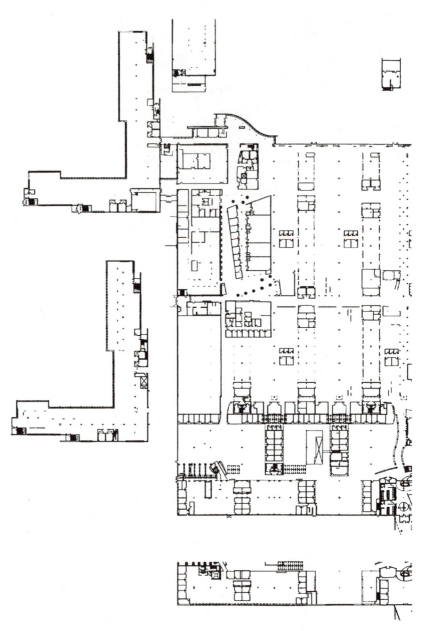

Figure CH.3.3   Plan of the vast 1-million-ft^2 Nortel Network headquarters.
(*HOK Canada.*)

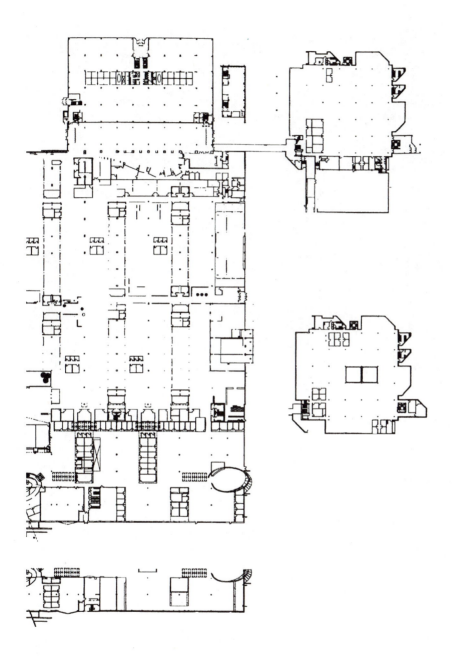

Figure CH.3.4   Business units select their own layouts and demarcate their area and town hall with colorful flags.

(*Image HOK Canada.*)

Case History 4. Andersen Consulting

Organization	Andersen Consulting (AC)
Location	Wellesley, Massachusetts
Completed	February 1997
Area	62,000 ft^2 (5,800 m^2)
No. people	700 and growing
Designers	Elkus/Manfredi Architects Ltd., Boston, Massachusetts

Everyone who works from Andersen Consulting's Wellesley base books a workspace just for the time it is needed. Administrative and support staff who are permanently located there book their own spaces for a month at a time. Consultants, who are often out of the office far more than they are in, book a workstation by the hour. On arrival at the building, they find their files already waiting for them at the desk. A team of concierge staff help make this happen. They were hired from the hotel industry to apply to offices the skills and services that are automatically assumed to be available at the best hotels. Andersen Consulting's aim was to create an office building in which services would be available to ease the hassles of people leading busy lives. The concierge staff are the people who make it all happen—they arrange dry cleaning, clothes pressing, and car washing, buy birthday cards, and send off flowers for their busy clientele. To the company, this is seen as an important quality-of-life benefit that may assist in the recruitment and retention of the high-caliber consultants on whom the business depends.

Another important ingredient that shapes this office is the desire for collegiality and easy communication between people. This is achieved by the following:

- Dedicating much space to team and social areas such as the town forum

- Positioning whiteboards liberally around the building for people to readily share their ideas

- Building internal walls from large glass panels so that everyone knows who is in and whether or not they can be disturbed

Ready access to partners is one of the benefits of this building. No longer boxed in behind opaque walls, there is enhanced employee collaboration and cross fertilization of ideas. The workspaces vary from 120 ft^2 (11 m^2) glazed offices known as *acoustically private areas* to the typical 8-by 8-ft standard workstation, to small touchdown benches or tiny booths (Fig. CH.4.1). All workstations have desktop-level power—data and telephone outlets—allowing users to commence work readily at any location.

The original intention for the Wellesley building was to use traditional space allocation based on seniority. The company was moving from expensive space in downtown Boston with a loose density of 250 ft^2 (23 m^2) per person in which senior partners enjoyed offices of up to 400 ft^2 (37 m^2). Space and financial economies were goals of the move. The company did a major review of its accommodation strategy for the worldwide staff of 40,000 who kept growing at an alarming rate. Finite space in buildings could never keep up with the unrelenting demands of business

Figure CH.4.1 Glazed rooms, or "acoustically private areas," can be booked by the hour when privacy is required for meetings or heads-down work.

(Photograph: Elkus/Manfredi.)

teams to house a few more people every few weeks. AC's 1996 Paris office rocked established space practice by creating an office hotel operated by a professional concierge team. Benefits were less space per person, capacity to house extra numbers as growth required, and more interaction between partners and staff who could now better contact one another in an open environment. The traditional space plans for Wellesley were discarded at the eleventh hour and the office hotel emerged.

The building itself is an older building onto which additional space was added. This provided the opportunity to create a new, open stairway, leading to the forum, coffee area and travel shop area on the middle of three floors, the place to meet (Fig. CH.4.2 and 4.3). Conference rooms, meeting rooms, huddle rooms, and team areas abound. Storage has been rationalized down to two file drawers for senior staff and half that for more recent joiners. The process of change was excellently handled by Andersen Consulting who informed staff what was planned throughout the planning and move process (Fig. CH.4.4).

Figure CH.4.2   Bright colors and varied materials distinguish the coffee and break areas from the work areas.

(Photograph: Elkus/Manfredi.)

Figure CH.4.3   Shared areas are intended to be warm, welcoming, and relaxed in their furnishings and finishes.

(Photograph: Elkus/Manfredi.)

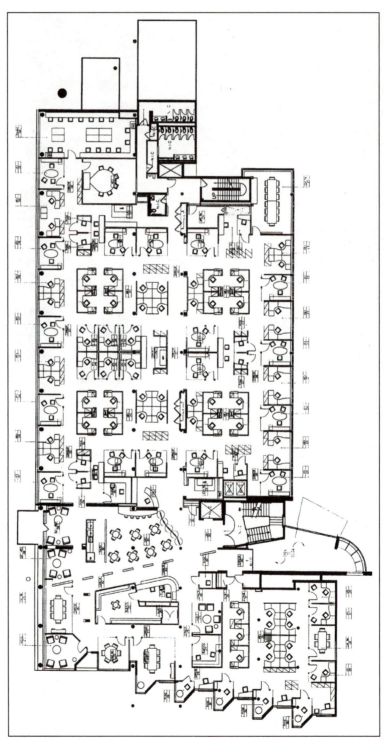

Figure CH.4.4 Plan of the second floor level showing the town forum, coffee area, and travel shop near the new stairway and a variety of workstation types.

(Elkus/Manfredi.)

Case History 5. "Location Free" Means Fewer Changes

Organization	MCI Telecommunications, Rally Center Project
Location	Boston, Massachusetts
Completed	1995
Area	40,000 ft^2 (3,700 m^2)
No. people	220
Designers	HDB Architects, Inc., Boston, Massachusetts

MCI's Rally Center in Boston broke the mold. It provided an office that did not have to be reconfigured as soon as the paint was dry. For five years it has continued to serve the sales teams that are based in this area without any change in the layout. To achieve this, a new approach to office provision was used. It involved giving new and better facilities, and taking away some familiar "givens." In order to implement radical change effectively, great care was taken with the process. MCI's human resources group was closely involved and surveyed the workforce to find out what they actually needed. The team wanted to know how long people were at their desks or elsewhere and what they did there. The HR team carried out a "gorillas in the mist" approach, watching to see what was happening. The designer devised a survey where people wrote down where they were, what they were doing, and when. A team of enthusiastic MCI staff helped to ensure that the briefing was right during the whole project.

The result is a new set of spaces including several that are new and attractive. There is the coffee area where people can relax and chat or do a bit of work, the "Hearth" where people can gather—and where training takes place (Fig. CH.5.1). There are team areas, small brainstorming spaces for groups. All these were provided for the staff as facilities for their benefit. Adjacent to team areas are clusters of heads-down desks. This is where the "taking away" happened. These desks, intended for the peripatetic sales force, are nonassigned (Fig. CH.5.2). People lost their own desks, an acknowledgment of the fact that they rarely used

Figure CH.5.1   The coffee bar and Hearth area are used both for relaxed meetings and social contact, and sometimes as a training area.

(Photograph: Joanne Devereaux.)

Figure CH.5.2 Most members of staff use unassigned workstations where they can sit down and pull up a wheeled table to work at.

(Photograph: Joanne Devereau.)

them, as had been discovered in the predesign stage. Desks vary in design. Some are straightforward desks, others are wheeled tables that can be repositioned as needed. Storage for peripatetic users is a set of wheeled baskets that are stored in a unit with shelves above the basket stack. Assembled and developed for this project, the company that made them—Egan in Canada—subsequently marketed them as part of their range (Fig. CH.5.3).

By being careful at the outset to find out what would really work, and by bringing the staff along with the new designs, this building has stood the test of time. Though the users have never expressed themselves as eager fans of unassigned desks, it still works for them, through all the changes that have taken place in the company. It acted as a prototype for other new MCI offices, though few were as

Figure CH.5.3   A cheap and effective solution for storage for itinerant staff was put together for this project and then marketed more widely by the supplier. The lightweight baskets are easy to move to the desk when paperwork is to be done.

(Photograph: Joanne Devereau.)

well researched. The initiatives that did not take the same care with preliminary work and that did not try to help educate the users have been somewhat less successful. Major change is difficult to absorb. It is fun and a challenge for the design and project team, but in the end the result exists to support the user population and the organization (Fig. CH.5.4).

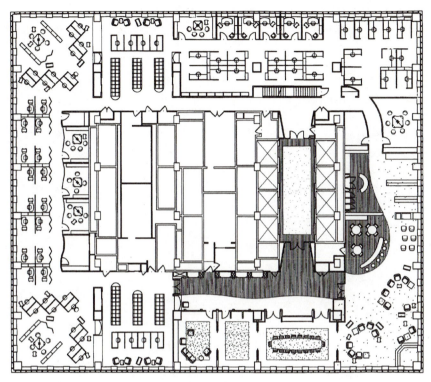

Figure CH.5.4   Floor plan of the center.

(Hoyle, Doran and Berry--HDB, Inc.)

CASE HISTORIES

Case History 6. Repair and Renewal to Bring Hope

Organization	National Minority AIDS Council (NMAC)
Location	Washington, D.C.
Completed	1995
Area	7,500 ft^2 (700 m^2)
No. people	44
Designers	CORE, Washington, D.C.

A pair of four-story row houses, floodlit at night to show the bright purple trim on the windows, stands out as a symbol, a beacon, in the heart of a transitional area of Washington, D.C. (Fig. CH.6.1). The National Minority AIDS Council, known as NMAC, is appropriately located here, highly visible to the minority communities it exists to serve the Black, Hispanic, Asian, and other groups represented in this culturally mixed area. The building had been partially burned out, and abandoned since 1968. The semiderelict building has been brought back into use, and at the same time its costs have been kept to a minimum. NMAC realized that their work would carry on longer than had been obvious when they were founded, so they needed to move to more permanent premises. They were looking for ways to become better connected to the community and chose this location deliberately, enabling them to be very obvious and close to their clientele.

The first issue was to understand what was salvageable of the building. Fortunately much of the structure could be reused. "Sister" joists were inserted alongside the existing

Figure CH.6.1   A victim of riots, the burned-out shell of two brownstones was transformed into the new headquarters of the National Minority Aids Council.

(*Photograph: Michael Moran.*)

floor structure to enhance their strength. Where brickwork was damaged, it has been patched with sheets of shiny metal. The building itself provided a framework for the low-budget solution that still looks fresh after five years. Every element has to work hard; nothing is included simply as a design feature. The working areas are stripped down to the basics, and simple materials have been used (Fig. CH.6.2). The brick walls were cleaned and left exposed. The spaces are fitted out around the perimeter with fixed blockboard work benches. Designed for four workplaces, they can easily accommodate a few more at times when needed. This enables interactive work to take place easily, symbolizing that through cooperation, help can be found for AIDS sufferers (Fig. CH.6.3). The perimeter arrangement allows the furniture to do double duty as the wall, moving fit-out dollars into the construction budget to help reduce the overall

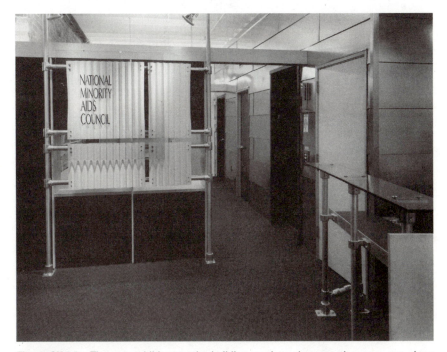

Figure CH.6.2   The new additions to the building, such as the reception area, use clean lines and simple materials.

(Photograph: Michael Moran.)

Figure CH.6.3   A tight budget encourages creative maximization of space. Shared desks are designed around group interaction.

(*Photograph: Michael Moran.*)

cost and allowing a better financial arrangement as capital expenditure attracts better tax credits than furniture. The materials in the reception are inexpensive—steel and ply-wood—but provide a fresh and interesting environment.

Fullest possible use has been made of the existing build-ing. It was extended as far as possible within the site, to provide maximum capacity. Disabled access is at the side, avoiding the need to negotiate the stairs up to the tradi-tional front door, entering at basement level where there are shared facilities, including a conference room that can be enlarged by sliding aside the wall between it and the lunch room (Fig. CH.6.4). The top floor was where the main fire damage had occurred, so a new roof was needed, and the opportunity was taken to raise the ceiling height by leaving the barrel vaulted timber roof exposed (Fig. CH.6.5).

Reuse of a derelict building enabled NMAC to afford the project and position itself among the people most needing its help. The bright colors that distinguish the internal areas functionally—red for circulation, green for shared areas, blue for public spaces—and liven up the façade create the lively and positive image that the client wanted and needed in this run-down and depressed area. A building that was a dead hulk for many years has taken the lead in the regen-eration of this area, where there are now many adaptive reuse projects in process.

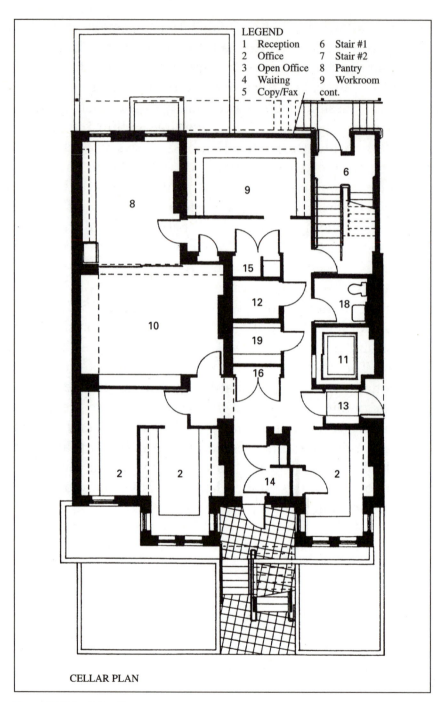

Figure CH.6.4 Cellar plan.

(*CORE.*)

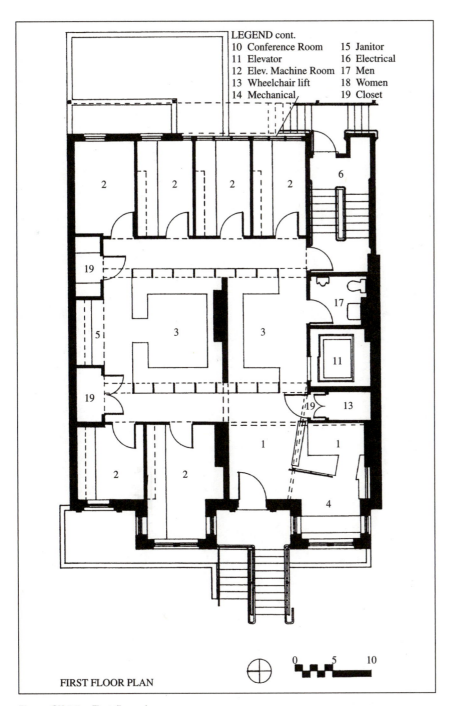

LEGEND cont.

10	Conference Room	15	Janitor
11	Elevator	16	Electrical
12	Elev. Machine Room	17	Men
13	Wheelchair lift	18	Women
14	Mechanical	19	Closet

FIRST FLOOR PLAN

Figure CH.6.5   First-floor plan.

(*CORE.*)

Case History 7. From Corporate Office to Creative Warehouse

Organization	Campbell-Ewald West
Location	Los Angeles, California
Completed	August 1998
Area	20,000 ft^2 (1,900 m^2)
No. people	100
Designers	Carmen Nordsten Igonda Design, Los Angeles, California

When the Michigan-based Campbell-Ewald advertising agency decided to open a new office in Los Angeles, they identified several requirements that the building needed to meet:

- An image of stability yet with West Coast appeal

- Large space for everyone to gather

- Improved team collaboration

- Comfortable workstations

- Showcase for customers

- Move within six months

The building chosen as the new West Coast headquarters is an 11-story mirrored-glass cube in Santa Monica built about 20 years ago. It had been used as the base for a legal firm; hence, it had many small offices around the exterior walls, a rectilinear grid, and low suspended ceiling. This layout would not work for creative teams whose environment of choice would be more akin to a large, free-flowing studio space with varied atmosphere.

New plans were rapidly developed by the Carmen, Nordsten Igonda Design team. Almost all the private offices were brought into the interior of the building, apart from those of the CEO and creative director whose offices are on building corners. The rectilinear grid is subtly distorted in several important locations. Low ceiling tiles were removed to expose the full ceiling height, the service ducts, and cables. Raw concrete floors were polished, then left as the finished surface. Workstations were located around the perimeter to give natural light and a view. Floating acoustic ceilings are built over workstation clusters. Uplighters give a soft form of indirect lighting to avoid glare. Conference tables are placed between each set of four workstations for creative teams.

At the reception, clients are greeted with a maple media wall showing videos made by the agency, and cantilevered display shelves (Fig. CH.7.1). The main conference room has a rear projection room and is set up for video conferencing, display boards, and computer access (Fig. CH.7.2). Lighting conditions can be varied for different presentation modes. Another conference room has a two-way mirror for use with focus groups.

Models and computer renderings of the proposals were made to show the rest of the company what was planned and to earn budget approval. The space that has emerged is tasteful, minimalist, serene. Distant views to mountains and sea give the local context. Materials are not in themselves expensive but have been carefully composed to shape an attractive and peaceful work environment.

Figure CH.7.1 The reception is a showcase of the work of the agency for clients, with display shelves, a media wall for videos, and dramatic views.

(*Photograph: fotoworks—Benny Chan.*)

Figure CH.7.2 The conference room is set up for rear projection, display boards, video conferencing, and computer access. Lighting conditions can be varied for different presentation modes.

(*Photograph: fotoworks—Benny Chan.*)

Figure CH.7.3   Glazed offices are away from the windows; people in open-plan workstations share conference tables.

(Photograph: fotoworks—Benny Chan.)

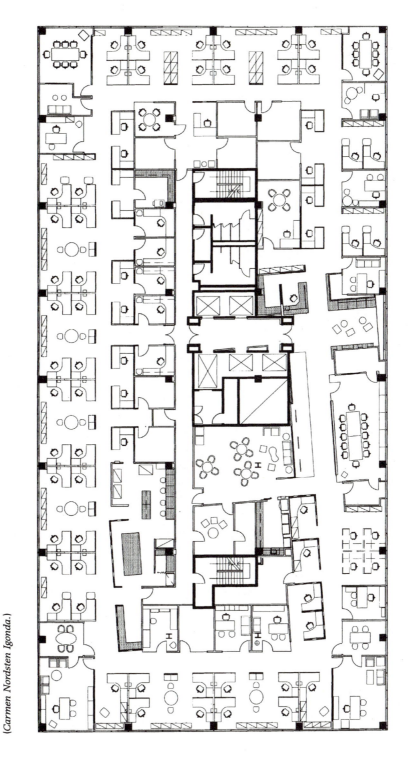

Figure CH.7.4 Plan showing open workstations around the edge with most enclosed rooms located in the middle. This reverses the layout of the previous occupants, a legal firm, who had enclosed offices all around the edge. *(Carmen Nordsten Igonda.)*

Case History 8.
Quadruple Whammy
Generates Property Savings

Organization	Arthur Andersen
Location	Boston, Massachusetts
Completed	February 1997
Area	108,000 ft^2 (10,000 m^2)
No. people	700
Designers	ADD, Inc., Cambridge, Massachusetts

It was only by fully understanding their existing office building that Arthur Andersen could set in motion a series of decisions to realize huge property savings. For 10 years, the Boston office occupied the top floors of a prestigious office tower with spectacular bay views. With the views came an awkward geometry—a circular tower intersected in plan by a rectangular core with an irregular column grid. Pie-shaped rooms around the perimeter uncomfortably accommodated rectilinear furniture. Even big rooms felt tight and poorly arranged. Columns in the open area commonly intruded upon efficient space planning. And the whole building felt less attractive and airy than it might have as only the private offices enjoyed daylight leaving more junior staff to work in the darker building interior. Though the floorplates were large—normally an advantage for communication between groups and accommodating change—the benefits could hardly be appreciated because of the poor plan.

The clients employed four fundamental strategies to realize space efficiency. First, they moved to a building with a lower rental per square foot. Second, the new building floorplate allowed for efficient layout so every square foot rented could actually be productive. Third, only a few different workstation sizes were used, giving greater flexibility and efficiency over time. Fourth, audit and consulting groups who are often out of the office, used high desk sharing ratios so considerably fewer desks than people were needed.

The new building was the headquarters of a large bank, constructed in the 1960s. The floor plan is a simple rectangle with cut away corners, a rectangular inner core, and one row of inner columns (Figs. CH.8.1 and 8.3). The col-

Figure CH.8.1 Enclosed offices are located around the perimeter of the building in this office space, which is planned efficiently within a rectilinear grid.

(*Photograph: Richard S. Mandelkorn.*)

umn grid has been intelligently built into the walls of private offices and meeting rooms so as not to intrude into the space. Private offices, 130 ft^2 (12 m^2) in area with some slightly larger, have glass fronts to allow daylight to the interior. Each façade is interrupted at least once with open areas to bring daylight and views to the rest of the floor. Eight corner rooms are finished in the same way to be used interchangeably as either conference rooms or senior offices (Fig. CH.8.2). Open workstations measure 6 by 8 ft (1.8 $\times$ 2.4 m) for people who spend a long time in the office or 6 by 6 ft (1.8 $\times$ 1.8 m) for those who are often away. All workspaces include infrastructure that will allow for growth and change into the future. The efficient rectilinear grid of the floor plan is altered by the new internal stairway that

Figure CH.8.2 Eight, light-filled corner rooms are furnished to be to be used as conference rooms or senior offices.

(Photograph: Richard S. Mandelkorn.)

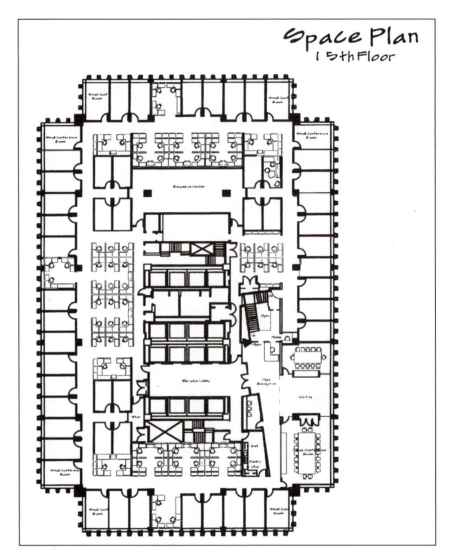

Figure CH.8.3 Typical floor layout.
(*ADD Inc.*)

has been sliced through the building so that people can
readily move between floors, to encourage interaction and
communication between people in different departments.
Visitors are greeted in a special reception area away from
the main flow to ensure confidentiality and invited into pre-

sentation rooms. In the subbasement of the building, Arthur Andersen has created an administrative floor for training rooms, graphics, reprographics, mail, library, central filing, and travel services (Fig. CH.8.3).

The clients are incredibly pleased with the project. They wanted people to be proud to move into the new office despite the altered location and views. The strategy seems to have worked. More space has now been taken on additional floors within the building for expanding teams and new projects.

Case History 9. Doing More with Less

Organization	Bates USA
Location	New York, New York
Completed	March 1999
Area	250,000 ft^2 (23,000 m^2)
No. people	700
Designers	STUDIOS, Washington, D.C.

Early strategic decisions suggested that Bates USA, an international advertising agency, should move out of the historic Chrysler Building in midtown Manhattan to a different location and building that would return better value for money. Bates was at the point of merging several different advertising agencies so the move provided the perfect opportunity to define the new culture that should be created. For several months Bates and their consultants strove to articulate the new requirements. They defined the main business drivers now and in the future, the different work flows and work processes, the technologies, and space and human resource issues. Objectives for the move were agreed upon: The company wanted to "celebrate the creative process," to improve the work process by increasing interaction among the many different teams, and to provide a "home" where work could occur in a wide range of settings. To continue to work effectively, the business required some special spaces: a large client presentation center and conference rooms, a library for access to shared resources, and a space for staff to meet together—the tradition of a bar being open every evening (Fig. CH.9.1).

The right building proved to be a large 1930s light industrial building in the less prestigious garment district, seven floors of which would be occupied by Bates. New bathrooms and air-conditioning were added. A coffee bar with cybercafé benchtop facilities was built into every floor,

Figure CH.9.1   Corporate culture is aided by bringing different groups together on projects and by a bar that is open every evening.

(*Photograph: STUDIOS Architecture/Andrew Bordwin Studio, Inc.*)

in full view of people using the main glass-enclosed staircase (Fig. CH.9.2).

Space in the building that Bates had previously occupied was very generous. To meet their objectives, the company had chosen the route that would give cheaper space, and less of it to each person. That demanded that most people work in the open. Previously, 80 percent of workstations were private offices and 20 percent were open. The aim was to reverse the balance. Only one person in seven was to have a private office, and everyone else was to have a cubicle. Two

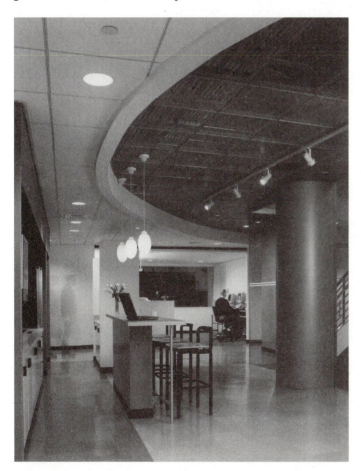

Figure CH.9.2 Cybercafé benchtop facilities next to the coffee bar facilitate rapid communication.

(*Photograph: STUDIOS Architecture/Andrew Bordwin Studio, Inc.*)

workstation footprints in the open were used, 7 by 7 ft (2.1 × 2.1 m) and 7 by 9 ft (2.1 × 2.7 m) (Fig. CH.9.3). Within these, a wide variety of furniture is assembled to meet the needs of different work teams. The height of the panels between workstations varies from standing privacy to seated privacy depending on how much the group needs to interact and how much they need to do solo work.

The result is a flexible, dynamic environment that will support Bates through organizational and technological change (Figs. CH.9.4 and CH.9.5). Colors are neutral in the work areas, creating a calm, soft interior that complements the colorful cacophony of the streets outside. The process of change was greatly aided by communicating the plans to employees before the move via lectures and seminars, and preparing an etiquette guide for the new office.

Figure CH.9.3   Three workstation footprints are used: one for private offices and two for work areas out in the open. Within these, a wide variety of furniture is assembled to meet the needs of different work teams.

(Photograph: STUDIOS Architecture/Andrew Bordwin Studio, Inc.)

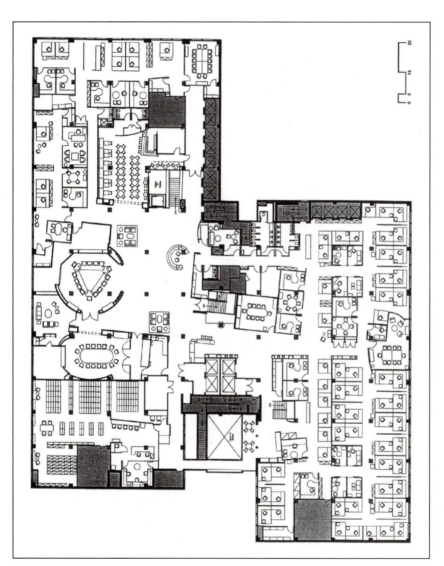

Figure CH.9.4   Plan of entrance floor including reception desk, waiting areas, presentation facilities, cafeteria, library, and central filing.

(*STUDIOS Architecture, Washington, D.C.*)

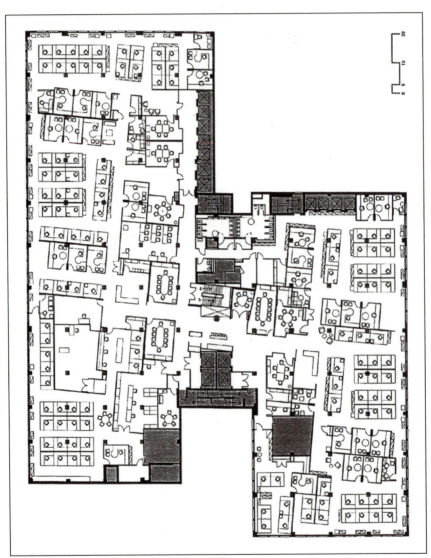

Figure CH.9.5   Plan of typical upper floor, showing workspaces grouped into neighborhoods with equipment hubs, quiet rooms, and conference and project war rooms.

(*STUDIOS Architecture, Washington, D.C.*)

Case History 10. One Size Fits All for Organizational Effectiveness

Organization	Alcoa Headquarters
Location	Pittsburgh, Pennsylvania
Completed	August 1998
Area	242,000 ft^2 gross offices (22,500 m^2)
No. people	400
Designers	The Design Alliance, Pittsburgh, Pennsylvania

"Architecture and space design can make a significant contribution to organizational effectiveness," says Paul O'Neill, chairman and CEO of the Aluminum Company of America. According to O'Neill, Alcoa's new headquarters "really changes the way people relate to each other and takes away the symbolic stuff of who's important. This is about encouraging the free flow of ideas."

Alcoa abandoned the 31-story tower that had been its home for 45 years to move to this 6-story, purpose-designed office block overlooking the Allegheny River, once dirty and industrial but now reviving as a place of leisure (Fig. CH.10.1). The old building was cramping the company's potential. Earlier attempts had been made to increase direct communication in the old HQ by taking top officers out of their walls and into cubicles. This was helpful, but the small floorplates still blocked interaction between teams. The decision was made to seek a new building.

People move through the new building on escalators rising through an atrium so they can see one another, and stop and chat, rather than changing levels by using an enclosed elevator (Fig. CH.10.2). A kitchen next to the landing signals the interaction space on every floor. Near reception is a news stand and a café open to the public. The main cafeteria opens onto a waterfront terrace for al fresco dining. A new public park allows employees and others to walk down to the shoreline. The $67 million investment improves the city as well as the corporation. Alcoa donated its vacated high-rise building so that it could be used as a regional resource center to house economic development agencies.

Figure CH.10.1 Alcoa's new corporate headquarters, gracefully curving along the Allegheny River in Pittsburgh, restores the riverfront from its industrial past and creates a radically new environment for the company.

(Photograph: Hedrich-Blessing.)

Figure CH.10.2 The internal atrium rises through all six office floors and links departments by escalators for ease of communication.

(*Photograph: Hedrich-Blessing.*)

The new building signals the importance of its product—the façade and internal furniture and fittings employ aluminum wherever possible.

One intention was that the new building should be open and nonhierarchical (Fig. CH.10.3). Everyone including O'Neill has an identical workstation measuring 9 by 9 ft (2.7 by 2.7 m), and nobody works further than 45 ft (15 m) from the windows. Floor heights, greater than for speculative office buildings, draw more light and views to the workstations. White noise helps to mask

Figure CH.10.3 There are few enclosed spaces except for conference and meeting rooms. All public areas and most workstations enjoy river views.

(*Photograph: Hedrich-Blessing.*)

unwanted noise at the desk. The only doors are on conference and meeting rooms enclosed in glass walls.

The building took five years from the decision to build to finish, with two years on site. A year-long communication process before the move ensured that everyone knew what was happening, had visited the building, and had played a role in selecting their furniture. Storage was rationed in the new building by a careful "paper-wise" program—people were told they could take only what they could carry. Every decision was made for a business purpose, part of a management strategy. O'Neill elaborates: "Alcoa Corporate Center was designed to make the organization more effective. It is different from most office buildings in that we started the design with business ideas, not architectural ideas. Our design principles grew out of business and organizational goals."

Case History 11.
Fundamental Change on a
Gradual Basis

Organization	West Group
Location	Egan, Minnesota
Completed	1999 and ongoing
Area	1,200,000 ft^2 (111,500 m^2)
No. people	4,500
Designers	Perkins and Will, Minneapolis, Minnesota

A skyscraper lying down is how you could describe it. This is a very large building, comparable to a 50-story sky-scraper in area and population, on only six floors but well over a half-mile long (Fig. CH.11.1). Less than 10 years old, this facility is undergoing considerable change, albeit for its original owners. It was built to a speculative office standard to house the West Group, a privately owned publishing house specializing in legal reference material, when they outgrew their downtown St. Paul offices. Now the new CEO, Brian Hall, who came in when the firm was purchased by Thompsons a couple of years ago, is pursuing his credo that "facilities are for people." With this philosophy, Hall aims to be the "employer of choice" in this area of very low unemployment. Along with many shifts in the nature of West Group's product, such as moving to publishing CDs, radical changes in the building use and design are being implemented—gradually, gently, and while the building is in full occupation.

The initial approach was to consider the strategic aspects and to find a way to humanize what had been a somewhat forbidding prospect. The plans had previously placed enclosed offices in a ring around the glazed wall. The various different grades had different-sized rooms including an ultragenerous executive suite, enclosed and remote from the rest of the workforce. The majority of people sat in unrelieved open-plan working areas where they could see from

Figure CH.11.1 From the outside the immense length becomes apparent, which on the inside has been transformed to a more human scale.

(Photograph: Jerry Hass.)

one end of the building to the other—over 1,000 ft (100 m), an uninterrupted sea of workstations.

The solution has been an incremental, many-layered approach. A reduction in the number of enclosed offices and a move to get the directors "off the glass," away from the windows, was one of the objectives, as well as a simplification of the number of workstation standards. With 4,500 employees, most of whom would be in the open, there was a real need to use design to break up the monotony. Equally important was the decision to provide a new and forward-looking range of services for the office population. These would be located on Main Street, the route through the whole building at the fourth-floor level (Fig. CH.11.2). The street is therefore full of incident. There is the office cafeteria, and also a coffee shop, Coffee.com, run by Caribou Coffee. It is unusual, if not unique, to find

Figure CH.11.2   Main Street runs throughout the building, linking workspaces and a series of shared facilities. West online is on the fifth floor.

(Photograph: Dana Wheelock.)

an independent retail coffee company located within an office organization's own space (Fig. CH.11.3). Within this coffee area there are semienclosed circular meeting areas allowing people hitherto used to feeling that "if you are not at your desk you are not working" to enjoy working in a more relaxed environment. This central meeting zone is more effective in this respect than the informal areas in the departments, where people tend to prefer formal meeting areas. There is a learning center known as "TU" (Thompson University) and a retail outlet run by West Group themselves that sells gifts, handles mail and laundry, and includes a bank and a training area. There is a Town Hall with seats for about 200 people with multi-

Figure CH.11.3   A privately run coffee business provides refreshments all day in Cafe.com, which is located off the central circulation street.

(Photograph: Dana Wheelock.)

media communications, a forum for departments and employees to meet and interact. Last—or rather first, as it is the first thing you see as you step out of the main elevator—the executive suite is now visible, opened up for all to see. The designers have signaled the various services, defined landmarks, and given different areas and departments their own local identity. This has been done by accent color: insets in the carpets, strong color on small areas of walls or ceilings, the introduction of curves in the patterns, and special lighting being used to articulate portions of ceiling. Similar devices are used to mark special places, concentrating on locally used meeting areas, print rooms, and storage areas along Main Street (Figs. CH.11.4 and CH.11.5).

The need to relieve the impact of the sea of open plan desks on the 160,000-ft^2 floor plates led to these first steps in the transformation of the working environment. Over half of the building is still to be finished, and at the same time the next initiative is underway. The old furniture was largely reused, and that has allowed workplaces to retain some of their old character in parts of the building. The next phase will consider the workplaces in more detail, considering a change from 8 by 8 ft (2.4 × 2.4 m), to 7.5 by 7.5 ft (2.3 × 2.3 m). This slightly smaller size will allow a better fit with the building dimensions. This will enable about 15 percent more workplaces to fit into the floors. In parallel, the furniture itself is being considered. The aim is to find or develop a range that will enable gradual change to take place. Those departments that wish to configure their workplaces on familiar lines will still be able to do so, but gradually layers will be "peeled off" to create a simpler, more flexible, and uniform pattern for the future, as departments adjust to the new environment. Signage is also being reconsidered and will be integrated with the new and livelier image, giving greater

WEST GROUP
"D" BUILDING LEVEL 4

SCALE

15   60
0   30

Figure CH.11.4   Plan of Level 4. The principal shared resources are on Main Street on this floor.

(*Perkins and Will.*)

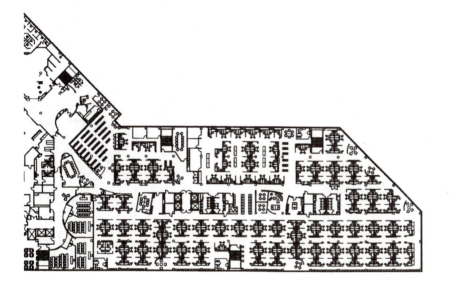

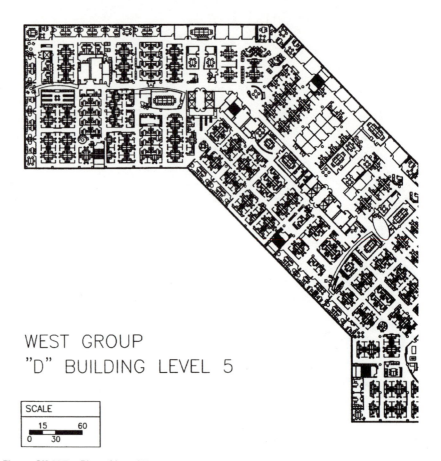

WEST GROUP
"D" BUILDING LEVEL 5

SCALE

| 15 | 60 |
| 0 | 30 |

Figure CH.11.5   Plan of Level 5.

(Perkins and Will.)

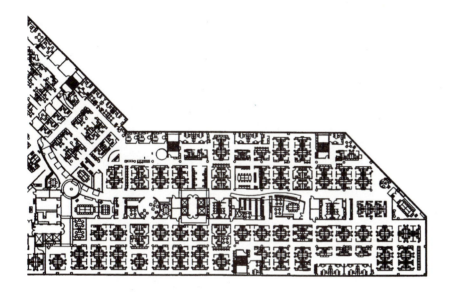

visibility to the shared activities as well as to different departments.

It has taken two years to get this far. Both the organization and the designers are learning from the process, and West Group will continue to change and benefit from the new flexibility that the present and future developments of the project will bring. It has been accepted by all concerned that culture changes slowly and that buildings are not necessarily a quick fix.

Case History 12. Caves, Cubicles, and Creativity

Organization	Silicon Graphics, Inc.
Location	Amphitheater Technology Center, Redwood City, California
Completed	May 1997
Area	500,000 ft^2 (46,500 m^2)
No. people	2,500 and growing
Designers	STUDIOS, San Francisco, California

A "fifth building" open to the skies forms the center of SGI's Amphitheater Technology Center, the third major R&D campus for this fast-growing software house (Figs. CH.12.1 and CH.12.2). In this carefully crafted outdoor space, people can be reenergized by sitting in the sun, playing ball games, or eating lunch together. The design intention behind the whole campus is to create a place that fosters creativity so that products can be rapidly developed and speedily brought to market. The academic campus was the pure design image—diverse buildings set in a safe and attractively landscaped pedestrian environment. Main circulation routes alternate between indoor and outdoor spaces.

Throughout the four-building campus, coffee bars and games areas provide staffers with "hangouts," which, it is hoped, will be the birthplace of new ideas. Whiteboard table-

Figure CH.12.1   Landscape shapes the campus.
(*Photograph: Michael O'Callahan.*)

tops and a generous supply of pens in the foyer and coffee areas encourage impromptu brainstorming sessions (Fig. CH.12.3). Elsewhere, comfortable chairs and additional whiteboards create collaborative lounges where people from different parts of the organization can meet and share ideas.

This is a place for serious fun. Amenities on site include a fitness center, library, volleyball courts, and parkland donated to the city by SGI. A fleet of bicycles is freely available for people to move from this campus to SGI's other buildings in the vicinity. A "cafetorium," the Ozone Café, is

Figure CH.12.2 Protected outdoor space as the "fifth room."
(*Photograph: Michael O'Callahan.*)

a combined cafeteria and auditorium with banquette seating for up to 500 people. Conferences and training are accommodated in a special facility (Figure CH.12.4). Services and structure are exposed, lending a loftlike character to the space. Much of the parking for 1,600 cars is underground so as not to litter the place with cars.

Workspaces are of two types. First, there are "caves," small "hardwall" offices measuring 10 by 10 ft (3.0 × 3.0 m), located in clusters across the deep floor plan, for development engineers who need to do focused academic-style work. Second, for technology groups, there are open workstation cubicles, most of which are 8 ft 6 in (2.6 × 2.7 m) by 9 ft or 12 by 9 ft (3.7 × 2.7 m). Executives as well as nonmanagerial people work from there. Colors drawn from SGI's product lines are used to accent the groups. Workstations have

Figure CH.12.3   The whiteboard table in the foyer is designed to allow creative moments to be recorded.

(*Photograph: Michael O'Callahan.*)

Ethospace spines with full cable management, linked to a "hummer," a custom-designed patch/data panel that allows easy recabling for workstation moves. Furniture is Action Office by Herman Miller. Floor plans divide the whole into neighborhoods of about 70 people sharing a large family kitchen and bar, which is the focus of the local group. SGI keeps growing so STUDIOS is now completing the next phase, Crittenden campus, which will be developed along similar lines. This will be launched in early 2000.

Figure CH.12.4   A double-height presentation space with bleacher seating for staff gatherings.

(*Photograph: Michael O'Callahan.*)

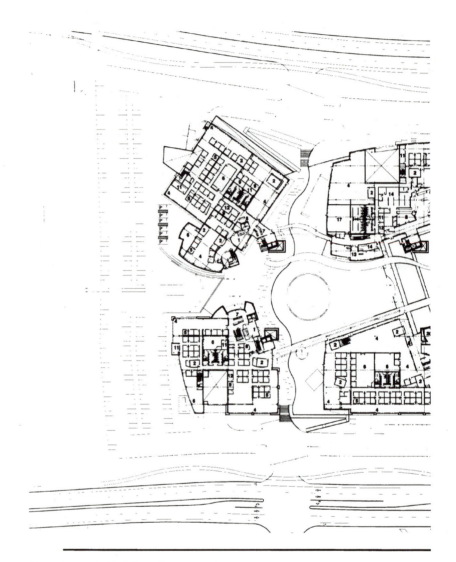

Figure CH.12.5   First floor plan.
(STUDIOS Architecture, San Francisco.)

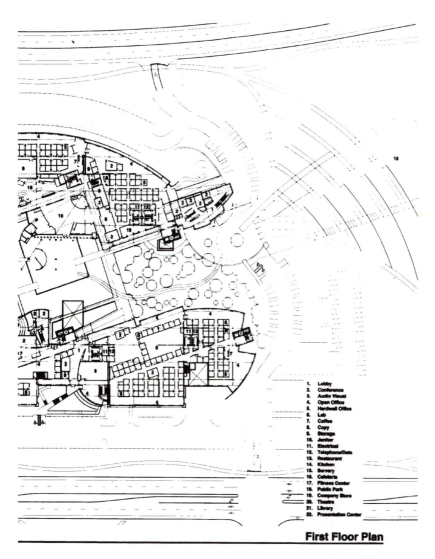

1. Lobby
2. Conference
3. Audio Visual
4. Open Office
5. Hardwall Office
6. Lab
7. Coffee
8. Copy
9. Storage
10. Janitor
11. Electrical
12. Telephone/Data
13. Restaurant
14. Kitchen
15. Servery
16. Cafeteria
17. Fitness Center
18. Public Park
19. Company Store
20. Theatre
21. Library
22. Presentation Center

First Floor Plan

0   32   64   128

Case History 13. Enclosed Offices for Education First

Organization	Education First (EF) North American Headquarters
Location	Cambridge, Massachusetts
Completed	November 1998
Area	160,000 ft² gross, 144,000 ft² net (15,000 m²) gross, 13,400 m² net)
No. people	600 approximately
Designers	Elkus/Manfredi, Boston, Massachusetts

Education First has decided that small offices for one or two people still have an important place in their operations. The company began in Sweden and now works in 34 nations promoting cultural and language exchange to break down geographical and psychological barriers. Group or independent travel programs, au pair services, high school exchanges, and language learning software are its products. Staff are mobile, young Generation X people with at least two languages who operate in competitive groups mostly transacting telephone sales. Six to eight people make up a typical team, supervised by people drawn from among their ranks who wish to keep communication lines open.

To provide support for this work process, supervisors were given offices of their own around the window wall, and adjacent inboard team rooms were created (Figs. CH.13.1 and CH.13.2). By using extensive areas of glass in the intervening walls, supervisors can both see and be seen by their teams. In their previous building, the architecture did not support their team process. The aim in the new building has been to use internal walls to create more of a team identity, hence the walls and the variety of colors to demarcate one team from another.

In moving to a new building the aim throughout was to create the sort of environment that would attract and retain young people to accept a job at EF and then remain. This was achieved by devoting a lot of space and budget to four atria rising through the building, to many shared areas, and designing attractive social spaces. The double-

Figure CH.13.1 Enclosed offices for team leaders hug the perimeter of the building, giving visual connection to the internal team rooms.

(Elkus/Manfredi Architects Ltd.)

height reception area makes a dramatic impact with bright blue sculptural chairs designed by Tom Dixon and an abstract sculpture of home, symbolizing protection, hovering over sofas and coffee tables (Fig. CH.13.3). Conference rooms, named after the cities in which EF operates, are a visual treat. Capellini manufactured most of the furniture, selected to evoke European style and sophistication, which is part of the EF corporate culture. In the words of the design team, "people who work at EF love the place as soon as they walk through the door—they're amazed at the amount of space for teaming, the social areas, the atria. The architecture supports them in the work they do."

Elsewhere materials and furniture are simple, not lavish. Polished concrete floors are used throughout, and suspended ceiling tiles are alleviated in places such as the coffee area by the insertion of translucent fiber-glass panels instead of the acoustic tile. The president's office was itself designed as a "corporate living room," a place with walls of glass—"no secrets." A contemporary feel, light and serene, was sought by the president and successfully delivered by the interior team (Fig. CH.13.4).

The building, newly built by a developer, was specially adapted for EF to a budget that was not extravagant, though it achieved a "huge bang for the buck." The whole project was delivered within 18 months from starting design.

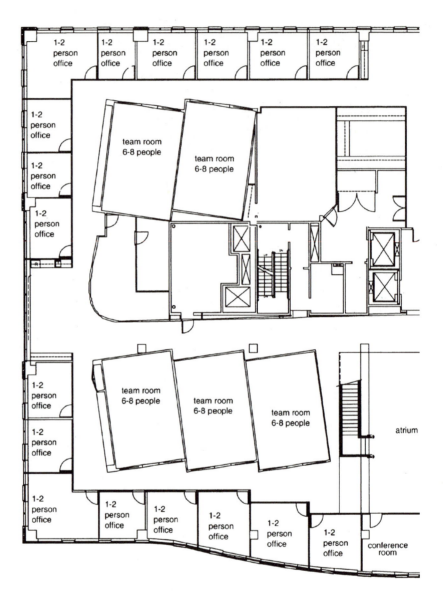

Figure CH.13.2   Seventh-floor plan showing typical layout of team rooms and one- to two-person offices.

(Elkus/Manfredi Architects Ltd.)

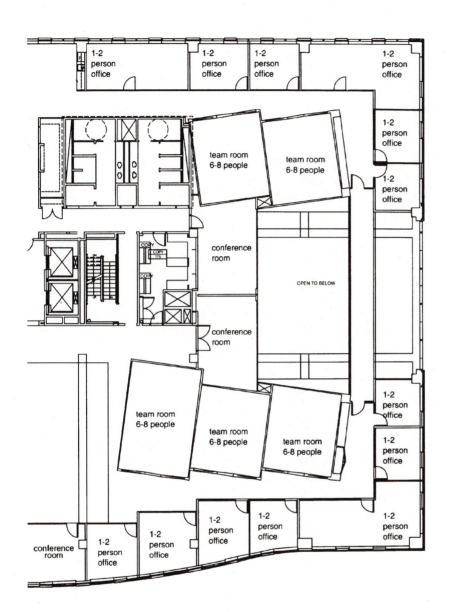

Figure CH.13.3   The reception impresses clients and staff with its airiness, sculptural chairs, Tom Dixon's "home" sculpture, and dramatic internal and external views.

(*Photograph: Marco Lorenzetti at Hedrich Blessing.*)

Figure CH.13.4   A contemporary feel, light and serene, was sought by the president and successfully delivered by the interior team.

(*Photograph: Marco Lorenzetti at Hedrich Blessing.*)

Case History 14. Classy Furniture Is Good Value

Organization	Publicis & Hal Riney
Location	San Francisco, California
Completed	June 1998
Area	120,000 ft^2 (11,100 m^2)
No. people	350
Designers	EHDD Esherick Homsey Dodge and Davis, San Francisco, California

The design objective was to create a pleasant, inspiring work environment for a hip, young, 350-person international advertising agency. Publicis & Hal Riney moved to a 1970s building with dramatic views of San Francisco Bay. A compressed program was met by streamlined decisions between a small client team, primarily two people who both have senior financial roles, and a tight design team who stayed with every detail of the project through the 10 months from sketch design to move-in. The building was stripped to its bare structure and walls—individual offices that hogged the views and light all around the perimeter were pulled down, and the low ceiling tiles with standard overhead fluorescent lights were junked. In their place the concrete ceiling was painted white, the concrete frame and columns were sandblasted and left exposed, and new services were installed and left in view. A new, dramatic, and inviting entrance was created, and internal streets linked the main elements within each floor. The open, airy quality desired by the client was maintained by placing private offices along the inner-core walls, leaving the views open for everyone (Fig. CH.14.1).

Furniture to complement this open, honest, even brutal shell had to be selected. Brilliant red leather le Corbusier armchairs with white Carrara marble coffee tables invite visitors to relax while waiting (Fig. CH.14.2). The maple reception desk was designed to house four computers shielded behind a perforated screen of satin finish

Figure CH.14.1   Open-plan workspaces are drawn away from the staggered window wall so that all users can enjoy light and view.

(Photograph: Richard Barnes.)

Figure CH.14.2 Red leather armchairs provide a splash of inviting color and comfort in the reception area.

(Photograph: Richard Barnes.)

anodized aluminum. On the next floor level, the client wanted a large, flexible space for client presentations and company parties that could also be used for project team meetings (Fig. CH.14.3). The company already owned a lot of Eames tables and chairs purchased for its earlier buildings and fully appreciated their design quality, durability, and elegance. Black leather and chrome Eames chairs furnish this space plus black granite tabletops on simple chrome legs, drawn from the company's existing inventory. In conference and meeting rooms, there are more Eames chairs and tables and Bellini rectangular and triangular maple tables, some renovated, some new. Vis-à-vis chairs by Citterio are used around meeting tables. Lounge chairs drawn from design masters of earlier decades, Aalto and Kjaerholm, are dotted about to encourage a break from the world of work.

What workstations would be appropriate? The client did not want a standard office system, did not care for corporate cubicles, and wanted furniture that would encourage openness, creativity, and communication. The design team explored several possibilities, considered then rejected a specially designed system, eventually selecting Vitra's Ad Hoc desks designed by Antonio Citterio with Memo spine wall by Mario Bellini and Tolomeo desk lights by Artemide. Three different workstations were chosen: a boomerang shape, a desk with a larger return giving more privacy, and a "unitable" that can be raised or lowered to suit the individual. Storage is contained within the spine wall, and in a mobile "pick-up" unit. The maple desktop is complemented by a perforated metal box to house the CPU, in one of four

Figure CH.14.3 The open edges of the workspace are comfortably and stylishly furnished and available for client presentation, project team meetings, and company parties.

(Photograph: Richard Barnes.)

colors. These colors in turn blend or contrast with the specially woven carpet in five colors. Small perforated screens give some privacy between people and shield the back of monitors from view (Fig. CH.14.4). These elegant, open desks demand a level of tidiness that not all in the company can meet, so a few more screens are now being installed. Within the glass-fronted private offices, Herman Miller Action Office units have been reconditioned, complemented by Eames or Citterio desks.

Rotating, brilliantly colored pinboards are a new piece of furniture invented by the interior architects especially for this project. The screens break up the long floor plate, subdivide workstation clusters into team zones, and give a useful surface for pinning work in progress for others to review.

Figure CH.14.4 The workspaces are furnished with light adjustable pieces of furniture that maintain the open feel of the large space. Small perforated screens give some privacy.

(Photograph: Richard Barnes.)

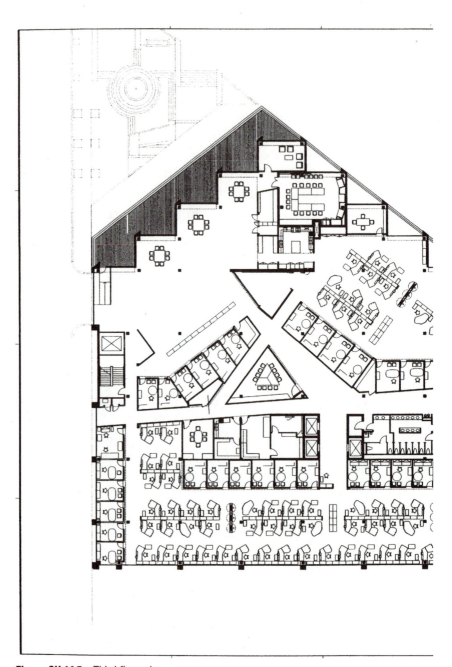

Figure CH.14.5   Third floor plan

(Esherick, Hornsey, Dodge and Davis–EHDD.)

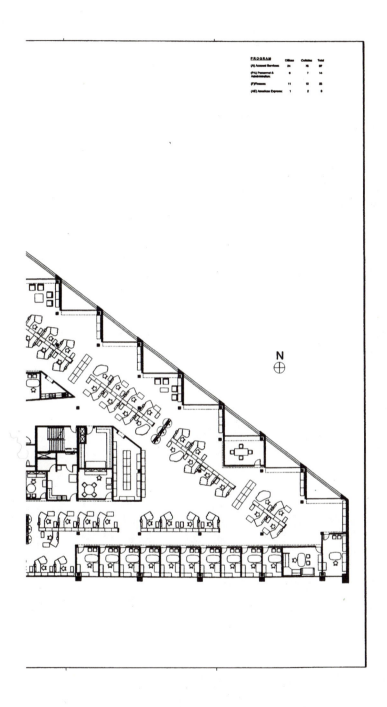

PROGRAM

	Offices	Cubicles	Total
(A) Account Services	24	70	97
(PA) Personnel & Administration	9	7	14
(F) Finance	11	12	25
(AE) American Express	1	2	3

N
⊕

In the words of the interior architect Briggs MacDonald, this was a "particularly enlightened client" who appreciated good design, was already used to working with excellent furniture products, and wanted to maintain high quality. The furniture budget was kept in check by reusing any items of furniture the company already owned that were attractive and in good condition, and refurbishing wood tabletops that showed signs of wear and tear. The remaining budget was used for workstations.

Case History 15. Playing Musical Beanbags

Organization	Rhino Entertainment Company
Location	Los Angeles, California
Completed	1994
Area	36,000 ft^2 (3,300 m^2)
Designers	Beckson Design Associates, Los Angeles, California

When a quirky company, whose business is to re-release music of the 1950s and 1960s, needs to replan its office, a traditional solution with cubicles and classy executive suites for the top people is unlikely to emerge. Rhino needed something utterly different. Beckson Design Associates articulated the philosophy of the owner and company. The corporate values are that companies should be creative, fun, and ecologically responsible—hence, recycled items are embedded into the floor, and recycled cassette cases form the main reception desks (Fig. CH.15.1). Making people feel comfortable is also important. The main gathering point is a multipurpose space next to the cafeteria, a "playroom" furnished with little other than beanbags (Fig. CH.15.2). "Beanbag meetings" are held there to keep everyone

Figure CH.15.1   Rhino's entrance immediately presents core values of the company—music, recycling, casual informality, and mixed styles from the 1950s on.

(*Photograph: Carolyn Cole,* Los Angeles Times.)

informed about company trends, and musicians occasionally give live performances there. A table-tennis table sits adjacent to the gym. In an industry with many freelancers, the aim was to create an environment that would feel like a special "club" where they would be made to feel welcome and part of the club and a place and company with which they would be pleased to be associated. In fact, 10 percent of the floor area is taken up by communal spaces for employees, but these are the crucial areas that most demonstrate company values.

Work areas comprise 45 percent of the area and are mostly open workstations. Standard desks from established furniture manufacturers felt too refined. A rougher image was wanted, and the selected approach was desks made from pegboard and other materials (Fig. CH.15.3). The building itself is newly built, with Rhino the first tenant. To

Figure CH.15.2 Beanbags furnish the open forum where staff meetings are held and musicians sometimes perform.

(*Photograph: Tom Bonner.*)

make it more dynamic, ceilings were omitted, services exposed, then new and varied ceiling planes inserted with varied light fittings. Circulation routes were set at angles zigzagging down the floor plate, and different colors were applied in different zones (Fig. CH.15.4). The building fit out was delivered in eight weeks on a very modest budget.

Figure CH.15.3   Workstations made of pegboard depart from the style found in a standard corporate office environment.

(*Photograph: Tom Bonner.*)

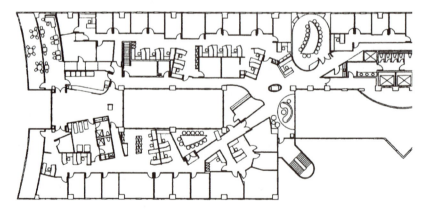

Figure CH.15.4   Plan of the Rhino office showing zigzag circulation and many shared spaces for meetings and employee gatherings.

(*Beckson Design Associates.*)

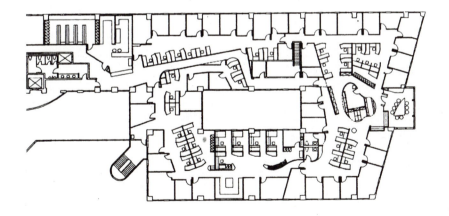

BECKSON DESIGN ASSOCIATES, INC.

Case History 16. Developing a Sense of Responsibility

Organization	Conde Nast
Location	Four Times Square, New York, New York
Completed	1999
Area	1,600,000 ft^2 (150,000 m^2)
Designers	Fox and Fowle, New York, New York

The new 48-story building on the corner of Times Square is a symbol of more than the regeneration of the New York office market. It is a building where the developers, The Durst Organization, and the design team, led by architects Fox and Fowle, have made a heroic effort to perform to the highest standards in terms of energy conservation, air quality, recycling, and building management. The building is also designed sensitively to fit into its environment, respecting the rather different visual conditions of its two main orientations, the neon-dominated Broadway and the more sober Bryant Park, showing that good design can be carried through on many levels.

The first step of the process was to achieve an efficient design method, which, as it always does, means efficient communication—for example, the use of electronic transfer of structural drawings, may have saved about half a million dollars. The team included several groups with specialist knowledge: National Resources Council, the Rocky Mountain Institute, and Consolidated Edison. They helped to address the important aspects of the design: how to achieve an excellent performance for the finished building (Fig. CH.16.1). Good daylight to the interior was helped by the use of low E glass, which allowed large windows without excessive heat gain. Energy consumption was kept down by better levels of insulation, by plant sizes that allow optimum running for the needs of any particular day, and by use of photovoltaic panels in place of regular glass panels on the south and east façades, which produce about 1 percent of the buildings's power. Good air quality was sought by a fivefold increase in the rate of fresh-air intake from 5 cubic ft per minute (cfm) to 25 cfm (14 to 70 liters per minute). A useful spinoff from this is the ability to use the very large air shafts needed for the ventilation system to bring in 100 percent fresh air to a floor that has been recarpeted or newly painted, before occupiers move in. The team also agreed to treat the construction process as one in which waste of materials, time, and energy would be kept to a minimum and health would be protected through control of dangerous materials and education of all concerned.

The tenants can benefit from all the knowledge and expertise generated during this project. The developers have provided a manual to help them understand how to get the most efficient, healthy, effective, and well-managed space for themselves. It addresses lighting, office equipment, indoor air quality, conservation of resources, and construction practices. It remains to be seen whether they will take up this good, unbiased, and helpful advice without having to pay for it. So far they are predictably unwilling to take on it board. The developers may find it necessary to offer more than encouragement, to demand compliance with some of the suggestions in the interests of ensuring that the building remains easy to manage in a responsible way.

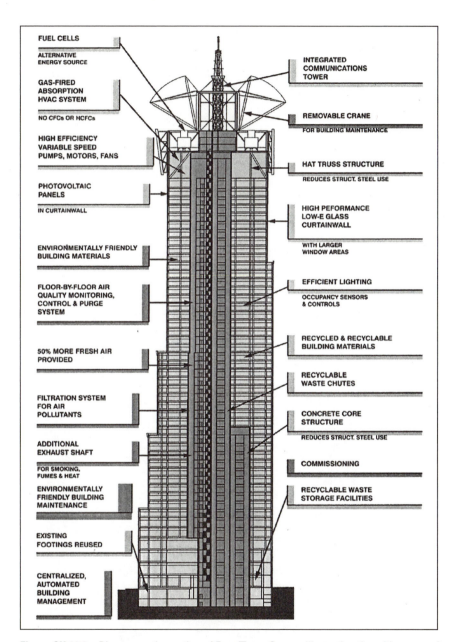

Figure CH.16.1   Diagrammatic section of Four Times Square illustrating the wide range of measures taken to improve the building's performance and to meet very high standards for energy conservation, air quality, recycling, and building management.

(*Fox & Fowle Architects.*)

The bottom line has benefited. The building may save in the order of $1 million per year simply in energy costs. That alone makes it a model worth pursuing. Other measures targeting responsible design set an example that others must watch and emulate.

Case History 17.
Waste Not Want Not

Organization	World Neighbors
Location	Oklahoma City, Oklahoma
Completed	1991
Area	11,100 ft^2, (1,000 m^2)
No. people	26
Designers	Elliot and Associates, Oklahoma City, Oklahoma

World Neighbors is in the nonprofit business of helping people who have very little, or nothing, to help themselves. Their building reflects the spirit in which they work with their "partners"—making the most of minimal resources, a necessity where the budget is tight and money is needed for more important things than an office fit out.

A 10-year-old speculative office building, which had never been occupied, was brought into use, recycled, and refurbished with simple, inexpensive materials and products, often themselves recycled. The layout is abstracted from the plan of an African or Asian village, and thus it avoids the rigidity of standard office planning (Fig. CH.17.1). The route that links the different areas, the departments, is delineated by adding a color stain directly

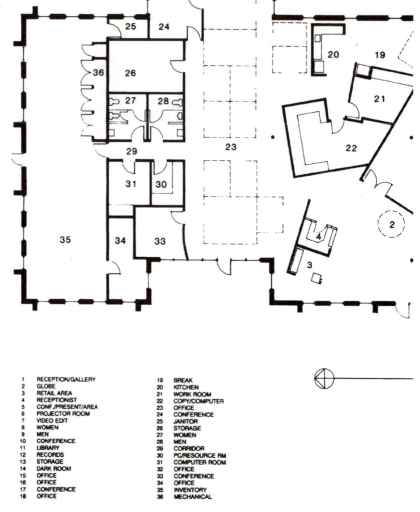

1	RECEPTION/GALLERY	19	BREAK
2	GLOBE	20	KITCHEN
3	RETAIL AREA	21	WORK ROOM
4	RECEPTIONIST	22	COPY/COMPUTER
5	CONF./PRESENT/AREA	23	OFFICE
6	PROJECTOR ROOM	24	CONFERENCE
7	VIDEO EDIT	25	JANITOR
8	WOMEN	26	STORAGE
9	MEN	27	WOMEN
10	CONFERENCE	28	MEN
11	LIBRARY	29	CORRIDOR
12	RECORDS	30	PC/RESOURCE RM
13	STORAGE	31	COMPUTER ROOM
14	DARK ROOM	32	OFFICE
15	OFFICE	33	CONFERENCE
16	OFFICE	34	OFFICE
17	CONFERENCE	35	INVENTORY
18	OFFICE	36	MECHANICAL

Figure CH.17.1   Floor plan that borrows from an informal African village arrangement.

(*Elliot and Associates, Architects.*)

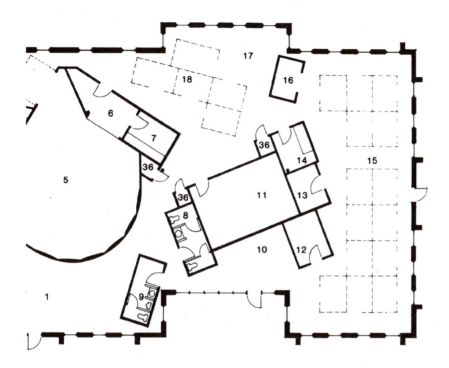

FLOOR PLAN

0   5   10   20

to the concrete as it cures. No carpets here—those are reserved for the workspaces. The roof, constructed from factory-assembled timber trusses, was already appropriate for the intended approach to the design. The interior walls are of oriented strand board, a cheap material, usually used where it cannot be seen (Fig. CH.17.2). There is a special effect in the WCs where the timber flake used for the boards is cedar (Fig. CH.17.3). This gives a special fragrance, which is trapped in the room as long as the door is shut. Over time the scent fades, but it can be revived simply by lightly sanding an area of the wall—a renewable effect. In the WCs other simple items have been incorporated. The lavatory basin is a simple, $8 stainless steel washing-up bowl with a hole in the bottom, fixed to a flat galvanized

Figure CH.17.2   In the reception area, just as elsewhere, the walls are of oriented strand board—unpretentious, functional, and friendly.

(*Photograph: Bob Shimer, Hedrich Blessing.*)

Figure CH.17.3 WCs are designed very simply to achieve maximum effect—right down to the built-in fragrance trapped in the cedar wall.

(*Photograph: Bob Shimer, Hedrich Blessing.*)

steel counter by the plumbing fittings. The mirrors in each WC are different, searched out in flea markets, secondhand. There are simple lights that can be bought from the local hardware store. In common with some other spaces, artificial light is not needed in daylight hours as light is borrowed from the skylights in the roof through the translucent double layer of corrugated fiberglass.

The reception area makes an immediate and relevant impact with its huge inflatable globe symbolizing the international scope and the name "World Neighbors" itself. An African stool forms the table for visitors, who sit on simple polypropylene stacking chairs. The office furniture is also all recycled—system furniture that has already served one organization has been reupholstered, using natural and neutral colors, and is given a new lease on life just as the people helped by World Neighbors.

Case History 18. Student Union in Ideas Factory

Organization	BBDO West
Location	Los Angeles, California
Completed	1996
Area	45,000 ft² (4,200 m²)
No. people	200 plus
Designers	Beckson Design Associates, Los Angeles, California

Team discussions over the net during a table tennis game is how people at advertising agency BBDO West now work. Management has realized that people are the greatest asset of this creative company. To help them enjoy work, the associated "play" areas are at least as important as the workstations in the new layouts created by Beckson Design Associates, despite taking up only 5 percent of the total space (Fig. CH.18.1).

BBDO occupied two and a half floors of a 25-story building. The aim of the refurbishment was to increase communication and interaction between different parts of the organization, to make the space feel completely new, and strip it of the staid gray granite, gray walls, gray carpet image. Today the carpet is a riot of technicolor patchwork

Figure CH.18.1   Part of the "student union," with table tennis, café, and bleacher seating for large team meetings.

(*Photograph: Tom Bonner.*)

carpet tiles. Unconventional displays of BBDO's advertising products allow clients to gauge the agency. Ceilings are open, structure and services are exposed, and lighting is indirect. Twenty meeting rooms are planned, and one, known as the "star chamber," has walls forming a star in plan (Figs. CH.18.2 and CH.18.3).

One workplace standard for everyone was introduced to replace the earlier hierarchical set. Traditional enclosed offices with everyone organized by department were abandoned, and people are instead organized into client core teams. Workstations are made up of industrial components—unistrut posts and laminate desks. There are many options for panel materials, each suited in a different way

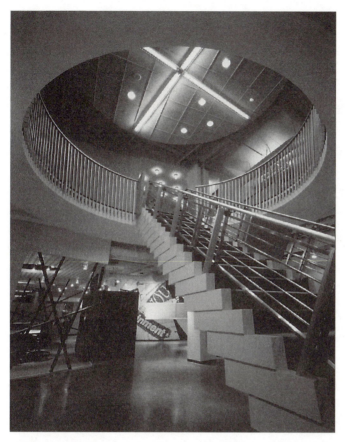

Figure CH.18.2   View of stair, circular balcony, and foyer meeting room.

(*Photograph: Tom Bonner.*)

for writing or display: chalkboard; perforated steel to which pictures may be tacked up with magnets; corkboard; mdf; boards composed of recycled banknotes; and tectum and dry-marker panels (Fig. CH.18.4).

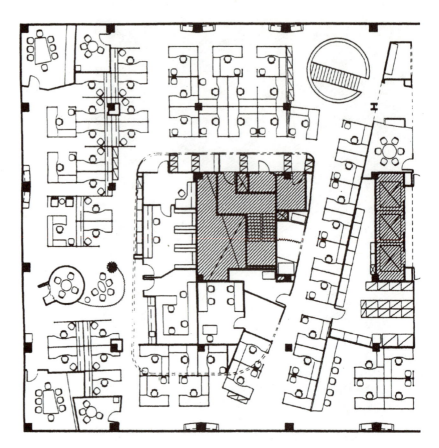

Figure CH.18.3   Plan of the two BBDO West floors showing the stairway connecting them. (*Beckson Design Associates.*)

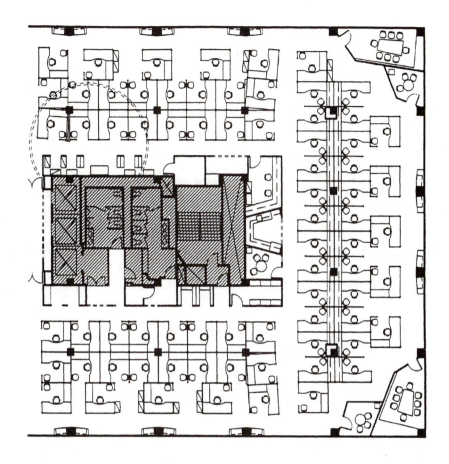

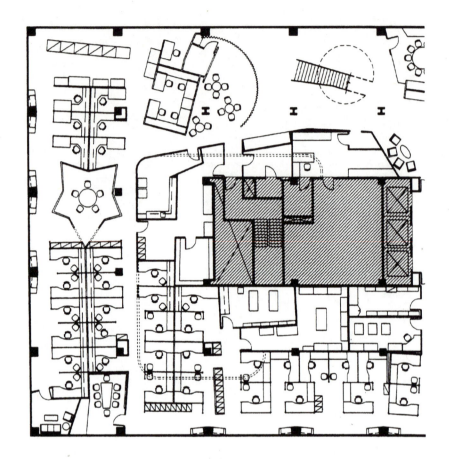

BBDO
WEST

Figure CH.18.3   *(Continued)* Plan of the two BBDO floors showing the stairway connecting them.

(Beckson Design Associates.)

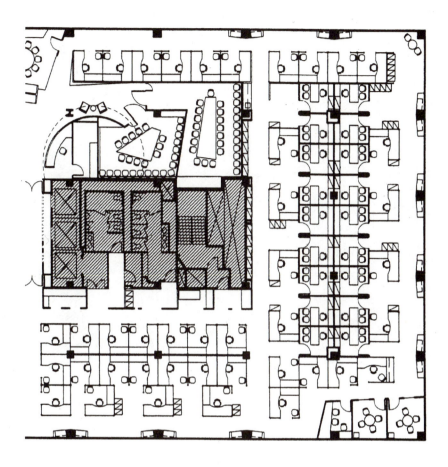

Figure CH.18.4   Workstations of Unistrut with a variety of infill panel, all selected for writing on or displaying works in process.

(*Photograph: Tom Bonner.*)

Case Study 19. Fun and Sun

Organization	TBWA/Chiat/Day
Location	Playa Vista, Los Angeles, California
Completed	1998
Area	120,000 ft² (11,150 m²)
No. people	540
Designers	Clive Wilkinson Architects, Los Angeles, California

A lofty warehouse has been transformed into a small town, a hive of activity housing over 500 staff in the headquarters of TBWA/Chiat/Day, the advertising agency that captured plenty of publicity for its previous New York City and Los Angeles buildings. In this one they seem to have struck a happy balance between a facility that suits their work style, and their play times too, and one that can let them expand and develop into the future.

The city planning image crops up frequently in describing office buildings. The introduction of many activities not considered to be "office," such as coffee bars, shops, banks, and fitness centers, gives weight to the idea of a "Main Street" from which shared amenities can be reached and where people can meet. Reinforcing this feeling is a range of structures along the street, of different numbers of stories, as you would find in a small town. Team meeting spaces, lightly screened in stretched fabric, are, as the designer Clive Wilkinson described, at the edges in the equivalent to "lower-value real estate" and can be transformed inexpensively to provide more workstations (Figs. CH. 19.1 to 19.3).

As all successful towns that wish to retain their young and lively population should do, this one has paid attention to the leisure needs of staff. There is a basketball court, a clubhouse cafeteria and a "park" with trees and small tables such as you might find in Paris (Fig. CH.19.4). An indoor basketball court is a fairly extreme example of a more commonly found amenity, a fitness facility—but probably much more popular and certainly good for people whose jobs are based on teamwork (Fig. CH.19.5). Its presence recognizes that people who work hard also need to play hard. Surfboards, a reflection of the local beach culture, were brought into their earlier building, under the guise of a large conference table. That conference table was transferred to this building when they outgrew their old space. Surfboards have a sufficiently large scale to hold their own in this large environment, and the theme has been continued into the bar.

As an advertising agency, TBWA/Chiat/Day has "toys" that accumulated after particular campaigns were over or that took someone's fancy and were bought for fun such as the tilt-a-whirl cars or the London telephone box that has been placed at the side of the park or the yellow bicycle that appeared with the yellow cliff dwellings. This "town" is flexible enough to accommodate varied leisure and support facilities that will serve TBWA/Chiat/Day now and that will accept the increased population if, as they plan, they expand by more than half as much again. That is the nice thing about shared amenities. They serve a wide range of people, and when they are as numerous as here, they can serve people with different tastes and preferences.

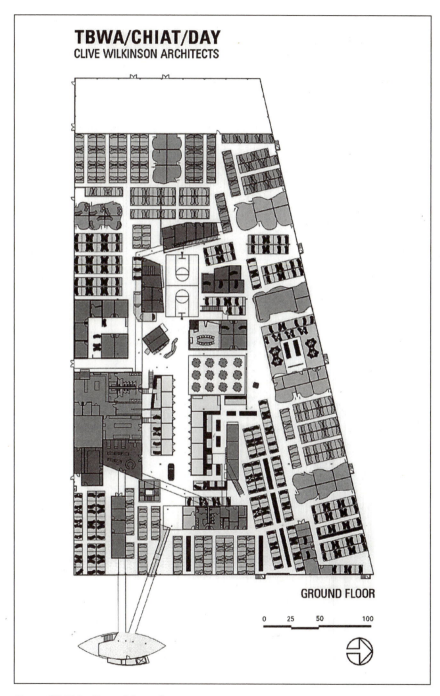

Figure CH.19.1 Ground-floor plan.

(*Clive Wilkinson Architects.*)

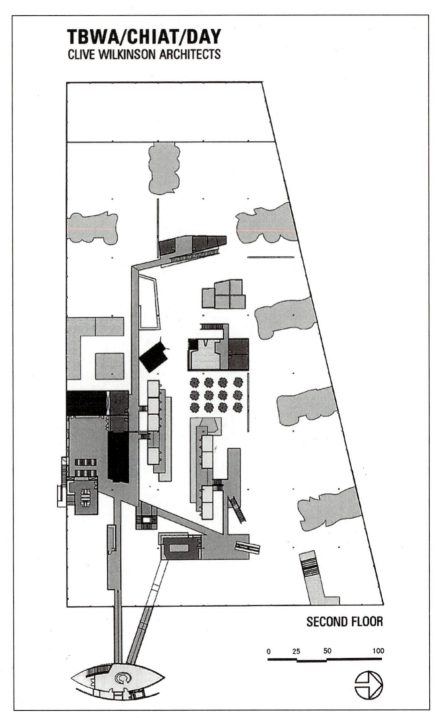

Figure CH.19.2   Second-floor plan.

(*Clive Wilkinson Architects.*)

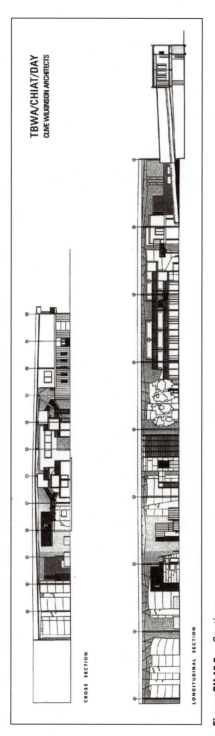

Figure CH.19.3.   Sections.

(*Clive Wilkinson Architects.*)

Figure CH.19.4.   Tables and chairs dotted among the trees in the park are well used for informal meetings, both work and social.

(Photograph: fotoworks—Benny Chan.)

Figure CH.19.5   The basketball court at the end of Main Street is overlooked by a large video monitor.

(Photograph: fotoworks—Benny Chan.)

Several different types of office space are needed here, again like the variety in a small town. The three-story cliff dwellings are designed for the copywriters and designers, the creative talent on which the business is based, who need privacy and pampering (Fig. CH.19.6). Open desk areas, filled with a specially designed desk, the Nest, developed in partnership with Steelcase, suit general uses (Fig. CH.19.7). Variety comes in the use of different colors—green, blue, and black—in different areas of the building. The design production office needed, and was given, a different sort of furniture altogether and an environment tailored to their preferences.

Figure CH.19.6 The design studio, where artwork is created and stored, is crossed by stairs connecting mezzanine levels.

(Photograph: fotoworks—Benny Chan.)

Figure CH.19.7 The Nest workstations, looking like a green orchard landscape when seen from above, were developed by the architects with Steelcase. Stretched fabric is used to screen meeting areas.

(*Photograph: fotoworks—Benny Chan.*)

As the population grows, new environments will be created, though always with a desk for each. No more virtual offices for TBW/Chiat/Day, at least not as they see it now. They pioneered some of the most celebrated and exciting examples of alternative offices in their earlier buildings—but not without pain. Their people are often at their desks, generate a great deal of paper, and depend on sparking off each other for creative edge. They are not the most obvious type for unassigned desks, hot-desking, or hoteling. With all its amenities, this building could serve an itinerant population well. But such groups do not have a monopoly of need for good-quality amenities. More and more people demand a way to make the work environment more fulfilling, to improve their life-work balance, and here it can be seen that provision of amenities is one way to do it. This population, where everyone has a desk of their own, is certainly happy with its new home.

Case History 20. Escape the Cube, Destroy the Box

Organization	Arthur Andersen, Human Capital Services
Location	Chicago, Illinois
Completed	May 1998
Area	13,000 ft^2 (1,200 m^2)
No. people	80
Designers	GHK, Chicago, Illinois

Rectangular buildings constructed with repetitive structural frames, rows of standard cubes or desks in parallel rows, acoustic ceiling tiles in standard square grids with standard overhead fluorescent light fittings, square carpet tiles laid in lines. That is how most office space is arranged, and Arthur Andersen's Chicago Tax office was no exception—650 people working in just the same mechanistic layout—at least until the Human Capital Services group, HCS, decided to destroy most of the office planning gospel. They wanted to think outside the box. By the time they had done so, neither cube nor box were evident.

Human Capital Services at Arthur Andersen is a part of the tax division but with an image quite different from the rest of the division—HCS is more like an advertising agency with a people focus. After being restructured, they wanted to express their new departmental image, use space efficiently, and to save real estate expenditure where possible. Designers GHK worked closely with the client team to create an innovative solution. Analysis of needs and test layouts were defined in parallel.

The result is a new layout and image that has truly changed the way HCS works (Fig. CH.20.1). Storage was rationalized in some cases by as much as 80 percent from 25 to 5 file drawers for partners, from 10 to 2 file drawers for other staff. Partners and managers moved from closed to open workstations of half the original area. Other staff relinquished their own private cubicles surrounded by high

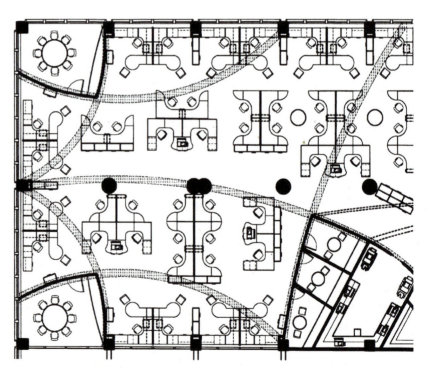

Figure CH.20.1   Floor plan. Curved walls, patterned carpets, and changes in ceiling levels and shapes transform a rectangular office box into a varied and attractive environment. (*GHK.*)

walls, to use any one of a pool of open desks with low screens (Fig. CH.20.2).

The appearance of the office is utterly altered by skillful interior design. Curved walls, carpet swirls, and variations in the height and pattern of ceiling materials have transformed the boxlike office (Fig. CH.20.3). A glazed circular meeting room sets the scene on entry (Fig. CH.20.4). Corner spaces are again used for meetings (Fig. CH.20.5). A family kitchen, open to the work areas, is the main gathering point in which birthdays and other special occasions are celebrated with cakes, cookies, sometimes champagne. Small quiet rooms and a library area can house heads-down work. Burnished aluminum ceiling tiles

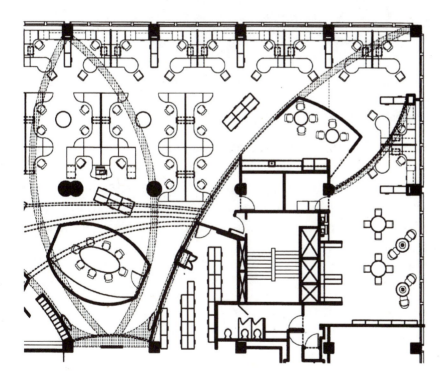

Figure CH.20.2 Two workstation standards are used: one for partners and managers, another for more junior consultants.

(Photograph: Charlie Mayer.)

and varied reflective surfaces add texture and interest to the environment.

The net result is an environment that reflects and encourages an atmosphere of teamwork, openness, innovation, and efficiency. Being outside the box has never looked or felt so good.

Figure CH.20.3 Ceiling forms have been altered, and reflective metal tiles give character and life to the open areas

(Photograph: Charlie Mayer.)

Figure CH.20.4 Curved geometry is introduced into a rectilinear shell, drawing staff and clients into the office.

(Photograph: Charlie Mayer.)

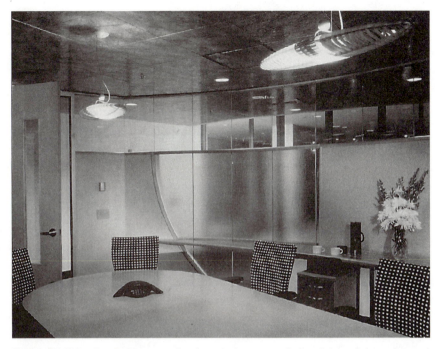

Figure CH.20.5 A consistent application of clerestory glazing brings light to internal rooms.

(Photograph: Charlie Mayer.)

Case History 21. Technology Plus Interior Design Equals Client Solutions

Organization	PricewaterhouseCoopers (PwC)
Location	The Zone, Philadelphia, Pennsylvania
Completed	February 1999
Area	20,000 ft^2 (1,900 m^2)
No. people	50
Designers	Gensler, New York, New York

The Zone is a setting unlike any other—a radical new form of office training and development center that employs theatrical lighting and new technology to help visitors rethink their business problems. PricewaterhouseCoopers created the Zone as a totally new way of doing business, a specialized drop-in center where technology-based solutions are demonstrated and developed for clients. It has three main purposes: First, it is a showcase for potential clients illustrating that PwC can solve their complex business problems; second, it houses training workshops for senior executives to embrace new technology; and third, it is a working area where integrated system solutions are developed.

The space draws you in to a touchpad kiosk in the entry and autopoles with Internet access to receive information quickly and easily. You are then drawn down a corridor leading to the presentation rooms that allude to the dynamic nature of technology—the space is constantly transformed through the use of sound, video, and lighting. Stainless-steel and terrazzo floor and wall surfaces reflect lighting that cycles between green, red, blue, and white spectra. Technobeams flit over the floor with changing images (Fig. CH.21.1).

Figure CH.21.1   Changing colored lights reflect on stainless steel and terrazzo to create an energizing and dramatic atmosphere.

(*Photograph: P. Warchol.*)

Visitors are given a wireless telephone on entry and access to the Internet, then escorted to presentation rooms equipped with the latest cutting-edge technology. Colored lights, multimedia, and backlit images provide all the color against neutral finishes and furniture. Four rooms are specially set up for four different economic sectors with different imagery and technology. The financial services room expresses key industry concerns of globalization and convergence. An illuminated global map fills one wall; on another is a large plasma screen; on a third are clocks from around the globe and an illuminated ticker tape of share prices plus a dozen monitors to display different systems simultaneously (Fig. CH.21.2). In the energy room, sequential screens demonstrate the effect of one computer program on

Figure CH.21.2 The financial services room has an illuminated global map, clocks, ticker tape of share prices, multiple computer screens, and furniture evoking Wall Street.
(*Photograph: P. Warchol.*)

Figure CH.21.3   The energy industry is symbolized by dynamic, restless furniture on wheels and sequential screens.

(Photograph: P. Warchol.)

another. The furniture is mobile for the group to configure as desired (Fig. CH.21.3). The consumer and industrial products room uses materials to represent different industries and a multitude of wall-mounted and ceiling-hung projectors (Fig. CH.21.4).

Presentation rooms have multimedia audiovisual equipment designed for easy use: video and data conferencing on screens; audio conferencing that can be activated from anywhere in the room so that people can move around the

Figure CH.21.4 Consumer and industrial products are shown through many different materials and computer images onto wall and ceiling screens.

(*Photograph: P. Warchol.*)

room freely instead of hovering over one speaker phone; electronic whiteboards linked to computers; and a wireless keyboard that can be used anywhere.

The data center houses 85 servers that bring all the required technology into the Zone. Six satellite dishes on the roof bring in 120 channels from around the world.

The aim of the PwC creator of the space, Scott van Valkenburg, was to invent an environment in which people's creativity could emerge, to let them feel at ease, to stimulate all senses, and to make people smile. "I wanted to give them an experience so that, at the end of a day in the Zone, they would be bursting to go home and tell their kids what they had done that day."

Case History 22. Inside Out

Organization	Bank of America Dealer Loan Center
Location	Las Vegas, Nevada
Completed	1995
Area	90,000 ft^2 (8,350 m^2)
No. people	400
Designers	Interior Architects

Bank of America set out to capture a large share of what was a new market for them, car loans. To achieve this, they needed a facility that would support their business in every detail. So they designed it inside out. The early planning took the form of a number of "vision sessions," large group meetings for 25 and more people. These sessions were forums in which the bank and specialists could work together to help define the brief. The technology that would be needed was the most important feature, as this was to be a data-driven paperless environment, using IT to enhance productivity and provide the market edge. Interior Architects participated from the earliest possible stage, before a city or site had been chosen, before there was a business case or any real project details. Taking part in the early stages enabled them to suggest to Bank of America a rather unusual concept—namely, that interior planning with a detailed layout should be prepared prior to the design of the building. The documentation they were to provide would be used to roll out a whole series of centers for car dealership loans if the business was successful.

At a very early stage, therefore, furniture decisions were made. The desk footprint was to be relatively small as the office was to be truly paperless so only a PC would be on the desk. It had to have a large monitor as split-screen format would be needed to give the operators sufficient information. Two furniture companies were contacted, told the requirements, and asked to come up with suggested workstation configurations. A choice was made, which then allowed the footprint to be defined, a 6- by 6-ft (1.8 × 1.8 m) workstation. The building was then planned around this module to be maximally efficient. The features that were to be incorporated were planned and laid out according to the client's vision and needs. When that was complete, a local architect, in the chosen city, Las Vegas, was brought on board to design the shell around the layout. Decisions until that point had largely been made unconstrained by the characteristics of any existing building. Ceilings that were 12 ft high (3.7 m) and large circulation spaces were incorporated to allow a sense of space and let light penetrate to give the staff a sense of space despite the small desk footprint (Fig. CH.22.1). The subfloor cable routes were planned for future flexibility. The structural grid was planned to accommodate the workplace footprint, but, to ensure freedom to move desks, the servicing grid is repeated at halfway points in both directions. This is essential as the "teaming" work style means that groups have to be continually reconfigured, which requires plenty of access opportunities.

Within three months of moving in, this new business had succeeded in becoming to all intents and purposes a paper-

Figure CH.22.1 The double-height lobby does double duty—to impress clients when they visit and to act as an information center and weekly meeting place for the staff.

(*Photograph: Beatriz Coll.*)

less office. There are no paper files, no bound manuals. All incoming mail and paperwork are immediately scanned and available on PCs. Security is exceptionally important as the center is wholly dependent on data safety. The valuable hardware is all on the second floor, out of reach of floods and protected from intruders. Standby power, sufficiently large to allow a second similar building to use the same unit, is located outside the building. Card-key control is used, and staff enter past a security guard.

The building acts as a showcase, an opportunity to bring customers and prospects to see what is going on. They enter the dramatic double-height lobby where they can catch brief sight of the office floors. After a presentation in the video conference room, they can step out onto a curved "stage" 3 ft high (90 cm), which provides an overview of the entire floor (Fig. CH.22.2). From here the colored panels at the desks identify the teams and are clearly visible so that the staff working for a specific part of the country can readily be pointed out to dealers from that area (Fig. CH.22.3).

The building has been a successful marketing tool, and the IT investment has been justified by productivity. The business has grown sufficiently so that a second similar cen-

Figure CH.22.2   Above the video conference room, informal meeting areas have a terrific view over the lobby and beyond.

(*Photograph: Beatriz Coll.*)

Figure CH.22.3 Groups of workstations accommodate teams, which are identified by colored panels incorporated in the supervisor's desk.

(*Photograph: Beatriz Coll.*)

ter has been built, based on the original documentation and adjacent to the first, on another part of the lot originally bought by the bank. "Inside-out design," giving an interior design firm the unusual role of designing the building, has worked. A clear understanding of the business started with deciding what technology would be needed to support the business process and how the staff would work. This enabled a very fast track project, eight months from starting design to occupation, to provide a launching pad for a successful business venture (Fig. CH.22.4).

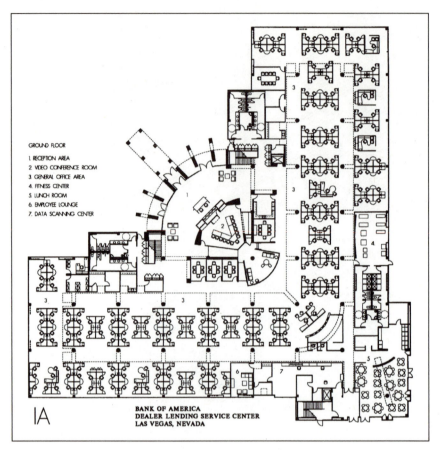

Figure CH.22.4   Ground-floor plan. Various staff amenities have been incorporated: a fitness center, a lounge, and a lunch room.

(*Interior Architects.*)

Case History 23.
Low-Energy Elegance

Organization	Commerzbank
Location	Frankfurt, Germany
Completed	1999
Area	1,300,000 ft^2 (120,000 m^2) gross
Number of people	2,400
Designers	Foster and Partners, London

A 46-story office block, laid out in relatively traditional German style, is a bold experiment in energy-saving design. Tall buildings in central city areas, dependent on many sophisticated systems, are prime candidates for extravagant energy use to keep them going. This one sets out to be different, and it gains brownie points for responsible behavior as well as coming out shining with style.

The building has been carefully slotted into the city grain, adjacent to the existing Commerzbank building, also a tall building. It shares a covered "Plaza" with its parent where a café and restaurant are accessible to the public as well as to bank staff. Other uses, such as apartments over shops, are also embraced by the base of the building (Fig. CH.23.1).

Higher up the unusual element reveals just how extraordinary this building is. In order to devise a system of natural ventilation that would allow maximum health for

Figure CH.23.1   The 46-story building fits into its city context by widening at the base and sharing space at ground level with its neighbors. (*Photograph: Ian Lambot.*)

the occupants, planting has been introduced, but not just a well-planted atrium or cascades of ivy from balconies but multiple "sky" gardens busily breathing out oxygen that is circulated to the people in the building as part of the natural ventilation system. On each face of the triangular building, every 12 stories, the office façade gives way to a plain glass wall slightly canted out to reduce reflections. Behind this is a garden four stories high open to the atrium (Fig. CH.23.2). The gardens on the different faces start at different floors, so that on each floor one-third of the plan is taken up by a sky garden. This means that all occupants are near a garden on their own floor to which they can walk, and also they are only one or two stories from others at the two other sides across the atrium, above or below them. The planting varies with the orientation to which it opens (Figs. CH.23.3 through CH.23.5).

The gardens are not just for looks. They are an integral part of the ventilation system, which, with all its features, is planned to save one-half to two-thirds of purchased energy costs. The system relies on a *breathing wall* and *stack effect ventilation*—that is, a double-skin wall with a 6.5-in (165-mm) cavity where the inner skin can be opened locally to allow people in the offices to bring in fresh air

Figure CH.23.2 Looking out into the atrium to see the ancient olive trees in a Mediterranean garden just below.

(Photograph: Ian Lambot.)

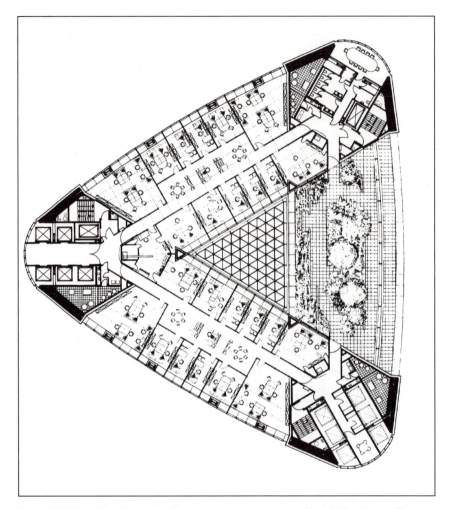

Figure CH.23.3   Plan of a typical floor with the more common Combi office layout. The corridor becomes wider in the center of the floor to accommodate the shared area for interaction.

(*Foster and Partners.*)

from outside or atrium air on the inner face. The glass screens outside the gardens can open at the top to balance the amount of fresh air coming into the atrium. Conventional convector heating under the windows, chilled ceilings powered by Frankfurt's urban steam mains, venetian blinds

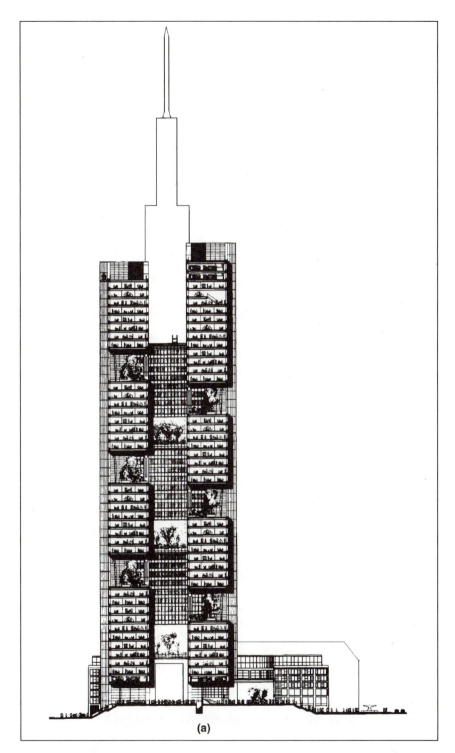

(a)

Figure CH.23.4a and b Building section (a) and diagram (b), showing the way in which the arrangement of atrium and sky garden space maximizes natural ventilation.

(*Foster and Partners.*)

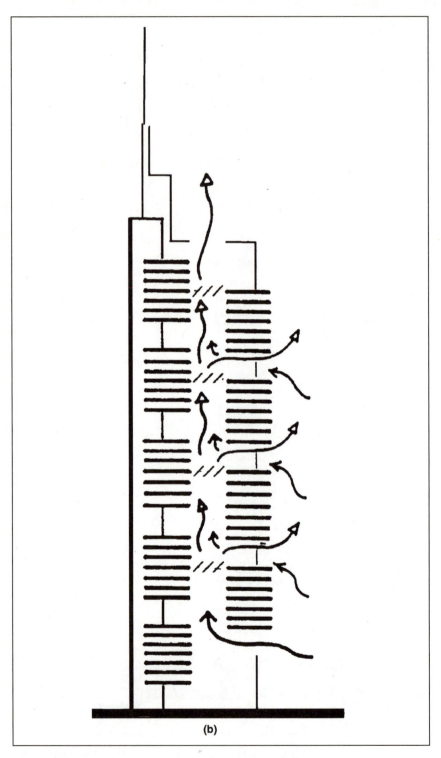

(b)

Figure CH.23.4a and b   Building section (a) and diagram, (b) showing the way in which the arrangement of atrium and sky garden space maximizes natural ventilation.

(*Foster and Partners.*)

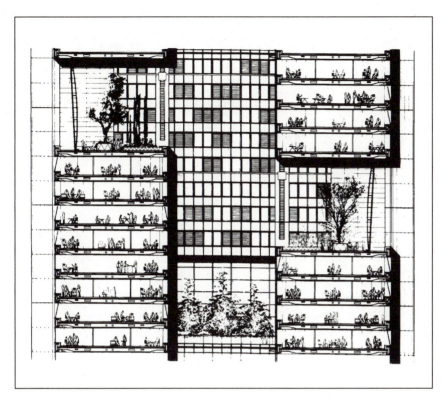

Figure CH.23.5 Section showing relationship of atrium to sky gardens. (*Foster and Partners.*)

in the window cavity, low-E glazing—all have a role in the temperature control, and a BMS balances the complex system modifying the outside conditions to suit the occupants. Other energy efficiencies include gray water from chillers being reused in WCs, use of only cold water in lavatory handwash basins, and automatic switches to turn lights off when spaces are unoccupied.

As a prototype, it is unreasonable to expect this building to out-perform the original aspirations, but the world needs more clients looking for responsible design and more examples to choose from when deciding on an energy strategy, so Commerzbank is to be congratulated on the project.

Case History 24. Value Added for Staff in an Unpromising Building Shell

Organization	National Electronic Warranty Company
Location	Great Falls, Montana
Completed	1998
Area	23,000 ft^2 (2,100 m^2)
No. people	220 workplaces
Designers	CORE, Washington, D.C.

It started out as a windowless box, a building that had housed telephone switch gear (Fig. CH.24.1). Now two floors have been devoted to a new call center, a 24-hour, 7-day facility with 220 workspaces and about 300 employees working shifts. This could have resulted in a dismal environment, with the usual rapid turnover of staff of anything up to 300 percent per year. This one is a bit different. People who work in call centers are generally not given many perks or facilities. Hours are spent sitting at a desk with a headset, a computer, and a manual—that is all. Most people who call in do so not because they are having a good day so staff stress levels may rise. In spite of the clear need to group people in formal functional teams and keep up the pressure for high levels of performance—the objective is that no caller is left on hold—the client wanted to emphasize the importance of employee comfort and provide a relaxed and positive atmosphere.

Windows have been inserted on the second and third floors of this building to bring natural light into some parts of the working floor and some special areas such as the large meeting room. There is also a small smokers' balcony on the second floor, open to the outside air, considered an essential facility by the client, despite the cost of making the opening. These openings were tricky as there had been several phases of construction all subsequently overclad, so it was not possible to know what would be found when opening up, and the costs stood in danger of escalating.

The approach to the design of the interior has focused on the psychological needs of the users. Standard call centers often have lay-in acoustical ceilings and light fittings providing high levels of illumination. Here much lower levels of lighting have been provided. The ambient light is low and

Figure CH.24.1   Three hundred employees are housed on the second and third floors of what was once a windowless telephone switch-gear building.

(*Photograph: Michael Moran.*)

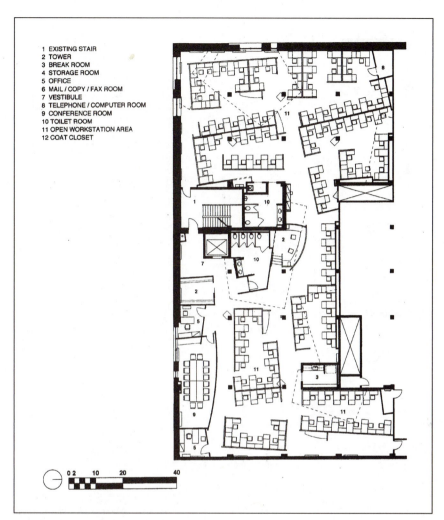

1 EXISTING STAIR
2 TOWER
3 BREAK ROOM
4 STORAGE ROOM
5 OFFICE
6 MAIL / COPY / FAX ROOM
7 VESTIBULE
8 TELEPHONE / COMPUTER ROOM
9 CONFERENCE ROOM
10 TOILET ROOM
11 OPEN WORKSTATION AREA
12 COAT CLOSET

0 2   10   20   40

Figure CH.24.2   Second-floor plan.
(*CORE.*)

indirect in the work areas, and it reflects off sections of lowered ceiling that are a dark blue. This was designed to prevent eye fatigue and to create a more tranquil environment. Darker and more saturated colors are used throughout to promote a soothing environment, which is needed in a job that is both stressful and of limited stimulus. Shifts arrive in five-minute increments, and every 6 months there is a

Figure CH.24.3   Third-floor plan—the smokers' balcony provides the only opening on this floor. It was costly, but the client insisted on providing it for staff.
(*CORE.*)

lottery for a reallocation of the time slots. Staff sit in rows facing their supervisor.

The work areas are more open than is sometimes found in call centers, with very low screens between people. This is intended to ensure that they talk quietly These screens are made of translucent material, further increasing the sense of openness. Acoustics do not seem to present a problem, the background noise of the mechanical system providing a level of white noise. As well as attention to the quality of the work areas, the design has incorporated a number of other facilities. A training room and a work out room as well as the smoking balcony are provided on the upper floor and an area for sitting at meal times and during breaks (Figs. CH.24.4 through CH.24.6).

The thought put into this design seems to have paid off. The turnover of staff here is far lower than generally found in call centers, about 40 percent, and there is a waiting list of over 200 people seeking employment. The client is sufficiently pleased with the results to be planning a second and much larger facility in the same town. The use of this building as a facility to which clients can be brought indicates that there is plenty of scope for greatly increased business in this area.

Figure CH.24.4 The supervisor's station shows how the intersection and layering of lines and planes generate a three-dimensional landscape within the existing envelope.

(*Photograph: Michael Moran.*)

Figure CH.24.5   The roof is exposed in some areas and lowered elsewhere to allow indirect light to bounce off it, creating a gently lit work area.

(*Photograph: Michael Moran.*)

Figure CH.24.6 Facilities for the employees have been welcomed, and staff turnover is low.

(*Photograph: Michael Moran.*)

Case History 25.
Internet Company HQ
Attracts Talent

Organization	Excite Headquarters
Location	Redwood City, California
Completed	July 1997
Area	88,000 ft^2 (8,200 m^2)
No. people	400, approximately
Designers	STUDIOS, San Francisco, California

Excite, Inc., a fast-growing Internet search engine company, was founded by a group of adventurous Stanford graduates interested in exploring the possibilities of the Internet. They needed a new corporate headquarters that would provide the technology infrastructure and the right environment for their evolving corporate culture. They needed to attract the best and brightest young journalists and engineers to create a dynamic new-media company for the twenty-first century.

A cavernous, obsolete warehouse, separated into two sections, was acquired (Fig. CH.25.1). The data center, located in a vast circular drum, was strategically placed in the center of the space, a symbol of the essential technology for a company in cyberspace. The center of the building is raised up on a platform, and all social and meeting spaces are elevated onto it (Fig. CH.25.2). A catwalk and stairways

Figure CH.25.1   The new headquarters for Excite was designed within an existing, tilt up concrete warehouse.

(Photograph: Michael O'Callahan.)

Figure CH.25.2   A platform raised 18 in (0.5 m) holds meeting, social, and group spaces and acts spatially as the key communications link.

(Photograph: Michael O'Callahan.)

connect to the upper floor. A brilliant red slide is an alternate way of changing level—a memorable attraction for potential new recruits who try the ride (Fig. CH.25.3). Once a week, everyone in the company is invited to a pizza lunch for quick dissemination of information in the central platform breakout area.

Open workstations measuring 8 by 8 ft (2.4 × 2.4 m) are high-quality cubes of neutral, calm gray. In contrast, brightly colored walls and billboards signal the communal areas. Glazed private offices for one or two people line the

Figure CH.25.3 The office space is punctuated by splashes of color and fun.

(Photograph: Michael O'Callahan.)

edges, allowing some daylight to enter. Though views are limited, a high level of natural light penetrates through the roof and the lofty spaces, reaching to 27 ft (8.2 m) high. All the services—cable trays and electrical raceways—are visible through the exposed steel trusses (Fig. CH.25.4).

This inward-focused plan is designed to use the building in the best possible way by providing high-energy places to congregate, surrounded by peaceful workplaces for people to concentrate (Fig. CH.25.5). Rapid exchange of information is facilitated. Advertising billboards further communicate new-media messages similar to the World Wide Web. And all this is achieved at a modest budget that does not drain resources from its mainstream business investments.

Figure CH.25.4   The design utilizes several workspace types: the semi-open-plan work-station, the enclosed office, and open mezzanine team spaces.

(Photograph: Michael O'Callahan.)

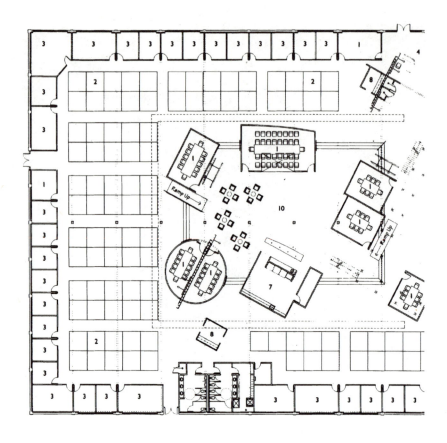

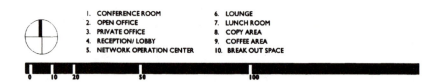

1.	CONFERENCE ROOM	6.	LOUNGE
2.	OPEN OFFICE	7.	LUNCH ROOM
3.	PRIVATE OFFICE	8.	COPY AREA
4.	RECEPTION/ LOBBY	9.	COFFEE AREA
5.	NETWORK OPERATION CENTER	10.	BREAK OUT SPACE

Figure CH.25.5   Ground-floor plan showing the 18-in (0.5 m) raised platform that collects a series of team and social facilities.

(*STUDIOS Architecture.*)

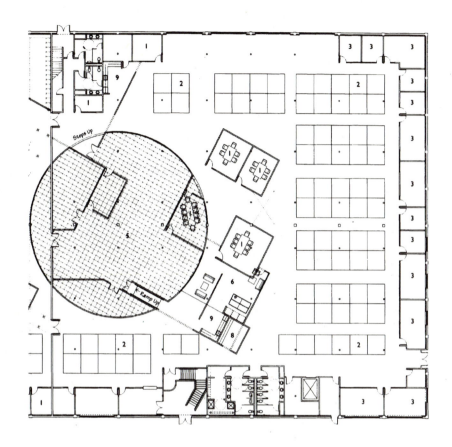

eXcite

PHASE I + II

Bibliography

Apgar, M. IV. 1998. "The Alternative Workplace: Changing Where and How People Work." *Harvard Business Review,* May–June, pp. 121–136.

Asensio Cerver, F. 1998. *Extraordinary Offices*. New York: Hearst Books International.

Bailey, S. 1990. *Offices*. London: Butterworth Architecture.

Becker, F. 1990. *The Total Workplace: Facilities Management and the Elastic Organization*. New York: Van Nostrand Reinhold.

Becker, F., and F. Steele. 1995. *Workplace by Design: Mapping the High-Performance Workscape*. San Francisco: Jossey-Bass.

Berger-Levrault, Nancy. 1984. *L'Empire du bureau 1900–2000*.

Brandt, P. 1992. *Office Design*. New York: Whitney Library of Design.

Brill, M., et al., and Buffalo Organization for Social and Technological Innovation (BOSTI). 1984. *Using Office Space to Increase Productivity.* Buffalo: BOSTI.

Brill, M. 1994. *Now Offices, No Offices, New Offices: Wild Times in the World of Office Work.* Toronto: Tekmon.

British Council for Offices. 1994. *Specification for Urban Offices.* Reading: B.C.O.

Building Research Establishment BREEAM/New Offices. 1993. *An Environmental Assessment for New Office Designs.* Watford: BRE Publications.

Clarke, A. C. 1973. *Profiles of the Future.* London: Gollancz, 1962; 2d ed., London: Pan.

Craig, M. 1981. *Office Workers' Survival Handbook: A Guide to Fighting Health Hazards in the Office.* London: BSSRS.

Curwell, C., C. March, and R. Venables R. (eds.). 1990. *Buildings and Health: The Rosehaugh Guide.* London: RIBA Publications.

Duffy, F. 1992. *The Changing Workplace.* London: Phaidon.

———. 1997. *The New Office.* London: Conran Octopus.

Duffy, F., A. Laing, and V. Crisp. 1993. *The Responsible Workplace.* London: Butterworth Architecture and Estates Gazette.

Eley, J. 1996. "Creating Flexible Workspace." *Facilities Management Guide,* no. 12, August, pp. 1–16.

Eley, J., and A. F. Marmot. 1997–1998. "Furniture." Six articles in *Space Management,* vol. 2, May 1997; vol. 3, August 1997; vol. 4, November 1997; vol. 5, February 1998; vol. 2/3, August 1998; vol. 2/4, November 1998.

Eley, J., and A. F. Marmot. 1995. *Understanding Offices: What Every Manager Needs to Know about Office Buildings.* London: Penguin Books.

Gorman, F., and C. Brown (eds.). 1990. *The Responsive Office.* Streatley-on-Thames: Steelcase Strafor/Polymath Publishing.

Handy, C. 1994. *The Empty Raincoat.* London: Hutchinson.

Harris, D. A., et al. 1991. *Planning and Designing the Office Environment.* New York: Van Nostrand Reinhold.

Hartkopf, V., et al. 1993. *Designing the Office of the Future: The Japanese Approach to Tomorrow's Workplace.* New York: Wiley.

Health and Safety Commission. 1992. *Workplace (Health, Safety and Welfare) Regulations.* London: HMSO.

Hendersen, J. 1998. *Workplaces and Workspaces: Office Designs that Work.* Gloucester: Rockport.

Kleeman, W. B., Jr. 1991. *Interior Design in the Electronic Office: The Comfort and Productivity Payoff.* New York: Van Nostrand Reinhold.

Knobel, L. 1987. *Office Furniture.* London: Unwin Hyman.

Laing A., F. Duffy, D. Jaunzens, and S. Willis. 1998. *New Environments for Working: The Redesign of Offices and Environmental Systems for New Ways of Working.* Watford: BRE and DEGW.

Lloyd, B. 1990. *Offices and Office Work: The Coming Revolution.* London: Staniland Hall.

Marberry, S. 1994. *Color in the Office.* New York: Van Nostrand Reinhold.

Marmot, A. F., and J. Eley. 1997. "Space Management for the Millennium." *Space Management,* vol. 1, February, pp. 4–5.

Mole, J. 1992. *Brits at Work.* London: Brealey, especially pp. 16–17.

Pélegrin-Genel, É. 1996. *The Office.* Paris: Flammarion.

Rappoport, J. E., R. F. Cushman, and K. Daroff (eds.). 1992. *Office Planning and Design: Desk Reference.* New York: Wiley.

Rayfield, J. K. 1994. *The Office Interior Design Guide.* New York: Wiley.

Raymond, S., and R. Cunliffe. 1997. *Tomorrow's Office: Creating Effective and Humane Interiors.* London: E & FN SPON.

Reiwoldt, O. 1994. *New Office Design*. Laurence King.

Steele, F. 1983. "The Ecology of Executive Teams: A New View of the Top." *Organizational Dynamics,* American Management Association, Spring, pp. 65–78.

Sundstrom, E. 1986. *Workplaces: The Psychology of the Physical Environment in Offices and Factories*. Cambridge: Cambridge University Press.

Tetlow, K. 1996. *The New Office: Designs for Corporations, People & Technology*. New York: PBC International.

Toffler, A. 1991. *Powershift*. London: Bantam.

Vischer, J. 1989. *Environmental Quality in Offices*. New York: Van Nostrand Reinhold.

White, J. R. (ed.). 1993. *The Office Building: From Concept to Investment Reality*. Chicago: Counselors of Real Estate.

Williams, B. 1995. *Facilities Economics*. Bromley: Building Economics Bureau.

Willis, C. *Form Follows Finance: Skyscrapers and Skylines in New York and Chicago*. New York: Princeton Architectural Press.

Wilson, A. 1994. *Are You Sitting Comfortably?* London: Optima Books.

Wineman, J. D. (ed.). 1986. *Behavioral Issues in Office Design*. New York: Van Nostrand Reinhold.

Worthington, J. 1997. *Reinventing the Workplace*. Oxford: Institute of Advanced Architectural Studies, The University of York.

Zelinsky, M. 1998. *New Workplaces for New Workstyles*. New York: McGraw Hill.

———. 1999. *Practical Home Office Solutions*. New York: McGraw Hill.

Index

Note: boldface numbers
indicate illustrations

About the Authors

Alexi Ferster Marmot is director of AMA, Alexi Marmot Associates, a leading office design firm based in London, England, and established in 1990. Among their clients are a number of large international companies, government agencies, and healthcare firms. She has a B.Arch in Architecture from the University of Sydney, Masters degrees in Architecture and City Planning, and a Ph.D. from the University of California at Berkeley. Before starting her own firm, she was director of research at DEGW, one of the world's largest office design firms.

Joanna Eley has a B.Sc in Architecture from the University of London and an M.A. from Oxford University where she studied Politics, Philosophy, and Economics. She is a director for AMA and has worked as a consultant for many other organizations including DEGW. She has 20 years of experience in architectural design, consultancy, and writing on architectural and business issues.

About the Authors

Alexi Ferster Marmot is director of AMA, Alexi Marmot Associates, a leading office design firm based in London, England, and established in 1990. Among their clients are a number of large international companies, government agencies, and healthcare firms. She has a B.Arch in Architecture from the University of Sydney, Masters degrees in Architecture and City Planning, and a Ph.D. from the University of California at Berkeley. Before starting her own firm, she was director of research at DEGW, one of the world's largest office design firms.

Joanna Eley has a B.Sc in Architecture from the University of London and an M.A. from Oxford University where she studied Politics, Philosophy, and Economics. She is a director for AMA and has worked as a consultant for many other organizations including DEGW. She has 20 years of experience in architectural design, consultancy, and writing on architectural and business issues.